RECLAIMING COMMUNITY

RECLAIMING COMMUNITY

*Race and the Uncertain Future
of Youth Work*

Bianca J. Baldridge

Stanford University Press
Stanford, California

Stanford University Press
Stanford, California

Printed in the United States of America on acid-free, archival-quality paper

Library of Congress Cataloging-in-Publication Data
Names: Baldridge, Bianca J. (Bianca Jontae), 1983- author.
Title: Reclaiming community : race and the uncertain future of youth
    work / Bianca J. Baldridge.
Description: Stanford, California : Stanford University Press, 2019. |
    Includes bibliographical references and index.
Identifiers: LCCN 2018038220 | ISBN 9781503606975 (cloth ; alk. paper) |
    ISBN 9781503607897 (pbk. ; alk. paper) | ISBN 9781503607903 (epub)
Subjects: LCSH: After-school programs—United States—Case studies. | Youth
    workers—United States—Case studies. | Social work with youth—United
    States—Case studies. | African American youth—Education—United
    States—Case studies. | Minority youth—Education—United States—Case
    studies. | Community and school—United States—Case studies.
Classification: LCC LC34.4 .B35 2019 | DDC 371.04—dc23 LC record available
    at https://lccn.loc.gov/2018038220

Typeset by Westchester Publishing Services in 10/14 Minion

Cover design by George Kirkpatrick

For Amanda & Leslie,
Pearlie & Mac Sr.,
& Bobbie.
To Zahra, Zion, and Mecca—for your light.

on writing — needs more story-telling

Contents

Acknowledgments   ix

Abbreviations   xiii

PART I: The Golden Era

1   Community-Based Youth Work in Uncertain Times   3

2   "The EE Family": Framing Race, Youth, and
    Educational Possibilities   28

3   "We're Not Saving Anybody": Refusing Deficit Narratives   76

PART II: Things Fall Apart

4   "Expanding EE's Footprint": Navigating Organizational
    Change   107

5   "The Family Is Dead": Corporatizing After-School   148

6   "It Was Never Ours": Race and the Politics of Control   175

    Conclusion: Reclaiming Community-Based Youth Work
    in the Neoliberal Era   201

Appendix: Methodological Reflections, Considerations,
and Accountability   211

Notes   225

Bibliography   237

Index   249

Acknowledgments

THIS BOOK WAS A LABOR OF LOVE for many years and would not have been possible without the dedicated community-based leaders, youth workers, and staff at Educational Excellence. Thank you for your labor and unconditional support of the many young people you served at Educational Excellence. You all were always willing to participate in interviews, open to my observations, and open to providing any kind of support I needed to complete the research for this book. Thank you for your candor and belief in the power of our youth. To the young people of Educational Excellence, you taught me much more than I could ever teach you. Thank you for letting me be a part of your lives.

I offer sincere gratitude to the staff at Stanford University Press. I am grateful for the editorial guidance from Marcela Maxfield, Olivia Bartz, and the entire SUP team. Marcela, thank you for believing in my work. I am grateful for your patience and tending to *all* of my questions and worries about the publishing process. I have deep appreciation to the anonymous reviewers that provided important feedback.

Throughout my adolescence I had many experiences that revealed the power of learning outside of school. Educators in my life like Ellen Petruzzi and June Thompson nurtured my passion for teaching and learning while showing me that school could also be stifling to education and learning. These women nurtured my early desire to teach and showed me that young people had the capacity to change the world if adults got out of their way. Through my early experiences in community-based youth programs, I developed strong skill sets that I carry with me today as an educator. At the same time, many of these experiences were scarring and harmful as a young Black girl. I knew in college and then in graduate school that I wanted to study community spaces that engaged young people like me. However, I knew these spaces could not be studied without deeply exploring their sociopolitical contexts and how the dynamics of race, class, gender, and power functioned within them. I'd like to thank early mentors in my career, Robert L. Allen and Velma LaPoint, whose wisdom, advice, and mentorship helped me think about these issues and led me to pursue graduate work.

Those early experiences negotiating race, power, and class within community organizations as a participant and educator led me to graduate school, where early ideas for this work were nurtured by the guidance of Amy Stuart Wells and a community of cheerleaders—James Alford, Ramatu Bangura, Tara Conley, Darnel Degand, Jacquelyn Duran, Jeffrey Henig, David Johns, Omari Keeles, Shamus Khan, Richard Lofton, Jamila Lyiscott, Michelle Knight-Manuel, Isabel Martinez, Ernest Morrell, Aaron Pallas, Allison Rhoda, Cati de los Rios, Yolanda Sealey-Ruiz, Karin Van Orman, and Miya Warner. My colleagues at the University of Wisconsin—Madison have been supportive advocates of my work, and for that I am grateful. To my colleagues in Educational Policy Studies—Mike Apple, Lesley Bartlett, Gloria Ladson-Billings, Jordan Conwell, Michael Fultz, Mary Jo "M. J." Gessler, Diana Hess, Nancy Kendall, Jacob Leonard, Adam Nelson, Bill Reese, Linn Posey-Maddox, and Walter Stern—thank you for every note, e-mail, and pep talk in the hallway. To Erica O. Turner and Kathryn Moeller: I can't thank you enough for helping me stay grounded throughout this process and for your feedback on portions of the manuscript. I'd like to especially thank Stacey Lee. Stacey, thank you for carefully reading the manuscript from beginning to end and for your constant support and belief in my work. To Rachelle Winkle-Wagner, who read this book in its early stages, I am deeply grateful for your early encouragement. John Diamond, thank you for the countless hours, days, and weeks you spent reviewing this book.

Thank you to the UW students I have had the pleasure to work with and learn from. You all have been encouraging and supportive throughout this journey. You all remind me of what's important. I'd especially like to acknowledge the dedication and hard work of Marlo Reeves and Ashley Smith, who helped assist me with last-minute tasks before publication. Thank you for putting up with all of my requests. I am also grateful for the generous support of the National Academy of Education/Spencer Foundation Postdoctoral Fellowship program for allowing me time and mentorship to move this book forward.

I am surrounded by amazing friends and colleagues around the country who have provided insight and critical feedback on my work. Those people are Derrick Brooms, Marc Lamont Hill, and R. L'Heureux Lewis-McCoy. To my colleagues, Jarvis Givens, Carl Grant, Saida Grundy, Amanda Lewis, Erica Meiners, Dave Stovall, Elizabeth Todd-Breland, and Mark Warren— conversations about the publishing process and writing helped me approach this book in new ways throughout the writing process. Our interactions had more impact than you know. I'd also like to thank Chris Lura for his feedback on multiple drafts of this book; I'm so thankful for your critical eye and validation. To Maisha T. Winn, Monica White, and Ron C. Williams II: your friendship sustained me throughout this process. You all knew exactly what I was going through as you were completing important books of your own. I'd also like to thank a group of friends whose encouragement, support, daily or weekly check-ins, and/or pleas for me to take care of myself while completing this book were helpful during very challenging personal times. These people are Fenaba Addo, Kendra Alexander, Brandelyn Anderson, Jamal Anderson, Angela Rose Black, Kshinte Braithwaite, Erika Bullock, Alyson Edwards, Sakeena Everett, Taucia Gonzales, Annalee Good, Keisha Green, Erica Hewitt, Amari Johnson, Tiffani Johnson, Ruth Latham, Justin Martin, Maxine McKinney de-Royston, Afia Dawn Opantiri, Shameka Powell, Shanta Robinson, Constance Samuels, Katy Swalwell, Shannell Thomas, Chizoba Udeorji, Cidna Valentin, Melissa Valle, Shirin Vossoughi, and Torry Winn. I'd also like to thank my late comrade Antonio Nieves Martinez. He was a true advocate for young people and freedom fighter. I'm grateful for his belief in my work from the moment we first met and during great moments of doubt early in my career. To the Diamond-Berry, Mullen, Udeorji, and Winn families: thank you for your encouragement and support along the way. To my sister-scholars— Keisha McIntosh Allen, Sosanya Jones, Terrenda White, and Blanca Vega— thank you for your encouragement, laughter, moments of levity, and reminders about the importance of joy. I know there are many others who have been supportive of this book and throughout my career that I might have unintentionally forgotten to name. Please blame my head and not my heart.

To my partner, John, thank you for showing me patient and gentle love. Your support and unconditional love have meant the world to me. Thank you for loving me through all my panics related to this book. To my big and loving family, thank you for your support and being the first ones to "see" me. I love you all and I'm still waiting on visits to the Midwest. My brother, Brandon Muhammad, your strength and courage inspire me. To my loving parents: Debra Myles-Baldridge and Mac Baldridge Jr., thank you for always believing in me. Your sacrifices have made it possible for me to do the work that I do.

Last, thank you to the millions of youth workers who sacrifice so much to guide and learn from young people. Your work is not invisible; it is critical and necessary.

Abbreviations

EE   Educational Excellence

HA   High Achievers (middle school program at Educational Excellence)

S2C   Step 2 College (high school and alumni program at Educational Excellence)

YL   Youth Lead (youth development and counseling program at Educational Excellence)

RECLAIMING COMMUNITY

PART I

THE GOLDEN ERA

1 Community-Based Youth Work in Uncertain Times

The quality of what has been created over the last 12 years. I'm worried about that just being destroyed . . . by someone who has no clue about their experience. I was thinking about this very thing the other day, and really the word "co-opting" just kept coming back to me. The work that we've done is going to be co-opted.

—*Walidah Thomas, Director of High Achievers, Middle School Program, 2007–2015*

ON A COLD RAINY Saturday morning in February 2008, I walked several blocks to the neighborhood of Dunbar, a historic area located in a busy, rapidly gentrifying region of a large city in the Northeast. I was on my way to Educational Excellence (EE), a community-based after-school program.[1] I had been invited by a friend to participate on a panel about college for a group of middle school students as part of the program's Career and College Day event. After walking the few blocks from the bus stop, I approached the large high-rise building where the program was located. The building sat on a large city block nestled between a fast food restaurant and a hair braiding salon, with a popular corner store located at the end of the block. I took the elevator to the seventh floor. Once the elevator doors opened, I was immediately struck by the loud, gleeful voices of young people talking and laughing throughout the halls. As I entered the room where my panel was to take place, I noticed the room was filled with mostly young, Black faces—some with enthusiastic expressions and others looking annoyed, likely due to the fact it was so early on a Saturday morning. In the room that day, I also noticed that the staff members and other adults present were mostly Black and therefore reflected the population of students in the program. As a former youth worker, I have spent most of my life working with and alongside youth in community-based after-school settings and cherished these opportunities.

During the session, my fellow panelists and I fielded questions about college majors and job opportunities, college life, and financial aid. A few students boldly asked us about our social lives in college. We assured them that life in college had many social opportunities. Some students were assertive and very clear about what they wanted to pursue in college or for their careers while others were a bit more uncertain. After the panel ended, I joined students for lunch and observed other panels. Throughout the day there was a strong, vibrant energy from youth workers and students in the program that spoke volumes about the culture created within the program.

A few months before my visit to EE, I had met two staff members/youth workers from the organization at a regional conference in the Northeast where they discussed their robust programming with youth unpacking race, gender, sexuality, class, power, and privilege. These themes were evident during my first visit to the program for the panel. Although I had volunteered in the past with other programs on occasion, the tone and culture of EE was different—more specific to affirming the identities of Black youth across diverse ethnic backgrounds. Youth workers there understood how political forces like racism and poverty affected college attainment, something which was a part of the conversation on panels that day. Staff members engaged students in highly effective ways that were fun, loving, and humanizing. Students appeared comfortable, engaged, and genuinely happy as some were gently nudged to ask questions of panelists. I was moved by my experience at Educational Excellence that day, and soon after I started volunteering. I was impressed with the robust after-school, weekend, and summer programming the organization offered, which included a number of academic, elective, and youth development courses—as well as emotional support through counseling—for middle school, high school, and college students. Over the next three years, I went from volunteer to after-school course instructor, to part-time youth worker teaching youth development courses to middle and high school students, to ultimately being a researcher studying the experiences of staff members. Each of these roles and experiences provided an in-depth exploration into a unique after-school community-based program and revealed youth workers' experiences as cultural workers, institutional advocates, and pedagogues.

In 2011, as part of my research on how youth workers' imagining of Black youth shaped their organization, I spoke with all youth workers and every support staff member, rummaged through program literature, and sat in on staff meetings. Based on this research, I learned that staff members went to great lengths to avoid deficit-oriented language, like "at risk," and shied away from media attention that positioned the organization or its youth workers as "saviors" or "heroes" to students, which is all too common in community-based youth work and in the non-profit sector. EE fiercely fought to maintain its affirming and asset-rich language, which describes youth by the skills and talents they possess. Youth workers called EE students "scholars" and framed students as "high potential" and "intelligent" on program literature and in media engagement. I found that youth workers at EE, who were predominantly Black, had a firm grasp of the complex political problems that informed the lives of the youth and families they engaged. Youth workers saw sociocultural, political, and emotional development as critical to students' academic success an intentionally took a comprehensive approach to youth development exhibiting radical care. Although there were differing approaches and attitudes among youth workers, they shared a belief in the humanity of Black and other minoritized youth. As has been found in research elsewhere among youth participants in community-based organizations, youth workers at EE demonstrated a belief that young people always had a critique of the world in which they lived and needed opportunities and spaces to share that critique.[2] Staff and students alike celebrated EE as a "family" dedicated to youth achievement and personal well-being. Former students describe the program as confidence boosting—a space that helped them sort out their multiple complex racial and ethnic identities and made them want to excel in all areas of their lives. "EE's youth development class on gender, culture, and stereotypes changed my perspective on the world, but more importantly, it changed my perspective [of] myself," shared a student alum on a questionnaire. Alumni of the program expressed the importance of being treated as someone with a "valuable opinion and voice."

Schools are not, have never been, and will never be the only site for learning.[3] For Black, Indigenous, and Latinx communities, schools have often been sites of suffering, terror, and cultural violence.[4] But these communities have a long history of "youth work" that not only tries to uplift youth but also strives to counteract the pernicious experiences minoritized youth have in schools and broader society. Within Black communities, youth work exists in a fugitive space—always fighting for a right to exist within the oppressive structures of anti-Blackness,[5] it is nevertheless an effort to create a space where students can escape those very oppressive structures. Over time, youth work in Black spaces has been focused on literacy and learning in ways that will help students to unlearn false histories taught in schools, to foster political education, and to serve as a buffer against anti-Blackness and violence, among other things. From the creation of Freedom Schools to the spaces of learning and cultivation of resistance that occurred through the Black Panther Party's Free Breakfast Program and within the Black Church during the Black Freedom Struggle, for example, community-based youth work has always been crucial to Black communities. As locations of protection, nurture, and resistance, these spaces were central for the edification of Black youth.[6] Yet throughout history these spaces have endured government infiltration and destruction, and tensions as a result of external political constraints and policies, as well as internal turmoil stemming from conflicting ideologies and strategies for maintaining self and community determination.

This book tells the story of both the power of community-based afterschool spaces like EE and the problems these spaces confront as they strive to determine how youth should be engaged. For ten years, under the leadership of Dr. Leah Davis, Educational Excellence was able to determine its culture and pedagogical approaches and define youth in humanizing ways. However, between 2012 and 2013, at the same time as shifts in the city's education system and neighborhood demographics occurred, EE underwent major changes in its leadership, which included the departure of Leah, and the organization's founder retained more control. These changes resulted in a series of organizational and personnel shifts that influenced the work experiences and morale of youth workers who remained. I returned multiple times between 2013 and 2015 to conduct follow-up interviews with participants, and learned that Walidah Thomas's fears noted at the beginning of this chapter came true. After major organizational shifts, EE was now "different," "noticeably whiter," and "just not the same." EE began to focus solely on "expansion," "serving more students," and "serving the underprivileged"—language that was not supported just two years prior. Stemming from these internal changes, the organization began taking up language reflected in broader educational reform efforts aligned with privatization and competition and displayed a singular focus on measurable and quantifiable outcomes. During my follow-up interviews, it became apparent rather quickly that the culture I had been so impressed by when I first visited in 2008, and then experienced myself during my subsequent research with the organization, was nearing extinction. The space lacked vibrancy, and the tension was palpable among staff members—the familial rapport that once characterized youth workers at EE was struggling to survive. There was minimal engagement between staff members, little joy, and a lack of expressed excitement about the organization and its future.

For the most part, during Leah's tenure between 2002 and 2012, EE successfully resisted widespread tropes of color blindness and deficit discourses about youth participants (discourses that the organization's founder embraced) through a variety of subversive tactics on the part of its leadership and youth workers. Leah's presence had compensated for years of suffocating paternalism by EE's founder, Richard Dunn. It came as no surprise, then, that Leah Davis's departure after ten years as EE's leader resulted in extraordinary staff turnover. Although EE sometimes succumbed to expressed contradictions in their work with youth prior to the turnover, after Leah's departure there was an unmistakable rise in organizational practices that aligned with broader education privatization discourse. This more business-like and corporatizing approach to youth work shifted the culture of the program, eroding its family-like atmosphere and causing a breakdown in staff relationships. Ultimately, the students' perception of the program shifted as the organization began expansion and as youth workers came and went.

This book examines the external and internal political forces that contributed to the changes within this community-based after-school program. Although this book closely explores one organization, the story of EE reflects a larger, cautionary tale of what can happen to community-based youth work in an era marked by market-based approaches to public education, education restructuring aligned with deep privatization, and racialized paternalism. Important scholarship has shown how public education and schools have been shaped by the effects of privatization discourses and reform efforts resulting in school closures, the proliferation of charter schools, a rise in alternative fast-paced teacher education programs, accountability solely measured by test scores, and restructuring in major cities throughout the country.[7] Yet there is little work exploring how these approaches inform community-based after-school programs. But these programs have been especially impacted, and the consequences of these broader changes include measuring the impact of the program solely by "numbers"—how many youths are served—and measurable "success" indicators, such as test scores, which breed competition and meritocratic ideals through racialized framing that positions Black youth as objects to be commodified, fixed, and rescued. An abundance of scholarship has shown how these programs are important for youths' academic, political, cultural, and identity development. Through a deep investigation of youth workers' experiences at one organization, this book shows how current reforms to public education are shaping community-based programs and what we stand to lose as a result.

Community-Based Youth Work: Possibility and Paradox

As the quote from Walidah Thomas at the beginning of this chapter suggests, EE was a space of great value and yet was filled with paradox. In this way it was emblematic of community-based youth work and the wider challenges of educational institutions shaped by broader political and social forces. Sociologists of education have spent considerable time examining how inequality is reproduced within schools and the ways in which students are stratified by race, class, and gender. Even more, the links between educational attainment and social mobility have been widely studied. However, sociologists of education have overlooked community-based educational spaces and the pedagogical strategies that youth workers employ. With few exceptions, scholars have paid little attention to the ways these spaces and the youth workers in them both challenge and reproduce racial disparities and their relationship to the academic success of students in schools. But, there is much that sociologists of education can learn from these spaces and from youth workers. As this book will show, community-based spaces are important out-of-school sites of education. Indeed, they are often beloved by youth and families, and have been celebrated for being structurally unlike schools. Yet these spaces are also sites of contestation over race, power, and ideology.

"Youth work" is often used interchangeably with youth development, out-of-school time learning, or community-based after-school/youth organizations.[8] As a field, youth work includes theory and practice of supporting children and adolescence, and encompasses the education, guidance, and mentorship of young people through a variety of settings, including after-school programs, community-based spaces including non-profit organizations, faith-based spaces, as well as youth detention centers, parks, and recreation centers.[9] Sometimes theorized as a third space—distinct from schools and families—after-school spaces are viewed as a site of development with opportunities for learning, play, socialization, protection, or care. Toward the end of the 19th century, the decline of child labor and implementation of compulsory education laws created the context for the emergence of after-school. Early spaces, like Hull House in Chicago, for example, engaged children in workforce development, English language development for European immigrants, informal education, civic education, physical education, and gendered work. As more women began working outside of the home, children would come home from school with hours of freedom before parents arrived.[10] For children living in poverty, this free time, and youth themselves, were considered a "problem."[11] And, so, even today, after-school time is widely regarded as a space prime for "opportunity" and "risk."[12]

At the beginning of the 20th century, churches and other faith-based organizations began setting up after-school programs in urban cities in the north.[13] Following the development of after-school programs offered in settlement houses like Hull House, Boy's Clubs and faith-based afterschool sites were established. Due to migration patterns, the structure of neighborhoods shifted and placed Black residents in contact with European children. Settlements and other after-school spaces were segregated as European families pulled their children from programs with Black children.[14] Black churches and Black settlement spaces in neighborhoods offered their own programming since they were excluded from other spaces. As previously mentioned, in addition to providing opportunities for play and leisure activities, political and cultural education were strong features of these spaces. The common history and dominant practice of American youth work has typically excluded Black youth and ignored the dimensions of youth work that have been highly valued in Black communities, historically and in the present.[15]

During the late 1970s and early 1980s, community-based programs emerged in urban centers in response to decreases in federal safety nets, underemployment, and underfunded schools as well as racialized and class-based legislation like the War on Drugs and the resulting mass incarceration and its impact on these communities.[16] The early deficit-framing of low-income youths as "problems" to be contained within after-school spaces became even more prominent as more programs developed with Black and Latinx youth in mind during this time. While many of these spaces developed by members of the communities engaged recognized the structural constraints to employment and the need for adequate and affirming educational experiences for Black and Latinx youth, the framing of after-school spaces as sites to control "male criminality and female sexuality" soared in the public's imagination.[17] Then, in 1994 (on the heels of national reports about the opportunities for youth development during non-school hours[18]), under the Clinton administration, the U.S. Department of Education granted millions of dollars to school-based after-school programs in rural and urban contexts through the development of 21st Century Community Learning Centers (21CCLC). Through 21CCLCs, the federal government allocates funding for states to distribute to schools and community-based organizations (some in partnership with schools) to provide after-school programming to increase academic achievement and access to higher education.[19] This marked an important moment in the history of community-based youth work as there was an explicit charge toward reducing "achievement gaps" and increased competition for funding. This competition for funding continued and was amplified under the Obama administration through initiatives like Race to the Top.

Community-based after-school programs—which traditionally have been designed to meet the specific needs of the community in which they exist— have been stable fixtures in many communities for generations and are an essential resource for many families as they provide working parents peace of mind that their child is safe during non-school hours, while also offering access to food, opportunities for learning, creative expression, identity exploration, and opportunities to hone various talents and skill sets.[20]

The adults who engage in youth work are referred to as youth workers, community-based educators, youth specialists, or some variation. Through the late 19th and early 20th centuries, these workers might have been local activists, educators, or members of faith-based institutions who usually worked on a volunteer basis or as part-time staff members.[21] Today, youth workers are still volunteers, part-time or full-time employees at a wide range of organizations. During the early 1990s, scholars of youth work wrote extensively about the heterogeneity of these spaces and lack of professionalization in the occupation.[22] In national surveys for youth workers, findings showed that training, specializations, credentials or lack thereof, changes from organization to organization, making it difficult to determine quality services.[23] Although some receive training, many youth workers have little to no training and there is a lack of infrastructure and understanding about the profession. Most concerning, many youth workers receive low wages for their work without unionization or uniform ways to carry out this work. However, the lack of uniformity also allows communities to define the work they do according to the needs of the youth they engage.

In many ways, these spaces have been important in the lives of youth and families. Research has shown that youth participants appreciate community organizations for their supportive environment and investment in them as "whole" beings, particularly for youth who feel rejected and are pushed out of schools.[24] After-school programs can be restorative spaces for students who are disconnected from schools[25] and can facilitate the development of social capital for young people and a deeper understanding of the social context in which they live and learn.[26] These spaces are recognized for their ability to design flexible youth-centered curricula and opportunities to meet the needs of youth who are over-disciplined and disregarded in schools.[27] The programmatic flexibility associated with community-based after-school programs is also linked to improved academic performance and psychosocial growth, reinforcing the value of imagining education beyond test scores.[28]

Youth workers play a significant role in the experiences young people have in community-based programs.[29] The relationships cultivated between adults and youths within these spaces are a critical feature of these programs. Opportunities for mentorship, positive relationships with adults (beyond teachers in schools and family members), and the social capital or connections adults can make on behalf of youth are celebrated features of these spaces. As the nature of youth work varies from after-school programs to detention centers to group homes to the streets, the day-to-day experiences of youth workers differs from one program to another. Turnover in the profession is high due to low wages, lack of opportunity for advancement, and the part-time nature of the work during non-school hours.[30] While some youth workers volunteer a few hours a week, some literally work twenty-four hours a day as they can be on call and needed by youth at any given moment.

Although community-based youth work is crucial to the educational and social experiences of young people, it should not be romanticized. Macro-level political structures, policies, and social forces inform all social institutions, and community-based youth spaces are not exempt. Youth work organizations are constructed and operate within a "field" that includes an array of political structures. Social forces such as racism, capitalism, and power function simultaneously and inform how community-based spaces are created, organized, and sustained.[31] For instance, organizational funding often informs how programs are constructed and are important to their survival. Historically, community-based organizations have operated as local and regional operations separate from schools and without federal funds; and, as a result, they were able to provide services and programs aligned with community interests and concerns, rather than being constrained by academic standards.[32] Without public funding, non-profit community-based organizations typically rely on foundations, donors, and grants—funding from outside the communities they serve—to sustain their work. However, they run the risk of mission drift as they try to appease donors and align their work with schools as a result of funding demands like 21CCLCs. Youth workers and community-based leaders often experience tension and conflict with donors over program values and visions, including how the youth served are viewed and engaged.[33]

Aside from funding and how the organizations are led, public discourse about which children are in "need" of after-school programs often positions these spaces and those who work in them as saviors. Race, and deficit framing more specifically, positions youth of color as needing to be "fixed," "saved," and "rescued" and racializes after-school spaces as being the kind of support these students need.[34] This need is often refracted through a deficit lens, framing these spaces as necessary because of an inherent lack among minoritized youth, rather than structural inequalities that create hardship for youth of color in schools and society. As such, after-school programs and community-based youth organizations are often positioned as places of containment and control for Black youth in urban contexts.[35] Although important research on the experiences of Black and other minoritized youth in after-school programs documents how aspects of their lives have been improved by their time in the program, the public and political discourse around these spaces often exude pathological undertones that depict Black youth as inherent problems and ignores deep structural barriers shaping their lives.

Even as greater attention has focused on the promise of youth work for a number of individual, community, and public goals, and on all of the documented benefits of youth participation in programs, the success of youth work is tenuous and cannot be taken for granted. Funding patterns, leadership, programming, pedagogical approaches, as well as larger political forces inform how youth work occurs. 21CCLC program funding continues to be the only federal funding designated specifically for after-school education, and even that is not assured as cuts to federal spending on programs are a persistent threat. Especially under the weight of political and economic forces like neoliberal reforms dominating public education and white supremacy, the important work of youth programs—and the flexibility, funding, and purpose that sustain these programs—is in serious jeopardy.

In the past three decades or so, research has illuminated the importance of school and community-based organizations joining forces in order to provide optimal opportunities for positive development for youth.[36] Schools and community-based organizations ultimately share the same set of students; however, there are philosophical and pedagogical differences that often and sometimes unfairly, pit these spaces against each other.[37] Milbrey McLaughlin found, in her work with a community-based program operating on the south side of

Chicago, that youth workers saw schools as not "respecting" or "valuing" their work with students, instead dismissing them as "mere fun and as having little contribution to the business of schools."[38] Conversely, youth workers respected the work of classroom teachers and, most importantly, understood learning as continuous across school and community organizations. Viewing these various spaces and roles as competitors is unfortunate because it dismisses the reality that youth have many teachers and mentors throughout their lives and throughout the many spaces they occupy. In a study of four community-based educators in California, Vajra Watson rightly argues that community-based educators "act as important alternative teachers and mentors in the lives of youth."[39]

Building on this foundation, my work positions community-based youth workers as pedagogues in their own right—with goals that sometimes overlap those of teachers but also constitute their own unique aims, knowledge, and teaching strategies. Youth workers are critical to youth development and are essential actors in communities.[40] This book closely examines youth workers—who they are, how they came to their work, their strategies for engagement, and the savvy ways they navigate complex economic, social, and political barriers in their work with young people. I also illuminate community spaces as dynamic institutions that stand on their own as distinct spaces from school. As noted in early history of after-school education in the United States, tensions with schools and wider views on education are not new.[41] However, as I explore throughout this book, given the pernicious racialized market-based reforms to public education, community-based youth organizations are vulnerable as these reforms shape the organizational and pedagogical practices of youth workers. The stories of youth workers illustrate how they navigate and disrupt broader deficit narratives that follow Black youth throughout their educational, social, and political lives, as well as how they negotiate complex racial and cultural dynamics occurring internally in their programs. Undertaken during a time of massive turnover at the organization, this research documents how a hyperfocus on expansion, competition, and serving more students shifted priorities of the program. Coupled with competing ideologies about youth in the program between new leadership and longtime program staff, these shifts shaped the organization's philosophical approach to race-conscious comprehensive youth work with predominantly Black youth in favor of neoliberal tactics of competition, individualism, and racialized control of youth workers and youth participants.

Racial Framing in the Neoliberal Era

Neoliberalism, as a term, has saturated political discourse in recent years. In the 1980s, it emerged as a form of political thought and a set of ideas that "reorder[ed] social reality."[42] As another iteration of capitalism, neoliberalism embraces the logic that all institutions within society will function at an optimal level if they operate according to the principles of markets.[43] Under neoliberal ideals, the State attempts to privatize "public goods," such that public resources are sold, commoditized, and ultimately treated as though they were private rather than public services. As part of these privatizing efforts, public sources, spaces, and individuals are commodified. Journalist Stephen Metcalf writes of the pervasiveness of neoliberalism as the way citizens are

> urged to think of ourselves as proprietors of our own talents and initiative, how glibly we are told to compete and adapt. You see the extent to which a language formerly confined to chalkboard simplifications describing commodity markets (competition, perfect information, rational behaviour) has been applied to all of society, until it has invaded the grit of our personal lives, and how the attitude of the salesman has become enmeshed in all modes of self-expression. In short, "neoliberalism" is not simply a name for pro-market policies, or for the compromises with finance capitalism made by failing social democratic parties. It is a name for a premise that, quietly, has come to regulate all we practise and believe: that competition is the only legitimate organising principle for human activity.[44]

Research on neoliberalism's impact on public education in the United States has been critically important to how schools have been reimagined and reconfigured through privatization and has revealed its constraining grip on the lives of administrators, teachers, students, and families.[45] Within the educational policy context, attempts to privatize public education have contributed to a proliferation of privately operated charter management organizations.[46] This has also led to increased school choice for families, but in a way that produces further inequality as choice is constrained for those who are poor and displaced. Corporate interests now influence public education, causing schools to operate like businesses and thus causing students to be treated as objects to be controlled, bought, and discarded.[47] What's more, neoliberalism and its alignment with and reliance on racism and settler colonialism generate very particular racial frames for communities of color in which failure and lack of opportunity become an individual problem devoid of structural constraints. In this context, community-based after-school programs are framed as sites of containment and control for Black and other minoritized youth.

Within sociological research, framing is defined as a mental construct and process that allows people to identify, make sense of, and label the individuals (and the communities from which they come), social interactions, and circumstances that enter their social worlds and inform their life experiences.[48] As Alford Young contends, framing within cultural sociology is

> directly associated with cultural properties. Hence, when doing framework analysis, investigators must be clear about the varied dimensions of culture, including values, norms, and institutional milieus that must be attended to and assessed in order to elucidate how and why particular frames emerge and what social, emotional, and cultural work they do for their adherents. These additional cultural properties must be attended to because frames are often constrained by the cultural resource base available to their producers. That base includes the extant stock of meanings, beliefs, ideologies, practices, values, myths, and narratives that such producers are aware of and can access to construct frames.[49]

Framing is more than description; it shapes the public's perception of a situation or group of people as well as how individuals make sense of their own social position. How we think about communities, public policies, political issues, and social problems is largely determined by the ways in which they are framed to us.

The framing of Black youth in deficit and anti-Black rhetoric has occurred in national political discourse for centuries.[50] "Youth" as a concept is a fluid social construction and is positioned as "other" to adulthood.[51] Adults, who designate the standards and conditions by which youth develop, shape the construction of youth as "other," and thus, youth in America have often been framed as problems and burdens to society.[52] There is a particular meaning and connotation made by the construction of "Black" and "youth." Black youth have been framed by deficit narratives that distinguish them from other youth. These deficit narratives depict Black youth in media and national political discourses as lacking and as inherent "problems." Such narratives follow them through all aspects of society, especially within education. Deficit framing can lead to a host of effects on the public perception of Black youth. Furthermore, the "framing" of Black youth is tied to how Black youth are imagined by others.[53] Imagining is not just how we envision or think about youth but also how we view what is possible for their lives.[54] Framing and imagining overlap and are intertwined because how we imagine others is shaped by the ways in which they are framed to and for us. For this reason, minoritized youth have historically been targeted for after-school programming as a preventive measure and a place of containment for those considered "at risk."[55]

The youth workers who participated in this study face dilemmas that shape the ways they are able to carry out their mission, construct their vision and imagining of youth, and frame their pedagogical practices and their interactions with youth. Pauline Lipman argues that under neoliberal reform, "disinvestment in public schools, closing them, and opening privately operated charter schools in African American and Latina/o communities is facilitated by a racist discourse that pathologizes these communities and their public institutions."[56] As a racialized neoliberal project,[57] this pathologizing rhetoric creates a narrative that frames Black youth throughout educational discourse with themes of deficiency that warrant "saving." As part of the larger project of neoliberalism within the educational policy context, business leaders and private companies swoop down to "save" schools by closing them and replacing them with schools that are part of predominantly white-controlled charter management organizations.[58] As part of a continuation of long-running ideologies of whiteness and anti-Blackness, private and white then becomes synonymous with "good" while public and Black becomes synonymous with "bad."[59] This narrative ultimately shapes the damage-centered research[60] and public discourse used to define Black youth's educational trajectories as well as the social services designed both to control and to support them.

Indeed, the rhetoric and labeling used to describe individuals and communities is important; and the rhetoric targeting Black youth as receivers of compensatory and after-school programs has a long history tied to policy interventions steeped in discourses of deficiency.[61] For example, Martinez and Rury provide an important historical analysis of commonly used terms to describe the educational history of Black and Mexican youth—from "culturally deprived," to "culturally disadvantaged," to "at risk." These problematic terms fueled policy agendas and compensatory education programs.[62] Although initially intended to be race-neutral, targeting all groups who were poor, these terms eventually became closely tied and linked to Black and Mexican American communities.[63]

During the late 1950s and into the mid-1960s, labels such as "culturally deprived," "culturally disadvantaged," and "disadvantaged" found their way into political and educational discourse framing Black and Mexican American students.[64] These labels incited national debate over structural constraints that prevented Black youth from achieving educational and social mobility versus cultural and familial explanations for low academic achievement and limited social progress. As these terms eventually faded, the 1983 report *A Nation at Risk*[65] gave rise to the label "at risk," which is still common (though often criticized) in many education policy and research circles. The struggle to find more positive terminology to describe Black youth and the challenges they face in education proved to be difficult then and continues to be difficult now. The neoliberal state is simultaneously "caring and ruthless," resulting in the positioning of nonprofit youth programs that both affirm and reproduce deficit narratives about minoritized youth.[66] These narratives not only establish a particular understanding of youth of color, but they also shape the public's understanding of who needs after-school programming and what that programming should look like. The ways Black youth are framed and how they are imagined informs the sets of policies and practices that affect their lives. It shapes the expectations educators have of them, and it influences the ways in which educators interact and engage with them. The educational climate we are currently in and the rhetoric used to define Black youth in urban contexts, the spaces they occupy, and the social and educational struggles they endure warrant close attention and redefining.

This book allows youth workers to voice their critique of the current educational climate and the subsequent framing of Black youth. Youth workers at EE strived to avoid deficit-based rhetoric, and as a result their funding, which rewards rhetoric steeped in damage and stories of struggle, was constantly in jeopardy. Against the backdrop of the surrounding neighborhood restructuring, longtime staff members departed en masse, and EE succumbed to the very deficit rhetoric it had actively avoided for so long.

Racism is inherent to the neoliberal establishment;[67] its relationship to and reliance on racism, capitalism, and patriarchy shape educational policy, opportunity, and narratives about race and academic achievement in very particular ways.[68] Although analyses of class are often used to critique neoliberalism as an economic doctrine, scholars have asserted the ways in which race functions as a dimension of neoliberal governmentality.[69] In many ways, racism carries out the work of neoliberalism, by reproducing and reshaping racial subjects. This occurs through the historical and contemporary power–knowledge relations that inform the racial discourses used to govern communities of color through patterns of control and paternalism or how communities govern themselves.[70] Therefore, we must examine carefully what race means in the context of neoliberal changes to education and social life. The language of neoliberalism projects notions of meritocracy, individualism, and the belief that everyone has access to the "open" market. In reality, these notions fundamentally neglect structural violence and oppression inflicted on communities of color. Moreover, under these notions of meritocracy and "choice" to engage in the market, race becomes absent as a factor contributing to how people have access to opportunity, and racism is denied as a barrier to opportunity.

If we examine how market-based ideology currently shapes the ways that public education is constructed and operationalized, we see that Black youth in low-income settings are treated as subjects in an experiment within charter management networks.[71] Even more, hundreds of public schools have been branded as failing and closed, completely reorganizing neighborhoods in cities like Chicago, Philadelphia, New Orleans, and New York City.

As a racialized project, neoliberalism pretends to offer equal opportunity and access to social mobility but often operates within binaries of "good" or "bad," "skilled" or "unskilled," using racialized coded language that de-emphasizes the role of race (color blindness) to focus on "character" and "ability."[72] As a result, after-school community-based organizations are often positioned as containment spaces for youth of color in paternalistic ways. People often see them primarily as ways to "keep kids off the street," implying that Black and other minoritized youth are prone to engage in criminal behaviors without supervision. Community-based after-school spaces are often seen as places where young people experience certain levels of freedom to just be themselves without draconian rules. Yet these spaces can function as a space of control and surveillance for Black and other minoritized youth. Rhetoric espousing meritocracy and notions of individualism ignores structural oppression and opens the door for damage-centered and deficit-oriented rhetoric and policies that position minoritized youth as needing to be contained, controlled and, ultimately, saved by community-based organizations.

The Study

Educational Excellence was founded in 1989, with the purpose of providing mentorship to youth in Dunbar to help them access competitive colleges and universities. Richard Dunn, a wealthy white real estate developer, founded and funded EE. Under the leadership from 2002 to 2012 of Leah Davis, a Black woman, former classroom teacher, and school administrator, the mission of the organization broadened. The goal of assisting youth in getting to college through supplemental academic support remained primary under Leah's tenure, but it expanded to become a comprehensive program that provided students with access to "youth development" programming, which included social identity development, service learning, activism, and personal counseling. The socio-cultural and emotional support became central to the organization and a critical factor in helping students get to and through college.

Youth participants voluntarily attend Educational Excellence (although many might have been made to attend by family members) and were accepted between their sixth- and tenth-grade years. Students who wanted to attend EE had to apply. The application process included a short essay; a meeting with the admissions director, Ms. Allan, and their parents or guardians; report cards; and test scores on state exams. As part of a "continuum," students remained members of the program through their completion of college and participated in programing for alumni as college students. Roughly 73 percent of students in the program are categorized as female. Ninety percent of students qualify for free and reduced lunch. A few hundred students (middle, high school, and college) are served annually, with a 100 percent college acceptance rate, and 95 percent of students graduate from college within six years.

Educational Excellence began as an organization targeting youth living in Dunbar and initially enrolled mostly Latinx students. Over the years, the de-mographics shifted, making the racial/ethnic breakdown 76 percent Black and 24 percent Latinx at the time of my study. Most students are racially Black and make up a variety of ethnic backgrounds that include ancestry in the Carib-bean, Latin America, and Africa. The majority of Latinx students identified as Dominican and would likely be perceived as racially Black (or multiracial) by larger society in certain contexts.

Staff at Educational Excellence worked with students to help them distin-guish between and embrace their racial and ethnic identities. After courses in youth development, many Latinx students would begin to understand and embrace their African ancestry. Given that the majority of students served in the program were Black and staff members were majority Black, the program was often read as a "Black organization" by outsiders. Nonetheless, EE staff members recognized and affirmed the diversity within Blackness by helping students understand the complexities of their various ethnic identities.

The participants/staff members of EE in this study can be thought of in three categories: leadership, programs, or administrative staff. The leadership consisted of the executive director/CEO, Leah Davis; the director of finance, Cynthia Gladys; and the director of development, Patrick Denny. Within programs, there are three departments that facilitate after-school programming for youth participants: High Achievers (Middle School), Step 2 College/Alumni (High School and College), and Youth Lead (Youth Development and Counseling).

The High Achievers (HA) program was designed for middle school students. In this department, students come to the program two days a week for an academic class in English/language arts or math and for a youth development course taught by staff members in the Youth Lead department. The HA program consisted of a director, an assistant director, and a handful of after-school course instructors who were typically traditional schoolteachers during the day. Walidah Thomas, a Black woman who was born and raised on the East Coast and was a former middle school teacher, teacher coach, and community-based educator, served as the HA's department director. Alongside Michaela Delgado, a Dominican and Puerto Rican East Coast native who served as the assistant director/coordinator for middle school programming, Walidah designed culturally responsive academic courses that attempted to engage students in real-life experiences while improving their writing, reading, and math skills. After students completed their eighth-grade year in HA, they entered the high school program, Step 2 College.

Step 2 College (S2C) included all of the high school students in the program. Students in the ninth and tenth grades participated in academic, elective, and youth development classes. As eleventh graders, students took a college-level class at a nearby college. During their junior and senior years, students participated in workshops on the college application process focusing on things like financial aid, asking for letters of recommendation, writing personal statements, and choosing appropriate colleges based on students' goals, career aspirations, grades, and family needs. During the first phase of study from 2011 to 2012, Step 2 College was directed by Terry Niles, a Black man from the East Coast. Alexandria Jimenez, an Afro-Latina Southern California–born community-based educator, served as the assistant director/coordinator for Step 2 College and the alumni program. Her main responsibility was working with high school seniors on the transition to college and maintaining contact and providing support to students enrolled in college. Omari Anderson was hired as a coordinator assisting the S2C programming.[73] Together, Terry, Alexandria, and Omari worked to make sure that students had the support they needed to stay in college. They also closely tracked their application process, often helping them navigate difficult circumstances in their high schools.

Youth Lead supports both High Achievers and Step 2 College. Created by Monica Matthews, the director of programming, and led by Dr. Faith Davenport, Youth Lead provides youth development classes, which include courses on social identity (race, ethnicity, class, gender, and sexuality), critical media literacy, and making healthy choices. Youth participants stopped taking youth development courses after the first semester of their tenth-grade year. As juniors, students in the program could apply to be a Youth Lead intern, where they would work alongside a youth development instructor teaching ninth graders. Interns would help set up classrooms, facilitate discussions, and sometimes assist with teaching. They could also apply to work on a youth participatory action research project (YPAR) where they helped to address an issue in the organization or within the surrounding community.[74] Later, as seniors, youth participants would take workshops on adapting to college life; Youth Lead staff, including Faith, Camille Kent, Solomon Modupe, and myself, led workshops. We worked with students to understand how their social identities may be challenged on their college campuses. Additionally—and perhaps one of the most unique features of the program—personal counseling was available for students in all grade levels. Faith was a trained psychologist and worked with a team of interns and a coordinator to keep case files on students who underwent counseling. Students were encouraged to attend counseling during difficult circumstances in schools, at home, and in their neighborhoods. In some instances, when students had more serious mental health challenges such as eating disorders, cutting, or depression, Faith and her staff would work with them and refer them to other locations for additional support if needed.

Each of these departments worked together to provide comprehensive support to youth engaged in the program. HA and S2C kept track of students' grades and sometimes communicated with students' teachers and administrators. Youth Lead staff members communicated with other departments when they saw a student facing a social or emotional challenge. The other staff members of Educational Excellence consisted of administrative staff, including assistants for the executive director and director of finance. Administrative staff members also included a handful of grant writers (permanent and temporary) and an admissions coordinator, a job managed by one staff member, Bernice Allan.

Research Methods and Researcher Role

In 2009, I secured employment as a part-time instructor for girls' programming within the Youth Lead department. In this role, I facilitated after-school courses for sixth, seventh, eighth, ninth, and tenth graders. In the summer of 2011, I began formal research with EE. I intended to study how youth workers identified and made sense of political and social problems. I sought to explore how their framing of Black youth, as a majority-led Black organization serving mostly Black youth of diverse ethnic backgrounds, informed the construction of their program and pedagogical practices. This study concluded in the spring of 2012. Next, between 2013 and 2015, I held formal interviews and informal conversations with youth workers who were previous participants in the study. The data presented in this book emerge from years of qualitative research, including participant observations and interviews with the full twenty-member staff at Educational Excellence between 2011 and 2012. After 2012, my follow-up interviews with key youth workers and new participants revealed the massive impact of the restructuring of EE. In 2018, I administered a survey questionnaire to former youth participants in order to gain insight into their experiences as students in the program and their thoughts about its transformation.

Qualitative researchers "study" individuals, communities, and phenomena in their own "natural settings, attempting to make sense of, or to interpret, phenomena in terms of the meanings people bring to them."[75] I chose a qualitative approach with ethnographic methods in order to learn and, in my case, relearn the cultural practices of participants at Educational Excellence and also to capture—while being immersed in the organization—the rich meaning making taking place there. With a critical lens, it was important for me to consider the social context in which participants operate.[76] Critical ethnographers have noted the importance of understanding participants in their historical, cultural, and social realities. Further, critical approaches to ethnographic work attempt to create social change through research by uncovering inequalities and problematizing them.[77] This epistemological frame was imperative for this study in order to understand how youth workers' thinking about, and practices with, youth were shaped by social, political, and cultural realities. Even more, it also considers the importance of my positionality as youth worker-researcher, which was essential to understand the ways youth workers made sense of social problems and their work with youth. EE, in particular, is an important space to study given that social and political problems are consistently problematized and analyzed within the program.

Researchers gain access to these sacred spaces and enter the lives of youth and communities to do research "on" and not alongside or with communities.[78] Given these practices, I was mindful of the importance of authentic and reciprocal relationships throughout the research process. I was honored by the trust my participants gave me and do not take the time they spent with me lightly. My role as both researcher and youth worker at Educational Excellence provided "trustworthiness" and a level of access I likely would not have received otherwise.[79]

By entering youth workers' "conceptual world,"[80] I immersed myself in the day-to-day flow of their lives at Educational Excellence. Because of this orientation in which my study is grounded, I was deliberate about being present in the space to observe youth workers and their practices as frequently as possible. During the first phase of research, between 2011 and 2012, participant observations occurred at program events for youth and their families over thirteen months, events during the holidays, middle and high school retreats, staff retreats, parent orientation meetings, curriculum planning meetings, and staff-development trainings. I wrote field notes before and after each workday. In order to triangulate participant observation data, every person on staff was interviewed individually and observed during (or in) staff meetings, organizational events, and while interacting with coworkers and students in the program. Three focus groups were held with staff based on the similarity of participants' work in the program (for example, all department directors, program coordinators, and volunteer coordinators). Additionally, I collected and analyzed program literature including annual reports, brochures, and course lesson plans in order to capture how students were framed within the organization and to others.

During the second phase of research, I made three visits between 2013 and 2015 to Educational Excellence to conduct follow-up interviews with youth workers who had previously participated in the study and who were present during the leadership transition (those who had left in 2012 or before were not asked to participate). Interviews were conducted with youth workers who were available and willing to be interviewed again. Interviews were also conducted with new staff members who were present during the restructuring. Previous participants were still employed at Educational Excellence, some had moved on to other organizations, and some were in between jobs. In 2017–2018, I developed and administered a questionnaire to former youth participants of Educational Excellence. The questionnaire asked alumni to reflect on their experiences with the organization and their time with staff members. Alumni were also asked if they had returned to the program since their graduation from high school and college and their thoughts about the changes made during the period of transition.

Overview of the Book

Chapter 2 tells the story of Educational Excellence and how it came to be. It covers the transformation of the program as a strict after-school academic program steeped in deficit rhetoric to a comprehensive program that includes emotional and social support as well as political education. This chapter discusses the competing framing (asset-based versus deficit) of Black youth among the organization's founder, Richard Dunn, board members, and current and new staff members in the program and the struggle to reimagine Black youth beyond deficit narratives rampant in the youth development and nonprofit funding world. Chapter 2 also explores how the trend toward neoliberal transformation affects the neighborhood EE calls home and the schooling experiences of youth in the program. This chapter captures youth workers' understanding of schools and how schools support and complicate their work with youth. Chapter 2 explores how youth workers become critical advocates and intercessors on the behalf of students, assisting them in navigating difficult school, family, and social barriers.

In Chapter 3, I examine how Black youth within after-school support spaces are often framed politically as "broken" and in need of "fixing." This chapter highlights the voices of youth workers as they navigate community-based youth work in the current national climate of education. It also discusses how the new leadership at Educational Excellence marked by education reform and the pressures youth workers felt to frame youth from a deficit perspective to compete for funding opportunities, political praise, and public recognition. This chapter describes how the common trend toward deficit framing is linked to the current neoliberal education market, which incentivizes community-based educational spaces to frame marginalized youth as socially, culturally, and intellectually deficient in order to successfully compete with charter schools for funding. In the words of Leah Davis and Monica Matthews, because "charter schools are the hot thing to invest in," traditional youth development programs have "disappeared from the landscape."

Chapter 4 discusses the departure of longtime executive director Leah Davis and its impact on EE. The context of EE and its cultural practices are reexamined through the new leadership of the organization. This chapter also explores the growing racial, class, and gender tensions between the organization's founder, executive leadership, and EE's board members. Chapter 4 examines the changing nature of leadership in the organization and its impact on the practices of youth workers, shifting priorities of the program, and the overall culture of the organization.

Chapter 5 explores how remaining youth workers strive to maintain strong and relevant pedagogical practices, familial-like culture, and an asset-rich ideology of youth in a new climate where organizational leadership is primarily concerned with funding, expansion, and greater exposure for the organization—without regard for the consequences for staff or student morale. As I illustrate, the camaraderie and relationships established between youth workers served as an anchor for accountability in the program. With relationships in jeopardy, accountability for resisting racist and deficit language withered and neoliberal expansion flourished under new leadership.

In Chapter 6, I examine the external pull (broader political and economic forces shaping public education) and internal push factors (competing frames of race, control, and paternalism between staff, the founder, and new leadership) that led youth workers away from Educational Excellence. Youth workers share their process for leaving the organization, what they learned during their time in the program, and reflections on challenging and rewarding experiences. Chapter 6 investigates the persistence of racism and neoliberalism within the current era of education that is eroding liberatory community-based spaces engaging Black youth.

Finally, in the Conclusion, I summarize the major findings of my research and highlight the major triumphs, challenges, and changes documented in the book. I make the case for researchers, policy makers, and community-based leaders to pay greater attention to the connections between racism, neoliberalism, education, and their impact on community-based youth work. I also place the story of Educational Excellence in a historical context of activism within Black communities who have long created alternative educational spaces for Black children to develop strong identities in a racist society. Through the lessons learned from Educational Excellence, I lay out a path for community-based leaders and youth workers to identify, name, and resist the complex dynamics of racism, anti-blackness, and politics that threaten their work with youth. Additionally, the conclusion lays out recommendations for both theory and practice that include (1) encouraging more scholarship that theorizes social location of community-based youth work and the deep pedagogical work that can occur within community-based after-school spaces that decenters schools; and (2) considering the potential effects of macroeconomic and social policies, such as education privatization, on after-school community-based spaces and cautioning against the erasure of the self-determination within community-based spaces as a result of the neoliberal turn.

Reclaiming Community

I employ "community" as a way of acknowledging the people and spaces outside of the structural boundaries of schools that have consistently fought for dignity and the right to educate Black youth. Understanding the social and political context of community-based educational spaces is critical for understanding how structural inequality is reproduced. As the threats to community-based youth organizations abound under the neoliberal era, the following questions arise: What educational spaces, if any, are free from structural and psychic violence against Black youth? Where can Black youth explore their multiple identities, think critically about the world around them, and be nurtured and guided by adults exhibiting radical care? What educational spaces can Black youth occupy where adults see them as fully whole human beings? Community-based youth organizations are these spaces, depicted as "places of refuge" against difficult school and societal circumstances. Yet as these spaces become increasingly vulnerable to market-based approaches to education reform, their efforts to expose youth of color to sociopolitical development and critical reflection on the worlds they navigate are undermined.[81] As community-based after-school spaces replicate the harms experienced in school, narrowing their support to standardized academic measures of success to appease funders, they lose their ability to nurture and affirm the identities of Black youth.

There are several outcomes that arise as a result of framing after-school spaces through a neoliberal lens. First, the capacity that after-school community-based spaces have for political, social, emotional, and cultural development for young people are dismissed, ignored, and overlooked in favor of only core academic support for students. As a result, the pedagogical possibilities within these spaces are neglected, thus narrowing the scope of these spaces and diminishing the skills and knowledge youth workers hold. Narrowing the scope and capacity of these programs also prevents Black youth from occupying spaces that nurture and affirm their identities. Second, community-based after-school programs run the risk of replicating harmful practices that occur within school. As flexibility is jeopardized, community organizations lose their autonomy to design and deliver programming in the way they see fit and in ways that meet the needs and interests of youth rather than being at the mercy of donors, foundations, and/or trends in educational policy.

Youth workers are an essential yet undertheorized and underutilized resource in education reform. They are typically thought of as important advocates for young people, yet their voices are seldom heard in important educational debates. Thus, youth workers' impact on young people's lives is not often acknowledged beyond nonprofit youth development circles. Given the long-standing research on the significance of after-school and community-based organizations on the academic and social lives of youth, greater theorization is needed to understand the social location of community-based youth work within the current education policy context and on the youth workers embedded within these programs. Sustaining, validating, and reclaiming community-based spaces for youth now is more critical than ever. As market-based approaches to education reform erodes public education, the necessity of protecting community spaces and the role they play in the lives of Black youth becomes increasingly urgent.

2 "The EE Family"

Framing Race, Youth, and Educational Possibilities

> This innocent country set you down in a ghetto in which, in fact, it intended
> that you should perish. Let me spell out precisely what I mean by that,
> for the heart of the matter is here, and the root of my dispute with my
> country. You were born where you were born and faced the future that you
> faced because you were black and for no other reason. The limits of your
> ambition were, thus, expected to be set forever. You were born into a
> society, which spelled out with brutal clarity, and in as many ways as
> possible, that you were a worthless human being. You were not expected to
> aspire to excellence: you were expected to make peace with mediocrity.
>
> —James Baldwin, The Fire Next Time

THERE IS NO SHORTAGE of imagery in film and television depicting poor Black young people in dire straits. From their neighborhoods to their families, images of suffering are ubiquitous. Black people in particular are often described as culturally and intellectually deficient. Whiteness is presumed to be the cultural and intellectual superior to all things as paternalism relies on white supremacy to portray non-white groups as being in need of saving or fixing by whiteness.[1] As a result, characterizations and images of Black youth being rescued or redeemed by white people are pervasive throughout American popular culture, politics, and literature. There is very little questioning of this positioning of Black people as needing to be rescued by whites or discussion of how white supremacy and anti-Blackness permeate the landscape and pose a constant threat to Black bodies. Even more disturbing is that very few critique the pervasive figure of the white savior or question its use as a strategy to accumulate wealth and land by dispossessing minoritized communities.[2]

In James Baldwin's epigraph, he captures the cruel yet very clear positioning of Black people in this country. For Black youth, the expectation of mediocrity, the limits of opportunity, and the denial of humanity by this country are real. This thinking has shaped every social institution, especially the system of schooling for Black young people. Written over fifty years ago, Baldwin's words capture the brutal honesty of how Blackness is imagined and treated even today. Theorists of anti-Blackness would argue that Blackness is not only shaped as a problem, in the DuBoisian sense, but also devoid of humanity.[3] In what Saidiya Hartman calls the "after-life of slavery," slavery is illegal under the law, yet there are everyday ways in which Blackness is positioned as slave, and agency, desire, and freedom are denied in contemporary Black life in America. From acts of police violence, to mass incarceration and inadequate schooling opportunities, there are countless examples of the ways in which Black bodies are rendered disposable and not worthy of care or protection.[4] The denial of humanity and disposability of Black life shapes the narratives and discourse about Black youth and the communities from which they come. How we imagine what's possible for Black youth is rooted in how we think about them.

Even within Black communities, Black youth and Black families can be depicted as problems. Geoffrey Canada, founder of the Harlem Children's Zone (HCZ), is regarded as an innovator in education. In one of his advertisements for his work with HCZ, Canada appeared in a commercial for its financial partner, American Express. At first glance, the commercial could be mistaken for a horror film. The black and white ad opens with an aerial shot of Harlem, New York. Canada's voice can be heard throughout the commercial speaking about the youth and families of Harlem. He says, "failure had become the norm in Harlem." He continues by saying "the schools were lousy," "violence was all around," "gangs were prevalent," and "families were falling apart." As images of students and the HCZ schools and programs appear, colored images replace the black and white ones. Although Canada pointed to problems like "lousy health care" and "lousy schools," many of the issues discussed centered on acts by the community and failed to identify larger structural and political problems. Throughout his career, Canada has become a media darling of the liberal Left and the business Right. His heightened media profile and his tendency to capitalize on deficit frames of Black youth in Harlem causes concern and conflict for many, yet I am reluctant to discredit anyone committed to trying to support Black youth.[5] Despite the effort that people like Canada make to improve educational experiences and outcomes for Black youth, there is a larger danger in a commercial like this. The imagery of darkness, the framing of Harlem and its residents as "problems" and lacking, and the positioning of Canada (alongside American Express) as a messianic figure fit a very troubling raced and gendered narrative that the political and social problems within majority Black urban centers are the fault of its residents and they need to be "lifted out" by some other entity. Even more, the presence of American Express also speaks to the intersections of racism, capitalism, and privatization further exacerbated by neoliberal ideology and its connection to and influence on education.

As an ideology embedded within every American institution, race and racism are pervasive forces that shape the experiences of all Americans and inform the educational experiences of youth of color in harmful ways.[6] As a socially constructed category, race continues to change and shift over time. In a post–civil rights era, notwithstanding the myth of a "postracial" era marked by the election of Barack Obama as president of the United States, racial rhetoric without the use of racist terminology continues to protect the pervasiveness of color-blind racism.[7] Neoliberalism is implicated in this process as it relies on particular assumptions about race and class while upholding privilege for those in power.[8] It touts equal opportunity while ignoring the impacts of structural inequality caused by racism and class disenfranchisement. As Henry Giroux argues, neoliberal racialized rhetoric "recodes itself within the vocabulary of the Civil Rights Movement,"[9] by asserting color-blind rhetoric rooted in meritocracy, thus making racism difficult to name. However, the steady reality of anti-Black racism evidenced by chronic high unemployment rates, consistent state-sanctioned violence against Black bodies, and continued subjugation to inadequate schools and disenfranchised neighborhoods prove to be significant barriers to social and academic progress.[10] As such, public discourse that frames and imagines Black youth informs how they are treated across and within the multiple spaces they occupy. Attempts to reframe and reimagine Black youth beyond suffering and deficit perspectives is critical to the story and transformation of Educational Excellence.

Educational Excellence and a Changing Dunbar

The story of Educational Excellence is as complicated as the story of Dunbar, the historic urban neighborhood in the northeastern city it calls home. The confluence of race, class, and power illustrated in Dunbar plays out within the organizational structure, culture, and transformation of EE. Dunbar is an intellectually and culturally rich setting to study a wide range of social and political processes. Dunbar has a long history of mobilizing for justice and equality as a center of Black cultural achievement. The building that EE calls home is indicative of Black excellence in academic, cultural, and political achievement. Iconic Black leaders and artists gathered to strategize, organize, and build community. At the same time, Dunbar receives national attention for disenfranchisement and poverty. In the public's imagining, Dunbar is both a culture-generating space and a place of marginalization. Although discourse about its disenfranchisement and marginalization is dominant, like many other cities in the United States, Dunbar is and has been much more economically and culturally diverse than common discourse suggests. Dunbar is also a source of pride for the participants in this study. As Faith Davenport, a native to the city and counseling psychologist at Educational Excellence says, "I just think of a place that carries a lot of history as well as a community that has a lot of needs that are not being met. . . . Historically speaking, I look at it as an African American community, rich in culture and history, but it's changed I mean in multiple ways."

Faith's analysis perfectly sums up Dunbar's complexities. The change that Faith is signaling is the persistence of gentrification in the city—"the return of the middle class and wealthy to cities, cities that through much of the twentieth century were markedly abandoned socially, politically, and economically."[11] The vast changes occurring in Dunbar include the transforming nature of public schooling characterized by the influx of large charter management organizations. Demographic shifts, stemming from gentrification and neoliberalism, make Dunbar an important place to study how race, place, and space change over time. Historically, Dunbar has been a predominantly Black and working-class neighborhood. But in recent years, it has experienced an exodus of poor residents and Black residents, as more affluent residents (white and people of color) rent and buy in the neighborhood. As property in Dunbar is increasingly bought by expensive large-scale chain restaurants and stores, and as white small business owners rapidly set up shop in the area, higher rent has pushed longtime residents and Black small business owners away. The average cost of rent for a two-bedroom apartment ranges between $3,000 and $4,000 per month, while the average monthly income is approximately $3,200 a month.

Gentrification is rarely discussed by scholars and residents with as much nuance as it deserves even though displacement of poor and working-poor residents in cities has economic, racial, and political consequences for neighborhoods, families, and individuals and their access to space, social mobility, and wealth.[12] The changing landscapes of neighborhoods within large metropolitan cities cannot be disconnected from how education is accessed and experienced. Neoliberal transformation has shaped every dimension of the Dunbar neighborhood—from the steady rise of charter schools to the influx of large chain restaurants and corporate retail chains. As such, Dunbar, a neighborhood world famous for its vibrancy and creation of Black culture, has shifted dramatically. Today, Black youth are growing up in a different Dunbar—one where gentrification has led to local businesses being replaced by high-end fashion boutiques, expensive restaurants, and trendy bars. Several youth workers featured in this book, who are native to the community and surrounding neighborhoods, note how many of the changes in Dunbar have shaped their work with youth and families. Some appreciate the benefits of having healthier food options that often come along with gentrifying neighborhoods[13] but are frustrated with the lack of reverence for the Black cultural vibrancy Dunbar is known for, which is reflected in Black bodies moving, working, and creating in the neighborhood. As scholars who study gentrification contend, class and race are inextricably linked; affluent gentrifiers of all racial backgrounds contribute to and support the process of gentrification.[14] As Mary Pattillo found in her study of Black middle-class life on the South Side of Chicago, Black middle-class residents supported the demolition of public housing in order to create more livable "desirable" communities.[15] At the same time, as affluent white residents descend on predominantly poor and working-class Black and Latinx neighborhoods, better services and resources appear, thus communicating to previous residents they are unworthy of such change.[16]

For youth workers at EE who are native to the area, the changes in Dunbar were met with frustration and worry of what would come next. On any given day, staff members would have conversations about the changes occurring in Dunbar. Alexandria, a California native and coordinator for alumni programming, saw the influx of high-end stores as a plan to get low-income residents to spend money on "frivolous material goods." Michaela, a native to the state and coordinator for middle school programming, said, "students talk about the change occurring in Dunbar often." I also observed students' frustration about many of the changes in the area. Some students expressed anger as they described tour bus lines carrying mostly white European tourists that cruise down major streets multiple times a day, as voyeurs of Black culture. They also noticed and spoke of the growing presence of white residents and higher-income residents in the area, which has resulted in more expensive restaurants and stores they no longer feel comfortable in or cannot afford to patronize.

In the five years following my initial engagement with Educational Excellence in 2008, the landscape of the Dunbar community dramatically changed, thus producing a very different space—one that is more white and wealthy and that does not seem to reflect the Black cultural vibrancy it once did. As expensive luxury condos, Whole Foods Markets, and high-end retail stores emerge, Dunbar has become a place of Black and poor suffering and a space of growing wealth and opportunity for those that have the means to live there. As I followed up with staff members between 2013 and 2015, many of them expressed how different Dunbar looked and felt to them. Upon visiting in 2013, parts of Dunbar were unrecognizable to me.

In the last decade or so, Dunbar has also been in a political spotlight due to educational innovations that have sought to provide comprehensive approaches to schooling by recognizing the importance of providing basic needs like health care and healthy food options for students within traditional school spaces. Dunbar is a compelling location to study because of the deep pockets of concentrated poverty,[17] which places Black youth at an educational disadvantage, despite its current population and economic shifts. In many ways, what is occurring in Dunbar is indicative of neoliberal transformations taking place in other cities like Philadelphia, New Orleans, and Chicago.[18] In part, one of the goals of this book is to acknowledge the significant role that social and political context plays in the construction, implementation, and day-to-day cultural practices within community-based after-school spaces engaging minoritized youth.

Change is constant; neighborhoods shift frequently, and they are expected to. However, neighborhoods are affected by macro-level political, social, and economic changes that shape, restructure, and reorganize them. As broader political forces change neighborhoods, micro-level patterns and processes orient residents and facilitate the creation of resources and services that no longer meet the needs of the original inhabitants of the neighborhood.[19] The neoliberal turn in politics has restructured how we think about education, and it has decimated neighborhoods in major cities. For Black communities, neoliberal influence in education and employment has created perilous effects on Black life.[20] As public education in this country shifts to a business enterprise (for example, education management organizations, and voucher programs), individual explanations for educational failure (that is, poor performance on standardized assessments, grades) are offered that are devoid of any structural explanations. Dunbar is draped by a shifting political and economic landscape that shapes not only the construction of EE but the lives of its leaders, staff, and youth participants.

A Deeper Look at Educational Excellence

The physical space Educational Excellence calls home is relatively small considering the fact that a few hundred students are served on an average day and when compared to the spaces of other large-scale youth programs in the neighborhood. Flags representing over a hundred colleges and universities cover the central area of the floor where staff members' offices are located. The remaining space is composed of six classrooms, a small library used as a meeting space, two computer labs for students, and a student lounge with walls holding laminated college acceptance letters from student alumni. Dull blue walls in this section are lined with students' artwork, essays, and photographs that capture students' and youth workers' experiences at program events throughout the city. One wall holds the entire history of EE's cultural learning program in which students have traveled to countries in South America, the Caribbean, West Africa, and Europe, where they engaged in cultural exchanges and action projects alongside other youth. The aesthetic features of the physical space send a powerful message to students that higher education is not only attainable but an expectation.

During the weekday, "the Floor," a term affectionately used by youth and staff in the program to refer to the EE program, is relatively quiet between the hours of 10:00 A.M. and 3:30 P.M. With a familial-like rapport, staff members can be heard throughout the hallways laughing or sharing stories during their lunch break about life in Dunbar and their experiences with youth. Between 3:30 and 4:00 P.M., students trickle in from their respective schools to attend EE's after-school programming, which begins at 4:30 P.M. As students arrive, youth workers greet them with a series of questions that often include, "How are you?"; "How was school today?"; and "Where's that report card I asked for last week?" As students wait for their classes to begin, they gather in the middle school or high school lounge as the smell of McDonald's french fries, sandwiches from the corner store, and snacks provided by the program fills the air. Some youths begin their homework, some catch up on reading, while others play board and card games with youth workers and adult volunteers. Between these hours, the volume in the space increases and the floor becomes full of energy and laughter. Staff members use this time to talk with students about their performance in school or attendance in the program or to assist students with personal issues. A few minutes before 4:30 P.M., youth workers begin ushering students to their respective classrooms for after-school programming. These courses range from academic classes that help students with English and writing through literature like Octavia Butler's *Parable of the Sower*, math classes on scale and proportion through architecture around the globe, elective courses on the role music played in the Black Freedom Struggle, or youth development classes about critical media literacy. As students go off to their respective classrooms, staff members who do not have direct engagement with students return to their office for meetings, to complete paperwork or other projects. A few minutes before students are dismissed (6:00 P.M. for middle school students, 6:30 P.M. for high school students), staff members emerge from their offices to greet students and ensure they get on the elevator and out of the building safely. After leaving "the Floor," some students gather in front of the building on the street or in front of the corner store rehashing what went on in their days. But this gathering is often short-lived as youth workers come back down the elevator to make sure that students leave the corner. Youth workers recognize that the streets of Dunbar are not safe for Black and Latinx youth to congregate as police officers routinely harass, stop, and frisk them without cause.[21]

The aesthetic features of Educational Excellence and the structure youth workers provide for students are important for the culture of programming, learning, and engagement at EE. From the moment young people step onto the floor, they see pictures of previous students' acceptance letters to college, they see college flags, and they are greeted by an adult interested in their lives in and out of school. In classes, students are challenged to think about their social identities, race, class, sexuality and gender (and the intersections between), and the ways in which they engage with media on a daily basis. They participate in courses that enhance their academic experiences with English and math through culturally relevant and youth-centered ways.

Defining education more broadly to include traditional core academic subjects, socioemotional learning, and sociocultural and political development is invaluable to how youth learn and deconstruct their social worlds. Though community-based educational spaces are philosophically and pedagogically diverse, relegating them to merely spaces of tutoring and academic support dismisses the role they can play in other important aspects of a young person's life. As a term, "community-based educational spaces" decenters school and highlights the agency and strength of community and the educators within them.[22] As many school settings across the nation perpetuate inequality and deficit discourses about Black youth, community-based spaces seemingly have the autonomy to redefine Black youth in more humanizing and restorative ways. Community-based educational spaces exist within this dialectic space where they have the ability to both disrupt and reproduce inequality.[23] For example, their relative autonomy but simultaneous reliance on the State or foundations for funding places them in a vulnerable position.[24] EE's deep focus on academic achievement and sociocultural political education is remarkable. However, funding from philanthropists and foundations also raises tensions and contradictions. At the same time, EE's focus on academic achievement and sociocultural political development is a form of both compliance and resistance to neoliberal logics of success. Further, the social and political condition of Dunbar and the larger city and state matters to the organization. In other words, just as the social context of schools matters to the experiences young people will have within them, community-based youth programs are also informed by their social context. The ever-changing landscape of Dunbar shapes the story of EE just as much as the people who lead the organization and the students and families who rely on EE for support.

The History, Social, and Political Context of Educational Excellence

Literature on community-based youth organizations often lacks deep analyses of how social context matters to after-school community-based youth work. For instance, broader social and educational policies shape the lives of youth and their families; and the influence of racism, hypersurveillance of minoritized youth, and other social harms that converge in the lives of students matter deeply to the learning experiences and outcomes of youth inside and outside of schools. Understanding the social context of community-based educational environments is important for those looking to work in and build spaces for and with youth and for those who desire to work with youth in these spaces. Although the youth workers featured in this book held different political leanings and understandings of the world, they held sophisticated understandings of how educational policies, race, gender, and class shaped how Educational

Excellence was framed and positioned next to other programs in the area. Even more, they understood how broader social, political, and economic forces shaped students' academic and social experiences in the program.

In the 1980s, the proliferation of arrests for crack cocaine, in part generated by the Reagan administration's War on Drugs, ravished Black cities throughout the country.[25] During this time, community-based nonprofit programs, including EE, were established through the support of the government as well as through the efforts of community residents in neighborhoods similar to Dunbar.[26] There are many national after-school agencies located in the Dunbar community, such as the YMCA, the Boys and Girls Club, and the Children's Aid Society—programs that support young people and the community at large. Such programs have a long history of supporting families and youth.

EE was founded in 1989 by Richard Dunn, a white and wealthy real-estate tycoon and philanthropist, with the purpose of connecting youth in Dunbar with adult role models who could encourage them to pursue higher education. Between 1989 and 2002, EE operated as a mentorship program during after-school hours designed to get youth of color into prestigious colleges and universities. EE developed partnerships with middle schools in Dunbar and offered after-school tutoring and fostered relationship building between youth and adults. After-school programs were designed for middle and high school participants. Richard recruited well-connected and wealthy colleagues in banking, law, and real estate and a few prominent academics to serve on the Board of Directors.

In 2002, Leah Davis was hired as the new executive director of Educational Excellence. Under Leah's leadership, the organization developed new recruitment strategies with tweaks to the program structure. As the demographics of the program shifted from Latinx to predominantly Black (with varying ethnic identities, including Dominican and Puerto Rican), EE began to market itself as a "college completion and youth development organization." Leah, a Black woman, was a former school administrator, classroom teacher, and east coast native. Leah felt strongly that a comprehensive and holistic approach to education was critical for the development of Black youth. This belief was rooted in her upbringing as she shared that her mother "wasn't counting on schools to educate [her]." In addition to changing EE's relationship to neighboring schools, Leah worked feverishly to change the narrative EE held of minoritized youth and their families.

With a kind face and sometimes stern demeanor, Leah took the education of Black youth seriously. Often described as a "visionary" by youth workers,

Leah provided direction for the staff in ways that sometimes came off as tough. During our first interview, Leah shared that deficit rhetoric such as "at risk" and "broken" were used frequently to describe youth in the program and was regularly displayed on the organization's literature. She also indicated that the staff was "unprofessional" when she arrived. In her attempt to describe Black youth in more humanizing ways and provide leadership to a highly "unprofessional staff," she was met with resistance by the organization's Board of Directors, Richard (EE's founder), and staff members. As a newer staff member, I often heard comments from longtime employees that "EE was out of control" before Leah's tenure as executive director. Curious about what "out of control" meant, I learned more when I interviewed Leah. The next section offers her perspective on EE at the time of her arrival, how she set out to transform the program, and her challenges and triumphs along the way.

Challenging Low Expectations and Deficit Rhetoric

Leah Davis was born and raised on the East Coast with family ancestry in the Caribbean. Leah's early educational experiences were spent in Afrocentric primary schools and in Black middle-class contexts. Leah's journey from school educator to nonprofit leader provided her with insight into how both students and parents were challenged by the education system in the city. Leah once worked as an administrator in a school that she described as being "forgotten by the city." After working in school contexts, she went on to pursue a doctorate of education at an Ivy League institution, while holding positions at various nonprofit educational organizations and after-school programs. A former colleague and friend encouraged her to apply for the executive director vacancy at Educational Excellence in 2002. Leah became the executive director of Educational Excellence at the age of 33. When I asked Leah to share her first impressions of the program and her initial attraction to the organization, she laughed and replied: "Nothing." Later she shared that she accepted the offer because it allowed her a unique opportunity to build and rebrand a program.

In our first interview, Leah was very candid in her description of the way EE "used to be" prior to her hiring as executive director. Within Leah's first two years as executive director, she fired the majority of the staff that was present before she arrived. She described an environment of total "chaos" led by an "unprofessional" staff. The first experience she shared with me was the moment she received her first piece of organizational literature. Leah explained: "So, one of the first pieces of printed material I got from EE . . . was a picture of a Latino kid and the caption said, 'If it wasn't for EE, I'd be in jail or in a coffin.'" Leah said that she held onto the brochure because she was not sure if anyone would ever believe her that it existed. "Yeah, I just have to keep it. Come on . . . you can't make this stuff up. And people might not believe you." This piece of literature reflects the deficit-oriented rhetoric often used to describe Black and Latinx youth. The trope of "if it wasn't for [fill in the blank], I would be in jail or dead" is all too common in youth development and in education philanthropy. This very type of positioning of Black and Latinx youth paves the way for saviors or messianic figures.[27] The framing of Black and Latinx youth as deficient and worthy of saving by after-school spaces and well-meaning white liberals is a phenomenon that perpetuates the belief in white saviors and white goodness and further designates Black youth and other minoritized youths as problems to be fixed or as threats to be destroyed.[28]

In addition to deficit framing of youth, Leah also talked extensively about the low expectations staff members held for students in the program, despite the organization's public assertion that the program promoted "high expectations" for everyone. In describing her predecessor, Leah suggested that "enabling" behavior among white liberals contributed to the lack of rigor and low expectations. She explained:

> So yeah, my predecessor was white and I think that [pause] there's a category of white liberal [pause] that is very enabling, and in the process of being enabling and apologetic, you fail to set a high standard for your kids. So, I think the kids who were destined to do well were doing well at EE. I think that the kids who were on the cusp didn't have the kick in the behind that they needed. The bar was just too low. It's like, you have a program called "high achievers" and you have really low expectations. So, it's like "well so and so mother's is so and so." So, what? We all have a hard luck story. You know, buck up, keep strong, keep it moving [laughter]. Not to be uncaring and unkind, but our kids don't have that luxury.

Upon hearing Leah's perspectives on the low expectations held for students in the program at the beginning of her tenure, I thought some might interpret her comments as being reflective of bootstraps rhetoric—perspectives devoid of structural explanations for the barriers youth of color endure in the U.S. public school system. As I would come to discover throughout my research, there was nuance as well as contradiction in the understanding of structural conditions and cultural responses to those conditions among EE youth workers.

Discussions of structural versus cultural explanations for underachievement, poverty, or lack of social mobility are often contentious and polarizing within sociological literature.[29] Despite the tension that arises from this discourse, EE youth workers conveyed an understanding of the structural constraints that shaped the educational opportunities for youth in their programming through their youth development curricula. At the same time, cultural explanations for academic challenges resulted in "personal responsibility" rhetoric by some staff members. There were moments where staff members used structural and systemic inequality as the major contribution to the experiences and performance of Black youth in schools. At the same time—sometimes in the same sentence—there were moments in which staff members' rhetoric reflected cultural pathological explanations and discourse that often created tension between staff members. Leah thought that Richard and those in power before her believed that Black youth were inherently incapable of meeting high standards. She also believed the bar was set low because of "enabling" behavior she attributes to white liberal guilt for the structural conditions that constrain opportunities for people of color.

When Leah began her tenure as the executive director, the department directors and youth workers in the organization underwhelmed her. In addition to Leah's assertion that youth workers set the bar too low for students, she also considered them to be highly unprofessional. Leah described an environment where the directors gave little oversight to staff members working directly with youth. I asked Leah to elaborate on what she considered to be unprofessional behavior. She discussed several issues upon her arrival:

> Uh, where do I begin? So, we had a counseling person, whose boyfriend used to come here at lunchtime and spend about two hours in her locked office and she was not fired. She cursed out the executive director and she was not fired. I had arranged for us to meet with the then superintendent of high schools from Dunbar and somehow she was going to be the staff person to go with me on the site visit and she came to work in a halter with no bra and was like "are we ready to go?" I was like, "I'm in my suit and I'm ready to go and you are not ready to go. So, I will." It was just stuff like that and I felt very disappointed to see people of color who should've known better, not raising the bar. Like, don't come to work in your cutoff jean shorts. If you want the kids to respect the work that we do, then act like you respect yourself. Be an example of what they aspire to. 'Cause they can get all that nonsense on [the] street before they come

upstairs. . . . There were a lot of young professionals here and they liked to hang out socially and they used to drink in the office before they went out so they could save on bar tabs. So, they all hated me. It was like "who do you think you are?" I was like "I think I'm the boss; you gotta go."

Other staff members agreed that prior to Leah's arrival, the staff was unprofessional. Although many might agree with Leah, it is hard to ignore the race, class, and gender-based undercurrent in Leah's workplace etiquette commentary. As Evelyn Brooks Higginbotham argues, the politics of respectability within Black communities is a set of very specific gendered and class-based practices that disavow particular "dress styles, leisure activities, and speech patterns" that ultimately disrupt the "metalanguage of race" evoked by those within and outside Black communities.[30] EE's desire for youth and staff to adhere to specific styles of dress and speech continued to surface throughout my research, sometimes in problematic ways.

In addition to battling an uncooperative and "unprofessional" staff, Leah also faced resistance from the Board of Directors that had approved her hire. Leah noted that many of the board members, the majority of whom at the time were white, had little insight into broader educational issues, especially those facing Black youth. Nor did they have a deep understanding of the social and political problems that inform the educational experiences and outcomes for students. The board also held deficit perspectives about Black youth and their families; many of their understandings of the problems plaguing the Black community in the area reflected the tone set by the founder of the organization, Richard Dunn. According to Leah and others, the board's deficit understandings of Black youth were reflected in the way they discussed youth and the work of the organization: "the first year was very hard. I think on one hand, I was battling staff . . . and then you had the board who was like, 'Why are you calling them scholars?' Like, 'They're poor kids, they're from the inner-city, you know we want to help them be a part of the mainstream,'" shared Leah.

Leah's resistance to the board's desire to move EE students toward "the mainstream" reflects a particular kind of raced, classed, and cultural discourse among Richard and the board rooted in deficit ideology about Black youth.[31] Here, mainstream represents middle-class white norms and values. As Barbara Beatty explains, the politics of popular expression regarding educational inequality, characterized by labels such as "culturally deprived," "culturally disadvantaged," and "at risk," has operated for decades. These terms, in their evolution from the 1960s to today, all evoke inherent judgments, perpetuate cultural pathological explanations for underachievement, and further designate what Black and Latinx students bring to educational spaces as different and therefore less than and lacking.[32] More specifically, compensatory education and after-school programs were thought to be important to help Black and Latinx students enter into "mainstream" culture—signaling the importance of white middle-class values by ignoring and diminishing the complex cultural forms and expressions of minoritized youth.[33]

Fighting a resistant staff on one side and a resistant board on the other proved to be a challenge for Leah. When I asked how she was able to continue working in such an environment, she explained, "I had a blank canvas." Leah shared that she wanted to mold the organization into the kind of program that truly held high expectations for youth of color and created a culture of excellence through knowledgeable, skilled, and professional youth workers. With her blank canvas, Leah spent her first few years as executive director "raising the profile on a national and international scale." When Leah became executive director, attendance was low and after-school programs were practically nonexistent:

> When I came to EE there were maybe under thirty kids in the middle school program; average after school daily attendance was like four kids . . . but there were fifty-six on the high school roster. I never saw more than maybe twenty-five, and certainly not all at the same time. So, you had an after-school program with no after-school and lots of individual successes, but not to scale.

Leah quickly made important hiring decisions to revamp the organization's youth programming. As part of her educational philosophy, she hired program directors who had backgrounds in education and extensive years in youth work outside of schools and who understood the importance of "whole child" and "student-centered" learning—meaning that young people's full lives as human beings were nurtured and their opinions were included in program development. In the first two years of her tenure as executive director, Leah created a new vision for the program, taglines, and logos. Within a few short years, EE began receiving local and national nominations for awards that highlighted nonprofit organizations working with youth in the city. The staff she would hire helped reshape the tone, purpose, and narrative of the organization.

Changing the Narrative

While being immersed in the day-to-day flow of the organization, youth workers and staff members can be heard referring to student participants as "scholars" or as being "college bound." Affirming and asset-rich language was embedded into all aspects of the program, including direct engagement with youth, on texts posted around the physical space such as in classrooms and hallways, and in program literature. Affirming language like "scholar" or "college bound" was second nature to youth workers and, as a result of the culture of the program, second nature to youth as well. To learn that the board resisted affirming language taught me just how divergent the framing of youth was within Educational Excellence among those responsible for advocating on behalf of the program to donors and foundations.

It also struck me that as an executive director who creates a vision and manages a staff, and who also works with the board to secure funding for the program, Leah was often placed in confounding and uncomfortable situations. As my conversations continued with Leah, other executive leadership members, and department directors, I learned that the resistance Leah experienced with the board was mirrored by her tense relationship with the organization's founder and largest financier, Richard Dunn. The relationship dynamic between Leah and Richard reflected a struggle for power rooted in race, gender dynamics, and paternalism that eventually led to Leah's resignation after ten years of service.

Leah and Monica Matthews, EE's director of programs, often discussed the contentious relationship with Richard as EE's major benefactor, founder, and active board member. There was a collective feeling and understanding about Richard among staff in the organization that he held paternalistic and deficit views of Black youth and the families from which they come. According to Leah, the twenty-one-member Board of Directors consisted mostly of supporters of Richard, and for this reason, the board often espoused cultural pathological explanations for the disenfranchisement of Black youth and families. EE's board was made up primarily of people from the corporate world, including banking, law, real estate, and some university professors.

On one late afternoon, staff and youth workers gathered for lunch as they normally did. Leah sometimes joined the staff for lunch as she did on this day. As everyone ate, a casual conversation ensued about Richard and the Board of Directors. Youth workers began discussing individual board members over lunch. The majority of them were described as personal friends of Richard who served on the board as a favor to him. Leah described the board as a conservative group and shared that she was "not always transparent" with the board because of their conservative positions on politics and social issues. I observed this lack of transparency occur in a few ways, including after-school course curricula and engaging students and staff in dialogue about race and structural inequality. For example, social identity development, which includes the study of race, gender, sexuality, and social class, were important in Leah's communication to the board, yet she downplayed how much these courses focused on systems of oppression. The more conservative components of the program, as described by youth workers, were often reframed in the classroom to be less conservative or laden with value judgments. To further illustrate, upon entering EE as a part-time instructor for girls, I was presented with a "pro-abstinence" curriculum intended for seventh graders. Solomon Modupe, the youth development coordinator and instructor working with boys, and I were uncomfortable with the title of the course, "Pro-Abstinence," because of the inherent values it validated. We both felt that a title that reflected making informed choices was a better approach to the course. Camille Kent, the coordinator for youth counseling and fellow member of the Youth Lead team, felt similarly, explaining, "I think we need to incorporate something else for when students get older because just thinking about students that I sit in the room with and do counseling with, they're [sexually] active. . . . I think we have to kind of incorporate some safety, because they're going to do it and I'd rather them hear it from a safe place where they feel comfortable." After some rallying, Dr. Faith Davenport, the director of Youth Lead, brought our concerns to Leah, who approved the course title change to "Making Proud Choices," a curriculum by Planned Parenthood. Through conversations with Faith and Leah about the initial findings from my research, I was told that the designation of "pro-abstinence" was a decision made and encouraged by the Board of Directors and Richard Dunn. As time went on, Solomon and I wanted to implement new curricula that would challenge the students to think even more critically about social institutions and structural inequality. Faith would often say, "well, you know how the board is," but would still approach Leah for approval, which she almost always granted. Curious about the level of power and control Richard had over some aspects of programming, through my interviews, I learned that he was always vocal in board meetings and received very little resistance from other members.

"The Problem with Black America"

"The problem with black America is that fourteen-year-old Black girls don't know how to keep their legs closed." According to Leah, Richard Dunn made this comment in a room of majority white donors, city officials, and other education stakeholders in the city. Leah sat in the front row, horrified as she was slated to speak after Richard. As she shared this moment with me, her voice bordered on indignant and humorous as she recalled the moment Richard looked directly at her. In that moment, Leah knew that her days as executive director of EE would soon come to an end. Although this particular incident took place in 2012, versions of this perspective were shared widely, through Richard's public speeches and essays. In a speech given at an Ivy League university in February 2011, Richard said,

> Black churches and community leaders, along with Black publications and Black radio and Black TV programs, must take the lead in changing inner-city child-raising practices, pleading with young girls not to have babies until they have completed their education, and convincing young men to assume responsibility for the children they father.

Considering remarks like this from one of Richard's speeches, the focus on "pro-abstinence" in the program as well as his public comments during the event Leah was present for are not surprising even though they were quite upsetting to her and other staff members. Given Richard's attitudes about Black girls and women, I spoke with Leah close to three years after her resignation from EE, in order to understand her perspective on her working relationship with Richard. Our conversation was illuminating.

Staff members often discussed Richard and Leah's contentious relationship. Leah shared that she had "dozens" of stories about things Richard would say about Black families, Black youth, and, in particular, Black women. Because he was someone with immense power in the philanthropic community, learning about Richard's deeply anti-Black perspectives about Black people is troubling but not surprising. The history of philanthropy in the nonprofit sector is deeply tied to paternalism and racism.[34] Ruth Gilmore, in a poignant essay about the "nonprofit industrial complex," discusses the ways in which nonprofits' dependency on relationships of financial giving is entrenched in neoliberal capitalist values that indirectly (and sometimes directly) thwart the rise of organizations that seek to create social change rooted in social justice frameworks. This point has been supported by other scholars, social activists, and nonprofit leaders;[35] the relationship between philanthropy, the capitalist state, and neoliberalism constrains organizations in ways that make community-based organizations particularly vulnerable to the power yielded by large donors and foundations.[36]

Richard goes on speaking tours throughout the country and abroad to discuss his philanthropic efforts. Many of his speeches and essays reflect cultural and individual explanations for poverty and underachievement within Black and Latinx communities. According to Leah and his own essays, Richard often argues for "the intellectual superiority of Jews and Asian Americans" and often compares their "successes" to the "failures" of Black and Latinx communities. In the same speech, Richard claims,

> The Chinese attribute their relative success to Confucian values like emphasis on education, diligence, merit, and reflecting well on the family. Jews traditionally attribute theirs to the high value they place on literacy, family cohesiveness, individual responsibility, and a focus on the future.

Richard's public speeches denounce Black "demagogues" who he believes promote "victimization," and his speeches ignore the social progress Black people have made, which he argues sends the wrong message to "inner-city youngsters":

> Prominent black demagogues usually look backward, rarely around them, and never forward, ignoring the remarkable progress that much of the black world has made, and also ignoring the factors that made such progress possible. The counterproductive message of victimization and militant despair sends the wrong signals to inner-city youngsters, whose conclusion is "Why try?" when the message should be constructive, pointing the path toward personal progress in a complex world.

When Richard made appearances during after-school classes, he often made staff members uncomfortable with his requests or when he shared his displeasure with certain activities. For example, Solomon, a youth worker supervised by Faith, recounted in an interview an occasion when Richard made a visit to EE with a donor. Some of the high school students were participating in a cultural history lesson on the connections between Dominican culture and African American culture in the city. A popular cultural center in the community that regularly celebrated Afro-Latinx history and culture was teaching students drumming linked to history and other art forms. Upon entering a classroom where the drumming was taking place, Richard became infuriated. Later Solomon found out from Faith, his supervisor, that Richard had angrily questioned Leah about her work in the organization during his visit. All future appearances at EE by Richard heightened directors' and youth workers' anxieties.

Given Richard's racial attitudes toward Black youth and families, it is not hard to understand why Leah was not always forthcoming and transparent with the board about the day-to-day pedagogical strategies employed during after-school courses and student retreats. In a discussion with Leah, she laughed as she recalled high school students Nasir and Jamal exclaiming, "Black people aren't paying for this? We're so revolutionary!" She responded, "I'm doing it on a sneak tip, so shhh." It is quite remarkable how the program itself was able to have such a strong stance on racial identity and social consciousness for ten years, such that youth often assumed that Black people financially supported the organization. In some ways, Leah's exchange with Nasir and Jamal represents the subversive nature of Black political resistance within diverse educational spaces. However, beyond Black political resistance, efforts from communities to exist in their own imagining of themselves are impressive considering the demands and pressure from foundations and donors. The right to self-determination and agency within marginalized communities has often been in conflict with white philanthropy where control is sought not just because of the power of money but also because of the power of race. James Anderson's seminal text about Black education in the South during Reconstruction, for example, provides a rich analysis of the ways Black communities created public educational opportunity and sought the resources of white northerners but fought to control the narrative of their communities and the right to educate Black youth in the way they saw fit.[37] Controlling the narrative of communities of color and having the freedom to educate youth in the way the community deems fit is an essential facet of self-determination and community agency.

Race, Culture, and Politics at Educational Excellence

From my years of working with community-based youth organizations, I recognized that EE was one of the few programs that unapologetically and successfully educated students about the significance of racial, cultural, and political identity in ways that were integrated into their academic identities. The pedagogical core of Educational Excellence is rooted in the understanding that "whole child" development should be central to youth work, especially for

Black and other minoritized youth. Scholars of community-based youth work have written extensively about the importance of nurturing the socio-cultural and political lives of youth of color,[38] yet oftentimes the social context of student's lived realities are ignored in approaches to youth development.[39] Social justice youth development has been a useful framework for understanding the process youth workers can utilize in guiding youth of color through social and political problems.[40]

During the mid-1980s through the early 1990s, research on adolescent development was largely dominated by psychology and focused on Black and Latinx youth as problems, and prevention efforts were focused on keeping them from becoming problems.[41] Later in the 1990s, youth development as a field began to highlight youth assets and acknowledged the strengths that youth already possessed. Known as positive youth development, this approach helped to reframe some research on youth from problem-driven to asset-driven.[42] As a result, positive youth development shifted commonly held assumptions about youth, policy, and practices by focusing on broader forms of development including emotional well-being, skill building, and recognizing youth as agents. Although positive youth development as an approach shifted scholarship on youth away from problem and prevention narratives, it has been criticized for not accounting for the social forces that shape the lives of youth of color in urban settings. As scholars Shawn Ginwright and Julio Cammarota explain, both models, problem/prevention and positive youth development, "[obscure] our understanding of urban youth of color more than they explain, because they assume that youth themselves should be changed, rather than the oppressive environments in which they live."[43] Ginwright and Cammarota, therefore, offer as an alternative social justice youth development (SJYD), which pays close attention to the relationship between critical consciousness and social action. They posit that although social forces are pervasive and powerful enough to impede the lives of youth of color, they can still challenge, contest, and resist these forces. SJYD mirrors Freire's concept of *conscientização* by recognizing that the conditions that surround the lives of young people are not immutable and can be changed through various acts of resistance.[44] The integration of critical consciousness and social action is essential for how youth make sense of the world and begin to change it.

Stemming from this scholarship, there are many scholars who have documented how community-based organizations have been important spaces for youth of color to develop tools to make sense of and deconstruct political and social problems in order to transform them.[45] The political education of minoritized youth has been a critical component of community-based youth work. Many community-based organizations have the flexibility to work with youth to develop their sociocultural identities and nurture their understanding of the world. As I and other scholars have argued, although it is important to understand the social and cultural lives of young people, this understanding should also encompass the social and political context from which they come.[46]

At EE, youth workers' dispositions and orientations toward social and political problems informed their comfort in discussing issues of race, power, and oppression. It allowed them to be candid with each other and with young people about the role of race in their lives. Youth workers should understand the importance of social context and how it shapes their family, school, and other positions and spaces they occupy. In conducting research with youth workers at Educational Excellence, I found that their broad understanding of the social context of schooling was not only impactful, but their intricate knowledge and critiques of formal schooling bolstered their attention to the experiences of youth and fostered the development of after-school classes and pedagogical tools that were in stark contrast to what students experienced in their school classrooms. It is important to note that EE youth workers' understanding of the school system as well as larger social and political problems was a function of their own social and cultural understanding of the world. Yet youth workers at EE were not monolithic in their thinking about social and political problems. In fact, disagreements about race and culture as these related to the academic outcomes of Black youth were often debated. One staff member, Terry Niles, the director of the Step 2 College program (and later the director of programs), prided himself on providing tough love and making decisions free from emotion in order to hold high expectations for students. His perspective was sometimes the outlier compared with others, yet dialogue among workers was encouraged and occurred quite frequently, usually prior to the arrival of students during the staff's lunch hour, in staff professional development meetings, or in informal conversations in the offices of staff members. For instance, during a focus group conversation among directors Faith Davenport, Walidah Thomas, and Terry Niles, a back-and-forth dialogue ensued between Terry and Walidah about the most pressing issues facing Black youth:

> TERRY: The question I always ask myself is it doesn't appear that Black Americans value education. . . . Just looking at statistics, white and Asians also, of

course economics plays a big role in that, it doesn't seem that education is valued as highly in, unfortunately, Black American households.

WALIDAH: We go can go into a history lesson around that. That's what complicates all these issues. It's not what you see on the surface. There's a whole lineage of issues from social to political stuff that plays into why people are doing what they're doing.

As I sat and listened to these conversations, I was often amazed at the level of comfort and ease with which youth workers disagreed with each other. True to a family-like atmosphere, youth workers and directors held intense conversations about politics, education, the state of Black communities, class, and sexism, and the list goes on and on. Very few political topics were off limits.

"Not Like School"   As a community-based after-school program, Educational Excellence deliberately tries to foster an environment distinct from school through the relationships cultivated between youth workers and students and through program culture and pedagogy. EE brands itself as an "asset-based" program—one that takes into consideration in the development of its programming the skills, gifts, and talents that youth already possess. Asset-based ideologies reject deficit notions of youth, believing that they do not inherently lack something that organizations or individuals provide. In their attempt to situate youth as powerful actors and creators in their own lives, youth workers at EE believed that their job as educators was to nurture the gifts that youth already possess and expose them to opportunities that would continue to support their growth. As Faith once said, "we're here to enhance, not fix young people." Educational Excellence's asset-rich approach to working with Black youth and youth workers' understanding of education as comprehensive—including academic, social, emotional, political, and cultural work—were central to the organization's cultural practices and pedagogical innovations once Leah, Faith, and Monica joined the organization. Drawing on their previous work with youth inside and outside of schools, these staff members can be credited with executing the asset-based and identity-affirming approach to EE's programming and engagement with youth.

Since its founding, Educational Excellence has formed partnerships with local middle and high schools in order to recruit participants. After the first few years of Leah's tenure as director, she redesigned the recruitment practices of the program and hired Bernice Allan, a longtime educator and former librarian, as the admissions director. As the eldest member of the staff she was referred to as Ms. Allan by staff and students alike. Ms. Allan was charged with expanding the organization's outreach to go beyond just schools to include various community spaces, including libraries and parent organizations (both within and out of schools), in order to reach a broader range of students. New youth participants often hear about EE through word of mouth, frequently from families of students already in the program. Students typically enter the program in the sixth grade and are considered members through their graduation from college. As Monica often said, "once in EE, you're always in EE." Monica and Leah often referred to EE as a "continuum" or, as others might describe, a pipeline, where there is a long-term investment and commitment to youth. Research has shown that sustained engagement with youth for longer periods of time can have greater results and outcomes for development.[47] When youth workers have the opportunity to work with students and families for a sustained amount of time, meaningful relationships can develop and youth workers can become knowledgeable of the multiple spheres of influence shaping the lives of youth. This model allows youth workers to track students' progress over time. At EE, the admissions coordinator, Ms. Allan, diligently worked to engage entire families in the program: "I also keep in touch with families. I grab their younger brothers and sisters, keep asking them how old they are, so that we have some families that have several cycles of [students at EE]. We have one family that has two kids in college, a step-daughter, [and] a granddaughter," she explained. The trust established in a long-term relationship engenders an opportunity that allows youth workers to create deep connections with youth.[48]

The intentional attention youth workers paid to race and its intersections with other social forces provided an important lens on schooling and education that made their approach in after-school courses relevant to youth participants. In addition to providing youth development courses where instructors discussed the social construction of and social reality of race, topics related to race and inequality were integrated into nonacademic courses quite frequently. Additionally, staff members held monthly professional development workshops, where they were asked on occasion to personally reflect on their own social identities, learn about social conditions that were going to be discussed with youth—such as the school-to-prison pipeline—and connect new learning tools to the social conditions youth experienced, conditions often rooted in race, class, and gender. In casual settings such as lunchtime, youth workers often engaged in conversations that ranged from serious political conversations about the "state of the Black community" or to discussions of Black cultural experiences in the area or at large. These conversations ranged from deeply personal and political to fun and lighthearted. Longtime staff members informed me that it took a while for people (directors, program coordinators, and course instructors) to get to this point of sharing and community building, in what would eventually be labeled as the "Golden Era of EE."

According to youth workers, the "Golden Era" describes the time when EE was predominately staffed by a group of youth workers who were politically and socially conscious and who were highly skilled and innovative in providing opportunities for youth. During a conversation with Monica, she shared that the deliberate focus on race had everything to do with the "characters in the room." In other words, the direct conversations about race, providing space and tools for youths to critically unpack social and political problems rested on those hired at a very particular moment in time. Youth workers' attention to race in their work with youth was critical and nuanced and, coupled with their understanding of educational problems shaping the experiences of youth in their program, aided them in the creation of their own pedagogical practices. EE's commitment to making youths' experiences in the program divergent from their experiences in schools was paramount to the organization's success as a comprehensive community-based program. These dimensions of Educational Excellence did not come into fruition until Leah was hired and was joined by department directors who shared her ideology about minoritized youth and who desired greater educational opportunity that was also culturally affirming.

Finding Youth Workers   Adapting to new employees, a Board of Directors, and the organization's founder, Leah was excited by her "blank canvas" to mold the organization into something extraordinary. In her first year, Leah also wrestled with racial and ethnic tensions within the Dunbar neighborhood and its impact on EE. Since its inception, EE had held partnerships and operated within some schools in the area in addition to occupying its floor in the high rise. At one particular middle school, Leah and staff members noticed that Black students were not represented in the EE program. Leah explained that a staff member at the school asked, "how come we don't have any Black kids and we're in [this region of Dunbar]?" Leah shared that after that question, "[the school was] less interested in partnering with us." She further explained the racial dynamics by saying, "the Dominican families had all of this stuff around who the

Black Americans were and how they were going to bring their kids down—which obviously was very offensive to me." Shortly after Leah's arrival, EE ended its formal partnerships with schools. The racial makeup of the program would fluctuate as the organization began serving mostly Black students. With this in mind, Leah found it important to hire competent Black and Latinx employees to reflect the racial/ethnic make-up of youth participants in the program.

Leah hired Monica Matthews, a former colleague, as director of programs who was responsible for creating a vision for after-school courses and all other organizational programming. Leah and Monica met through nonprofit circles around the city. Monica, a Black woman from the East Coast, came to EE with extensive experience in youth work and nonprofit management at a range of youth and community-service agencies. Raised by a grandfather who introduced her to the work of Paul Laurence Dunbar and other Black writers, Monica grew up with a love of learning, reading, a strong sense of self, and perseverance that she attributed to her work with youth. With a large smile and consuming vitality, other staff members often described Monica as a fun-loving creative genius or "mastermind." Upon meeting Monica for the first time, I was struck immediately by her energy, excitement, and passion for young people. As a trained theater actor, Monica's creativity was reflected in her vision for programming at Educational Excellence. As executive director, Leah focused on building and sustaining important financial relationships for the organization, while Monica supported the mission through its programming for young people. Monica also held extremely high standards for the ways in which curricula were implemented; engaging and innovative practices were an essential part of her expectations. She also believed in nurturing relationships with students. As a result of her leadership, the department directors (whom she supervised) also believed in hiring course instructors who understood minoritized youth as powerful actors and agents of change. The department directors, Terry Niles, Faith Davenport, and Walidah Thomas, had all been a part of the program from four to ten years when I began my research in 2011. With backgrounds in the criminal justice system, counseling psychology and research on race and racial identity development, and middle school teaching, respectively, these department directors set the tone for the youth workers they hired to teach after-school courses. Shortly after Monica was hired, Terry was hired to run the Step 2 College department, with Faith following close behind. Faith, alongside Monica, developed the Youth Lead department. About four years later, Walidah Thomas was hired to lead the High Achievers department.

Terry Niles, a Black man from the East Coast, began his career as a federal probation officer after completing law school. He developed a passion for working with youth after spending time working with young people in a faith-based youth group. Terry arrived at EE shortly after Leah and Monica in 2003. He came to EE because he wanted to help students who desired to go to college but did not have the "resources or tools to make it there." For Terry, going to college is just "what happened" after high school. Terry was known for his quirky and playful sense of humor and amazing rapport with students. At the time of my original study in 2011, Terry had been working with EE for nine years. At that time, Terry was directing not only the Step 2 College program but also the alumni program. During my follow-up study in 2013, Terry would transition to the director of programs.

Faith Davenport had been with EE for nine years at the time of the study. A Black woman and East Coast native with family roots in Dunbar, Faith had an extensive background in counseling psychology on race-related stress for Black Americans. As personal friends, Monica suggested that Faith interview for a director position at EE in 2003. Monica and Leah wanted to make the organization more comprehensive by adding opportunities for identity work and counseling. Faith's role as a psychologist was an added bonus and prompted the creation of the counseling component of EE.

Walidah Thomas, a Black woman also born on the East Coast, served as the director of the High Achievers department (middle school) beginning in 2007. She would later lead EE's expansion into another part of the city in 2014, which will be further explained in Chapter 4. Walidah came to EE as an experienced classroom and community-based educator. With a love for reading and writing, Walidah often created courses around topics of race, fantasy, and resistance to engage students. She used texts such as *Souls of Black Folk* and *Parable of the Sower* to help students with writing. With a love for technology, Walidah created opportunities for students to engage with digital media in after-school classes. At the time of the study, Walidah had been working with EE for four years. Once the transition of leadership began, Walidah would eventually be the last original director to leave the program.

Faith, Walidah, and Terry are all supervised by Monica and are the anchors of all the programming that occurs within EE. Each of these directors supervises a staff of coordinators, youth workers, or after-school class instructors. They design curricula, coach the teaching staff, meet with students' guardians, and work with each other to ensure that all students in the program have the

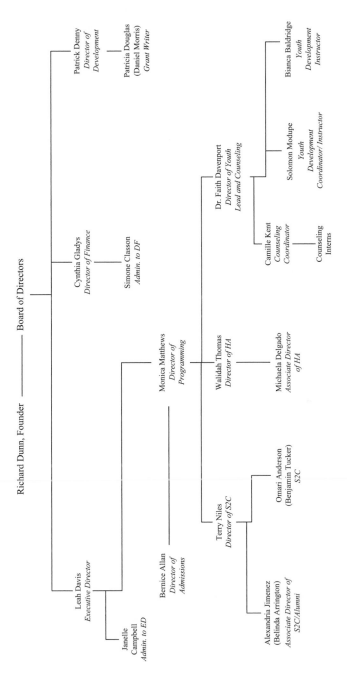

FIGURE 1. Educational Excellence, Organizational Hierarchy, 2011–2012

resources and support they need to be successful in school and in the program. With these core directors in place, several other youth workers and support staff members worked across middle school, high school, youth development and alumni programming.

Creating Structure and Pedagogy   Educational Excellence is divided into three specific departments: High Achievers (HA), Step 2 College (S2C), and Youth Lead (YL). Each department has a director, an associate director/ program coordinator, youth workers (full- and part-time), and after-school course instructors hired on a semester basis. At the programmatic level, EE provides youth with academic assistance, college preparation, state test preparation, psychological counseling, service-learning opportunities both domestic and abroad, and youth leadership and development training, which includes courses on social identity including but not limited to race/ethnicity, gender, social class, religion, and sexuality. Each department has its own goals that are aligned with the organization's overall mission to get students to and through college, recognizing that solely focusing on academics will not get or keep students in college.

The YL department was established to provide students with opportunities for social and emotional development through after-school courses, overnight retreats, and personal counseling. Prior to Leah's leadership, the program did not have a focus on social, cultural, and political development. As Faith shared in an interview, "academics are not enough to make you successful in life." Despite Faith's efforts and that of other staff members, it was believed by many in YL that funders wanted to fund only the academic components of the program and not programming offered by YL. The HA department helps students and their families navigate the city's high school choice system and helps youths develop quality applications for competitive high schools. Middle school students participate in a variety of elective courses, math and English courses, and YL courses, which focus on youth development, health, and critical media literacy. The S2C department focuses on helping youths access higher education. High school students also enroll in a number of YL courses, which are centered mainly on social identity awareness, self-esteem, social institutions, and service projects. During weekly classes, both middle and high school students take English and math courses, test preparation, and elective courses, which can include anything from art to psychology, law, and business. Both middle and high school students attend a daylong or overnight youth development retreat in the spring. High school seniors are taken on an overnight retreat in the spring semester to foster community building and prepare for college life. Throughout middle school and high school, EE takes students on college tours throughout the country. College students and alumni participants return to the program during their winter break for a special conference catered to their needs as college students. Information about internships and job opportunities is provided, and assistance is available to support students through social and emotional hardships they may be dealing with while away from home— like managing intense racial climates on their campuses and financial anxiety. As an insider and researcher at EE, I observed, attended, or participated in each of these courses and events during my fieldwork.

The executive leadership and directors wanted to ensure asset-rich framing; high expectations with regard to academic achievement and social awareness were integrated and woven throughout all dimensions of the program. Educational Excellence scaffolds students' learning in the program through academic and youth development courses that allowed students to hone essential academic skills and develop a strong sense of self. In their attempt to not make "after-school feel like school," youth workers taught traditional academic classes such as math and writing/English language arts (ELA) with themes that resonated with students' experience. In many cases, youths themselves chose certain themes through student surveys each semester. For example, there were ELA and writing courses developed around horror films, social movements and music, hip-hop, creative writing, and women's studies. Math classes were also developed as thematic courses like architecture and robotics. Both middle and high school students participated in elective courses during after-school hours as well. Elective courses were developed often and could be related to poetry, dance, and photography, among other things. Regardless of the type of course, instructors and youth workers are coached to create a classroom space where youth were at the center. Instructors provided brief overviews of topics, but class discussions and application to real-life experiences were primary for all classes.

According to EE's hiring materials for after-school course instructors, those with teaching credentials were preferred for academic courses like ELA and math, yet these teachers must teach their classes from a youth-centered perspective. This meant that instructors needed to center youth in their teaching and not take an authoritative stance as the sole bearer of knowledge. Classes needed to have a didactic component but also needed to have a significant portion of time spent on student discussions. These courses also needed to include examples from students' lived experiences. Many of the academic after-school course instructors taught in traditional schools during the day and taught at EE in the evenings and on weekends. During orientations for new teachers, program directors reiterate that EE imagines its students as emerging scholars and change agents. As such, courses cannot and should not feel like school in the traditional sense. Recognizing that schools are sites of suffering and trauma for Black youth,[49] EE was careful not to repeat some of the classroom processes found in schools like mundane worksheets or teacher-centered classrooms. I observed Walidah lead a new student–parent orientation for incoming middle school students, where she shared with attendees that course instructors have to be "willing to shed some of their teacher training" in order to adapt to the kind of pedagogy required at EE and in many community-based spaces. In an interview with Walidah, she offered the following:

> The students kinda recognize staff as authority figures, but at the same time, they know that we have high expectations for them so they can see us in a lot of ways, not too dissimilar from their families. They know we're going to push them. And at the same time, they know that they probably can develop some level of trust with us and they know that we are willing to have fun with them too; we can laugh and joke with them, but we know when, you know, at what point to do things. I think the teacher–student relationships tend to typically be the traditional relationships. You know, teacher as the authority figure, student is student. I think we try to push for teachers to kind of develop relationships, because a good educator knows that the relationships is [sic] the key through which learning is really happening.

Faith once shared in an interview that teachers must have a "youth development sensibility" in their approach to teaching. Although she struggled to find another description beyond "youth development sensibility," what I gleaned from her statement was that the approach needed to be about fostering relationships between youths and adults rather than perpetuating authoritative relationships commonly found in schools. After-school courses are infused with media, brief lectures, and group discussions that are often personal and political. Additionally, after-school courses can be loud; laughter can be heard down the hallways, and on most days, students are eagerly participating in discussions. These pedagogical tools disrupt the traditional relationship of adult as teacher and youth as learner. Youth engage in facilitation and teaching of their peers. And in discussion-based courses, adult instructors are looking to youths to share their insights about their experiences and are not positioned to always know the answer. In short, the pedagogy and organizational culture of EE supported the development of the "whole child" in that all aspects of a young person must be nurtured in the program.

Reframing Youth and Education   Monica, often energized by meaningful interactions with youth, believed that there was not much young people could not do. This attitude and approach to youth work filtered through to every aspect of the organization, creating a familial culture where honesty, critical reflection, and affirming attitudes about youth of color were central. No exceptions were made for those who did not share the same imagining of Black youth as staff members. As Faith explained during one of our interviews,

> You know there's a culture here, not just a general culture of what EE is about, you know there's a staff culture and there is an expectation and we are very, very particular with those that we hire. Keep in mind the fact that a lot of what we do is not only related to the organization but also related to the thinking and the belief of the staff. So, you can't hire someone who comes in and really does not believe in the young people, because it shows.

The familial-like culture established at Educational Excellence was solidified through a number of practices maintained by staff and students. From the first day I stepped on the seventh floor, the culture of the program was palpable. Staff members engaged youth in conversations that went beyond the superficial and tapped into their lives at schools, at home, and in their neighborhoods. Though staff members were energetic and fun loving with students, they also took their jobs as educators very seriously, striking a balance between high standards, flexibility, and love that contributes to a familial-like environment. This balance is captured through a conversation with Camille Kent, a program coordinator for counseling services in the Youth Lead department, as she says, "I think the staff as a whole makes it a point to get to know students despite what area we're in. I think that kind of contributes to the family feeling. Everybody should be kind of familiar . . . we all kind of make this effort to pull the students in that way."

In her role as the coordinator for the counseling program, Camille pays close attention to the psychological and emotional needs of students in the program. Faith supervises Camille, while Camille coordinates counseling interns and monitors case files for students. While Camille's job is to pay attention to all aspects of a young person's life, including the unspoken, as she states above, all youth workers at EE make an effort to get to know all students. Counseling interns in a local master's program staffed the counseling program at Educational Excellence. It is supervised by Faith, herself a clinical psychologist who specializes in mental health wellness and race. This counseling program went far beyond the services that youth and some adults are able to receive in Dunbar. The counseling component of the program essentially humanizes youth participants by recognizing that they are full human beings that require compassion and care.

The comprehensive approach to youth development at EE was made possible by the organizational culture and structure that was created during the beginning of Leah's tenure. Monica, who worked alongside Leah as director of programs, told me how the culture of the program was created by Leah and the staff members that Leah hired after replacing those she felt were not working in the best interest of students. Below, Monica addresses how her position evolved and how that position's evolution would become important in the broader development of a comprehensive program for student participants:

> There were silos between middle school and high school. And when we developed the youth development line and education line, there became silos between those groups. . . . And so, by having one person responsible for building a team of people around kids and programming, everyone became accountable for that child's success and their experience in the continuum. And so, a lot of the work that I do . . . was to build that culture of accountability, build a culture of understanding that we are a team. . . . I set up the case conferences. I said, "You know, it's not enough for counseling to know what's going on, and middle school and high school has no idea why this kid is acting crazy in class. You guys need to have monthly case conferences. You need to set up some system for referring kids to counseling as necessary. You need to talk about when you find out that parents are divorcing, as a middle school director, you need to let counseling know that so that they have that information, so they can be a support to the kid." . . . We just need[ed] to adjust our attitude about how the program worked.

Monica's comments reflect so much of what was unique and powerful about Educational Excellence. First, the continuum created in the organization through each department being accountable for students' academic, social, and emotional well-being is critical to the success of the program. The camaraderie and relationships established between youth workers at EE contributed to the flow of information between each department regarding students' needs.

This attention to all of the dimensions of a young person's life made it extremely difficult for students to fall through the cracks. There were clear lines of communication and camaraderie established between the staff that allowed EE to keep track of students' academic progress in addition to their home life and other experiences they might have in their neighborhoods. If appropriate, a member of the YL department would inform the academic staff about the everyday experiences or traumatic experiences that might have occurred that may affect students' attendance or performance in an after-school class or within their schools. Youth workers would often share information about students pertaining to deaths in their family, divorce, deaths of friends, physical or mental health concerns, and bullies at school or within their neighborhoods. Youth workers believed that these sorts of circumstances required additional support for students.[50] When I worked as a youth development instructor with young women, students would often say to me, "Y'all always know everything!" Indeed, this was true. While sensitive information regarding the mental health needs of students could not be shared outside of the counseling staff, assisting youth in navigating difficult school, family, and neighborhood circumstances was a large part of EE's work with students.

Second, Michaela's assertion shared earlier about students being aware of how the changes in Dunbar are not necessarily improving their circumstances is indicative of the youths' analysis of their community and the ways in which they are able to process their feelings and critiques (and develop them as well) within the context of the program. Through academic and youth development courses, youths often engaged the Dunbar neighborhood in class discussions, canvassing the neighborhood to document the number of healthy grocery stores or to note race-themed advertisements. These types of educational moments helped youths understand their neighborhood more fully and how larger social forces shaped their neighborhoods and schools. Staff members at EE not only offered space during classes and retreats to process Dunbar and other neighborhoods youths hailed from, they also provided support and advocacy for students when navigating challenging neighborhood circumstances that had the potential to disrupt their trajectory toward college, like unfair school policies, police surveillance, and gang violence. For example, Faith shared that a former student was jumped by a gang and while in the hospital contacted Terry before her guardians for support. I suggest that youth workers at EE provide a pivotal role of support, that they are cultural workers and also institutional agents working on behalf of youth.

The examples above reflect the attention youth workers paid to the social and political context of their program and the lives of youth participants. Their understanding of social problems including—but not limited to—issues of race, class, and political disenfranchisement were foregrounded in their programming through class curricula and pedagogy. Through this programming, youth were able to think critically about issues of race, class, and gender and the ways these forces informed their experiences within their schools, families, and neighborhoods.

Cultural Work and Institutional Advocacy

Youth workers are most often thought of as college-age young adults working in after-school spaces providing academic tutoring. Although academic tutoring is indeed an important component to youth work, our understanding of youth work is severely limited. Youth workers include those who mentor, guide, and teach youth in a variety of spaces including but not limited to nonprofit community-based programs, schools, youth detention centers, and summer camps.[51] Youth workers come to this profession from a variety of fields and entry points. Whereas many become involved while in high school and college, others receive advanced training in a wide range of disciplines, including sociology, social work, adolescent development, community psychology, counseling psychology, and education.[52] Because the qualifications and experiences of youth workers vary across specific organizations and cities, scholars of youth work suggest that the profession has been difficult to legitimize in the academy because of the lack of professionalization and credentials needed for the work.[53] The lack of professionalization and lack of uniformity as a discipline within higher education also makes this work difficult to validate in a society dependent on hierarchies, credentials, and elitism. I suggest that this difficulty in legitimization is in part a function of their exclusion in broader educational discourse.[54]

Those who identify as youth workers do not hold the same ideologies or possess the same skill sets as these things change from organization to organization.[55] Youth workers can be what Freire describes as "cultural workers," assisting students to identify and make sense of injustices in an oppressive society.[56] As cultural workers, youth workers often create spaces and opportunities for young people to process and critique the social and political problems they encounter.[57] Thus, community-based educational spaces become a critical space in which youths and adults foster relationships that assist young people in developing a consciousness and understanding about the world in which they live and, by doing so, foster youth engagement and activism.[58] Freire described this process as "praxis"—a marriage between critical reflection and action. Because community-based spaces for youth vary in philosophy and approach, understanding how youth workers conceptualize and understand the world around them has deep implications for how they imagine and interact with youth within these settings.

Youth workers are instrumental to community-based education, but there is a scarcity of scholarship that addresses how the educators within them make sense of their work with youth. Most important, community-based spaces have been pivotal in the broader efforts to assist youth, taking on what schools cannot, while positioning themselves as sites of resistance against structural forces and the symbolic violence that occurs within schools. Black civil society organizations, for example, were often established both organically and intentionally for the edification of Black communities but also in response to hostile forces that shape the life chances and outcomes for Black youth.[59] Youth workers in community-based educational programs serving Black, Latinx, and other minoritized youth today are positioned uniquely to meet the multiple and complex needs of youth in ways that schools are unable to due to the political constraints often surrounding schools.[60] Stanton-Salazar would describe this process as adult actors working on behalf of minoritized youth as institutional agents. Using a social capital framework, Stanton-Salazar defines institutional agents as "high status, non-kin, agents who occupy relatively high positions in the multiple dimensional stratification system, and who are well positioned to provide key forms of social and institutional support."[61] Though all youth workers at Educational Excellence may or may not be "high-status," their level of formal education and position within the organization helped students form a social network through nonparental adults who were committed to their academic and social success. Within literature on youth development and adolescent psychology, nonparental adults play a critical role in the development of youth.[62] In addition to playing a supportive role, institutional agents are able to use their cultural and social capital in tangible ways that allow youth access to particular spaces and experiences they would not otherwise have the opportunity to obtain.

I observed staff members intervene on behalf of students when they experienced difficulty with administrators or teachers in their schools or with the college admissions process. In one instance, Leah began accompanying a single father to advocate for a seventh-grade boy named Bekele. The school principal was targeting Bekele; several staff members believed and mentioned on a few occasions that this particular principal treated Black boys unfairly. In an interview, Faith shared that this principal had a reputation for "railroad[ing] Black boys." Leah attended parent–teacher meetings alongside his father and spoke to his principal and teachers to ensure that he was being treated fairly.

As a ninth grader, Bekele began having major difficulties and was in danger of being held back to repeat the ninth grade. In a late-afternoon interview, Faith appeared tired and expressed that there was "a lot going on." She shared that she had just met with Bekele's father, his older sisters, and two EE staff members. The meeting between EE youth workers and Bekele's family was an "all-hands-on-deck" situation as Faith explains:

> We have a child that has been left back; this is the first time we've ever experienced that . . . and we're like, what do we do with him? Do we just push him off? And so we just had the multiprong approach sitting here. We had the family here. We had the academic department here. We had the [director of programs] here. We had myself. When we came out of that meeting, we had a plan in place. . . . So, we all came together to figure out "what can I give to help?" You know, pull this child up. Or the analogy that was used in here yesterday was that he's flatlining and we're all like pumping to give him CPR, we're taking turns giving him CPR and that everybody has to chip in. . . . Someone's going down and we just as a staff, we can't watch a child go down and watch them drown. . . . I had two meetings like that yesterday, one with a young man and one with a young woman, where both of these kids were flatlining.

Faith also shared that part of the plan included getting Bekele evaluated for a learning disability, sharing strategies with the family, and regularly attending counseling with her as she noted that he was severely depressed. Upon hearing about this meeting with Bekele and his family, I was moved by the way the youth workers and Bekele's family joined together to provide support. One part of the plan to support Bekele consisted of creating an opportunity for him to experience some form of personal success. Youth workers created a volunteer opportunity where he worked with younger students and assisted staff members in organizing social events for the organization, so that he could "feel a sense of purpose," as Faith expressed. Coupled with individual counseling, in a few months, Bekele started to feel like himself again. He started seeing a tutor for some classes and volunteering for the program, allowing staff members to see more of him and work together alongside his family to meet his needs.

Much like Bekele, Nasir, a charismatic student who had been a part of EE since the sixth grade, is known for his humor, skepticism, penchant for asking difficult questions, and tendency to freestyle hip hop lyrics at random moments. Nasir was beloved by youth workers. Faith would always say with a smile that she "put a lot of work into Nasir" and that he had come "a long way" since the sixth grade. I worked with Nasir as a course instructor for a year. Nasir, an inquisitive teen, often asked me questions about college and graduate school. Nasir would spend a lot of time with Solomon, the Youth Lead coordinator and instructor for boys, exchanging music and talking about religion and political issues. With encouragement from his family, youth workers, and his peers or "crew" from EE, Nasir was eager and excited for the college admissions process. He had worked really hard throughout high school to achieve excellent grades and had tons of remarkable leadership experiences that allowed him to travel abroad several times. It came as a surprise to all of us that Nasir was wait-listed for every school he had applied to. After informing the staff that he had been wait-listed for a school where staff had connections, Leah, Faith, Monica, and Terry began calling their networks of people who were connected to the college to inquire about the likelihood of coming off of the wait-list. They made calls and wrote letters on Nasir's behalf. After a month or so, Nasir was moved from the wait-list and accepted to the college he would end up attending and graduating from. Although I do not know whether staff members' phone calls or letters led to him being admitted, it was powerful to witness youth workers employ their social and political influence on behalf of Nasir just to see if anything could be done to support him.

EE developed several cultural practices that were beloved by staff and students alike. One favorite is a ritual of announcing college acceptances. As EE students get accepted to colleges throughout the spring semester, they must go into the Step 2 College office and ring a bell notifying everyone on the floor of their acceptance. Everyone stops whatever tasks they are working on to come in to the halls to cheer, clap, and celebrate a student's acceptance to college. It becomes a beautiful moment to see all staff present and students from all grade levels applaud and celebrate with students who have been accepted. When Nasir was finally able to ring the bell, the joy youth workers felt could not be contained. Youth workers and students alike clapped, jumped, and cheered in the hallways for Nasir. Early during my involvement with EE, I did wonder what this practice might mean for students who did not get accepted to college. I later learned that according to the program's record at the time, all students who graduated from high school got accepted into college. Two-year or four-year college acceptances were publicly celebrated in the same way.

I note this example because it shows how youth workers rallied, encouraged, and utilized their professional networks to support a student. Youth workers at EE often stepped in when students' high school guidance counselors were slow or refused to send out transcripts or write letters of recommendation. Staff members at EE coached students on how to approach guidance counselors, called in favors to professors and employers to help students obtain internships while in high school or college, talked with students' families when appropriate, and hired alum when possible. Student alumni in college called staff members often as spring semesters came to a close in order to inquire about summer internships and employment opportunities.

Youth workers did everything in their power to navigate institutions that were too complex or foreign for students to navigate on their own. College was the expectation for all youth participants at EE. For the most part, all staff members supported this even if they understood arguments that "college isn't for everyone." Most staff members believed and discussed with students that very few people (especially poor and people of color) achieve social mobility without higher education (and that increasingly advanced degrees were necessary but even still not a guarantee for social mobility in today's economy because of the role race and class continues to play in access to social progress). Leah and others also recognized that the "college isn't for everyone" narrative was often communicated to Black, Latinx, and poor youth. Solomon Modupe, a youth development coordinator, was the only paid youth worker without a college degree. His lack of degree came up from time to time as a contradiction to EE values by some of the leadership. He was often described as a powerful teacher who connected the most easily to students. He was beloved by all, yet this conflict surrounding his lack of a college degree spoke to what some staff members saw as a contradiction and what others viewed as elitism.

While under Leah's leadership and the support of a transformative staff, youth workers created a culture of high expectations rooted in affirming language that recognized the strengths that youth possessed before entering Educational Excellence. Racial literacy and social consciousness building was an important anchor in the program that was integrated throughout every department in the program. Most important, understanding social forces and the implications they had on the academic and social experiences for Black youth was paramount to the work of Educational Excellence. Through this understanding, youth workers were able to advocate for students in ways that were vital to their academic success and that would help nurture the gifts and skills youth already possessed. Nevertheless, despite the forms of advocacy employed by youth workers, the asset-rich framing, and culturally relevant pedagogy used by youth workers, tensions and contradictions were present that caused some conflict between staff members.

Tensions and Paradoxes in the Golden Era

As a participant observer at Educational Excellence, I uncovered multiple tensions in the framing and imagining of Black youth that informed the pedagogical practices and relationships between EE students and youth workers. I witnessed and felt the complexity of youth workers' challenge to frame and imagine Black youth from asset-rich perspectives and not deficit narratives. I learned that youth workers at EE, like many other grassroots activists and educators, are forced to simultaneously work within and critique a system of which they are a part. Through my research, I learned the challenge of maintaining a program that fights against a dominant paradigm of Black youth as deficient, delinquent, or just in need of "fixing." Worse yet, so much of this framing comes from the very organizations that community-based programs like EE must rely upon for their very existence. These issues—and how youth workers see them affecting Black youth and their own pedagogy and engagement with youth—were paramount to their understanding of why they engage in youth work. There are two distinct processes that occurred within EE that reflect a disconnection between ideology and practice: (1) the conflicting definitions of academic success versus whole child development and (2) the raced and gendered cultural and behavioral expectations youth were held to by the organization.

In addition to the challenges youth workers faced with their Board of Directors, external funders, and larger political framing of Black youth in community-based programming, youth workers themselves also experienced internal tensions, which I argue are connected to their own understanding of the world. A critical effort of this book is to unpack youth worker's understanding of race and educational problems and how that understanding informs their work with youth. Youth workers' framing of and beliefs about the political problems facing Black youth are deeply connected and intertwined with how they think about and serve young people in Educational Excellence. Young people internalize the messages that are communicated to them both directly and indirectly through the institutions they occupy, the adults they encounter, and the society in which they live and learn.[63] Moreover, the framing of discourse has the ability to structure meaning and responses to social problems.[64] Therefore, exploring not only how the disposition of youth workers has been shaped by macro-level policy that uses deficit frames but also how structural inequality has shaped the context in which youth workers provide services to young people is critical. Working within a system of inequality shapes not only the schooling experiences of young people but also the conditions in which they live. Making sense of the way youth workers' imagining of youth seemed divergent from their actions was sometimes difficult to explain. Sociologists of race have argued that a racialized person's sense of self and response to the world can be contradictory or divided, particularly when operating in a system of white supremacy.[65]

Rejection, Respectability, and "Other" Black Youth

Liberatory education and youth work in the context of a racist, capitalistic, cis-heteronormative society is always susceptible to contradictions. Race-conscious work in particular is vulnerable to contradictions as white supremacy dominates institutions and the cultural practices within them, which are difficult to disrupt and destroy. As such, for EE, an organization where staff members understood how structural racism, capitalism, and patriarchy shaped their lives and the lives of their students, there were often moments of contradictions among some youth workers regarding the cultural standards students and some staff members were held to. As a predominantly Black staff who recognized how pervasive racist and deficit narratives shaped the educational and social lives of youth participants, they sometime engaged students through the gaze of whiteness in order to structure their behaviors, language, and styles of expression.

Despite EE's emphasis on asset-based approaches, deficit comments often surfaced in interesting ways. EE youth workers negotiated the process of creating distance between the programs they provide and traditional schooling. For many youth workers, maintaining a powerful critique of deficit framing of youth of color in schools is important; however, as I have learned through my research, some of the constraints traditional schools experience are similar to the constraints community-based programs experience, depending on their funding sources and orientation of program leaders and organizational culture. Even though EE youth workers' acts of resistance against deficit narratives and low expectations come across in their curricula development and pedagogical practices with youth, I also observed the ways in which youth workers formally and informally assess students beyond academics, including informal cultural practices. Student participants are expected to look, behave, and speak in a certain way that often limits or diminishes students' own cultural expressions. These same cultural expectations also apply to youth workers at EE. As a result, the same cultural processes that EE condemns and supports are often manifested in EE youth workers' framing of students, something that can be observed in the differences between what youth workers say *about* students and what they say *to* students.

For example, as students approach EE, there is a disrobing or cultural shedding that occurs—a shedding of identifying markers that might link EE youth with "other" youth within the surrounding Dunbar neighborhood. At any time on the EE floor, students are expected to speak "standard American English" during after-school courses, and they are expected to wear EE-"appropriate" clothing, which cannot include "sagging pants, midriff tops, too-tight clothing, short pants or skirts, spaghetti-strapped tops, and shirts with photographs or messages on them that are deemed inappropriate." For the most part, these are standard rules for most traditional school settings as well as some out-of-school settings—however, they are often gendered and they reflect particular cultural values and messaging communicated by adults to young people. Students and youth workers are also not allowed to wear any head coverings (with the exception of head coverings for religious observation, but cultural head wraps were not allowed). These dress codes are stated in the EE employee manual and are persistently communicated to students by youth workers on a daily basis. Students can repeat these rules and standards on command. Youth workers say they want students to have respect for themselves, and this is important given the ways in which Black youth are constructed and perceived in society. Be that as it may, the dress code is also present so that there are distinctions between EE students and *other* students on "the street" as some directors often expressed.

The idea that youth can "come as they are" to community spaces is often seen as being one of the many characteristics that sets these spaces apart from traditional school settings where youth, specifically Black youth, often encounter cultural clashes with school authority over their style, expressions, and identities.[66] But even at EE, there were consequences for students who do not conform to these rules. For example, if youth arrived in "inappropriate" attire, they would be forced to put on "ugly pants," suspenders, and shirts as a form of embarrassment to prevent them from breaking the rules in the future or risk being banned from certain trips. The ugly pants were typically a pair of large pajama bottoms with a busy color-clashing print. These were given to young women who wore shorts that were deemed too short, a skirt or a dress deemed too short, or leggings. Young men were sometimes given ugly pants or suspenders if they were caught in sagging pants. I often felt, as did a few other staff members—including Solomon and Camille—conflicted enforcing some of these rules, feeling that students were being shamed for various forms of expression. But staff members would be reprimanded if they did not have students adhere to the rules. Nevertheless, to avoid having students (mostly young women) wear the ugly pants and be laughed at by other students, some youth workers would look the other way or have them place their coats or scarves over their legs. Although this organizational practice was not enthusiastically supported by every single staff member, it was a practice that was maintained. While some students laughed and took it all in stride, many were upset and often challenged the fairness of the rules. Ultimately, EE created an environment where youth felt comfortable being in the space, yet this practice made the program feel more like school. Youth needed to "change" or "cover up" or risk experiencing a ritual of embarrassment. During interviews, some youth workers acknowledged that the "ugly pants" ritual or encouragement to speak Standard American English was the organization's way of preparing students for professional opportunities like internships, college, and careers—while sometimes reinforcing that students may be judged because of racism and class-based stereotypes. It was also an effort to ensure that students in the program were not mistaken for "other" youth outside of the program. This tension demonstrates the challenges and contradictions facing youth workers as they strive to guide Black youth in urban settings while recognizing the unfair criminalization that occurs and simultaneously trying to encourage their creative expressions as young people.

In this current political moment, time has shown over and over again that Black people in this country are targeted and rendered disposable at the hands of State.[67] State-sponsored violence and other structural violence including schooling inequality, continued neighborhood segregation and dispossession, and water poisoning are just a few ways that the State neglects the most vulnerable and contributes to the afterlife of slavery.[68] Over the last few years, as highlighted by Black Lives Matter, we have seen one too many Black youth viciously attacked and murdered by the police without consequence. In some of those cases, the public attempts to justify the murder of Black people by the kind of lives they lived; educational attainment, level of politeness, or what they might have been wearing are all used in the public's efforts to determine what the victim could have done to avoid conflict with the police. But time and time again—as more video footage surfaces of Black folks' interaction with the police—it is evident that clothing, time of day, full compliance, or the level of politeness an individual expresses has not mattered. Cries from some within the Black community have blamed Black youth for using the N-word, wearing sagging pants and hoodies, and other things, citing these as factors contributing to their violent arrests and killings. Yet, as we have seen, politeness, following directions, and what you look like do not matter as much as the color of one's skin. Attempts to center these explanations are steeped in anti-Blackness. This also holds true for Educational Excellence, where students were held to standards that bordered on the politics of respectability and anti-Blackness, even as they attempted to center and affirm Blackness.[69]

Solomon, one of four men on staff at the time of my first phase of study in 2011, told me in an interview about a fear he held, one that I would later learn was held by other staff members as well. Solomon's frustration with EE not understanding and accepting all that students have to navigate in their neighborhoods made him concerned that the organization would become irrelevant as it moved further and further away from addressing the struggles that students have to negotiate daily. Solomon explains:

> Every year it is becoming more and more clear that we are—and this is my opinion—that we are becoming more and more disconnected from what students are actually experiencing, and I think in some ways we are becoming irrelevant, and maybe closer to their parents as an institution than we are adult mentors, and confidants that really drives our success. We're losing that. I think those are the only things that we have that have been very successful for us. In addition to highly prioritizing excellence and scholarship and trying things that are new, regardless of what you feel you can do or not. We may not be relevant anymore.

This issue also surfaced during an interview with Terry, who said, "I fear that I am aging out of this profession because as I get older, I become less in touch with or I have to do more to stay in touch with what young people are doing, living, experiencing." These comments provide insight into the reflection some EE youth workers engage in as they try to understand their work with youth and better understand the students they serve. Whether or not Terry's feeling has to do with the growing age gap between himself and students in the program, these insights provide important clues to how youth workers conceptualize the struggles that young people are experiencing and how they are able to work through them despite their age, their racial and cultural biases, and their own understanding of the world. These blind spots humanize youth workers in some respects—but even if they can be seen as just flaws that are inherent in all people, these issues nevertheless have implications for organizational conflict and student engagement in community-based after-school programs.

Youth engagement with drinking, drugs, and sexual activity was a typical stressor for staff members. For anyone engaged in youth work, understanding how young people move in and through the world and the decisions they make requires compassion and support. The separation of EE students from other youth in their neighborhoods is a tension that some youth workers found problematic in how the organization imagines students in the program and how they frame those who are not in the program, creating an "us" versus "them" discourse. Below, Solomon discusses this tension as he explains how other staff members underestimate the power of structural forces that manifest in very real ways for youth in the program, as well as the common experiences that all teenagers endure as they come of age:

> The frustrating thing is that if we ask students how many of them are drinking, you know smoking or whatever, they would say no, even if they have considered it, tried it or whatever have you, and we really want to have a different relationship with them, but we're not accepting that's a reality, and so it's frustrating because it's like we are almost undoing the progress that we made with them, the relationship that we made because they know they can't be honest around us for fear of rejection from us, and that we would look at them in a different light.

Solomon captured a tension that is also very relevant to how Monica and other youth workers viewed an eighth grader's suspension from school for allegedly possessing cannabis. The reality that students could fear "rejection from [the staff]" if they engage in activities some staff members disapprove of in some ways seems contradictory to a program that builds relationships over many years. This fear of rejection students might feel from youth workers because of choices they make was clearly visible toward the end of my data collection period, when high school senior Xenia became pregnant.

Xenia had submitted several college applications (and was still very much in the process of applying) at the time her pregnancy was revealed. She has been a student at EE since the seventh grade; I met Xenia as a ninth grader and saw that she had made significant personal growth throughout her time in the program. Initially, she rarely spoke during after-school courses and hardly ever engaged with staff members unprompted. By her senior year, Xenia was much more vocal, became a bit more engaged with the program, and developed friendships with her peers. Xenia's pregnancy was quickly noticeable because of her small frame, and Terry suspected her pregnancy when he noted weight gain. When confronted, Xenia explained that she did not want to tell the staff and get kicked out of the program. To my knowledge, this was the second student who became pregnant as an active high school student in the program. Xenia, like the student before her, was told that when she started to show and appeared more obviously pregnant, she would have to stop coming to after-school classes. She was told that she could come only on Friday afternoons (a voluntary day for students who are in extracurricular EE programming). Youth workers did not want middle school students seeing Xenia walk down the hallways pregnant because it would send "mixed messages" to all students according to the leadership as was explained to me by Faith. Camille, Xenia's counselor, was infuriated by the remarks made about Xenia and felt like there could be another way of "not encouraging teen pregnancy" without "shaming" the student. Teachers at Xenia's school had already written her off as someone who had "ruined her life," according to Camille; and sadly, there were moments where Xenia felt written off by some staff members at EE. Program leadership and youth workers continued to support Xenia one on one even though she was not allowed to be on the floor during regular after-school programming. With the support of her family and with guidance from individual EE staff members, Xenia finished high school and is a college graduate.

Without a doubt, the response EE has toward pregnant students reveals a significant gender bias that leaves male students who were expectant fathers free to attend programming. While discussing this issue with staff members, Leah told me that removing pregnant students from after-school courses was a decision by Richard Dunn and the board and enforced by staff members. For Camille, Solomon, and myself, it remained one of the most disturbing practices upheld by EE.

Making Sense of the Contradictions

Making sense of these practices was challenging. Participants in this study advocated for race-conscious and affirming spaces for youth that celebrated Black identities and forms of expression, yet at times, some of their practices seemed laden with cultural pathological judgments. W. E .B. Du Bois writes of Black life as a paradox and suggests that navigating the boundaries and barriers of white supremacy is taxing for Black people.[70] As Du Bois writes, being Black in America and seeing oneself through the lens of others "is a peculiar sensation, this double-consciousness, this sense of always looking at one's self through the eyes of others . . ."[71] Sociological analyses of filtering one's thoughts, expressions, and actions through the gaze of whiteness have been helpful in addressing how Black and other minoritized communities end up with contradictory views of the world and political problems. Second sight helps explain the embrace of respectability politics and the emulation of whiteness by participants in this study. The reality of existing within white supremacist structures helps us understand some participants' contradictory practices and moments of internalized anti-Blackness—why they might simultaneously offer an analysis of systemic racism in schools *and* also question the investment in education by Black communities.

Youth workers at EE generally incorporated strong critiques about structural inequality with regard to race and academic achievement into their framing and pedagogy. They drew on understandings of racism and capitalism as the most salient factors shaping the educational and social experiences of youth in their program. Yet at particular moments of engagement with youth, some held and expressed contradictory views. Though some of these practices might have been shaped by Richard Dunn or the Board of Directors, some of the actions among youth workers were filtered through raced-classed and cultural ideologies. Making sense of the way youth workers' thinking and imagining of youth seemed divergent from their actions was sometimes difficult to digest. However, in the context of nonprofit sector, framing, and cultural pathological depictions of Black and other minoritized youth, these practices are very common. Dancing on the line of cultural pathological explanations for perceived failures of Black youth is typical in youth work and education more broadly. It is important to stress here that working within the context of white supremacy, coupled with racial neoliberalism's insistence on self-governance and self and community responsibility (and thereby obscuring structural oppression)[72] shapes how youth work is constructed and how youth workers engage with youth. Within this context, EE youth workers' actions toward students makes sense even as they are difficult to accept.

• • •

Over a three-year period, I observed EE take a strong position on race, the construction of Black youth, and a holistic approach to education and youth development—an approach centered on youth of color as whole beings. EE's construction of youth at the beginning of my time with the organization was rooted in a critical understanding of structural inequalities—including racial discrimination, mass unemployment, tough critiques of neoliberal education restructuring such as accountability through standardized testing, and mass disenfranchisement—that shape the experiences and academic outcomes of minoritized youth. Conflict, tensions, and contradictions were present, despite staff members' strong understanding of the structural constraints Black youth face and their culturally centered approach to programming. Youth workers' understandings and imagining of the youth they work with is uniquely tied to the ways in which they understand structural and cultural forces that constrain and enable social action. Thus, the dispositions and orientation of youth workers informs their sense making of themselves and their relationship to their social world but also how they make sense of, imagine, and interact with others. Further, these tensions and contradictions reveal the malleable nature of culture and practices within social organizations.[73] As with all organizations, the actors within them come with a set of dispositions and lived realities. And, given their access to control and power within an organization, they have the ability to shape and reshape cultural practices within the organization.

In the next chapter, I examine the tensions and struggles inherent in youth workers' desire to maintain affirming and asset-based framing in their quest to obtain funding. Prior to the changes in the program culture amid a mass exodus of personnel, though not without contradictions, EE was able to negotiate broader educational shifts rooted in neoliberal logics and engage in various acts of resistance in its program in order to maintain a race-conscious approach to social justice youth development. The contradictions, tensions, and resistance further illustrated in the next chapter are indicative of the current trajectory of education reform—a trajectory leading toward an educational path defined by neoliberal logics of academic success and educational change, thus narrowing the understanding of education and the imagining of Black youth.

3 "We're Not Saving Anybody"

Refusing Deficit Narratives

O N ONE AFTERNOON, I arrived on the floor to find Walidah, the director of the High Achievers department, frustrated. I always knew when Walidah was angry because the weight of the world was visible in her solemn facial expressions. Later that day, during a formal interview, she explained that she had been in phone meetings with a student's parent most of the day. She met with this parent multiple times as eighth-grade students prepared to apply for high schools in the city. One of the organization's goals was to successfully help students get from middle school into reputable high schools. The school selection process in the state and city was quite difficult for families to navigate on their own. Students across the city—of all racial, ethnic, and socioeconomic backgrounds—feel the pressure of this highly competitive race for seats in top public high schools.[1] For students of color and lower-income students, the process is even more daunting. The high school selection process factors in test scores, grades, and attendance records. Customized specialized schools require interviews or auditions. These processes are not always transparent; therefore, EE youth workers would intervene and guide families and students through this process.

Resources are allocated differently across school regions throughout the city, which more often than not leaves low-income students and families of color in schools that are underresourced. Most EE students resided in neighborhoods with regional high schools that lack basic resources and have low college attendance rates. As a result, EE students applied to "selective" or "customized" high schools. As the director of the middle school program, Walidah would provide a list of possible schools to students and families based on each student's interests, grades, and test history. According to Walidah, the "[customized] high schools"—some of the most coveted and selective schools in the city—use exams, while the "selective" high schools use interviews, grades, test scores, attendance records, and a lottery system. Although this process was a challenge for all students, EE believed that students lacked the necessary economic resources and social capital to effectively complete the school selection process.

Michaela, a Puerto Rican and Dominican woman from a neighborhood nearby Dunbar, served as the assistant director of the High Achievers department and reported to Walidah. She attended an elite private high school on scholarship near Dunbar and was appalled by the city's confusing and defeating public high school selection process. Michaela told me, "the high school process itself is so difficult, that unless you have someone who is working one-on-one with the family, it's just too hard." Parents were always grateful for the guidance they received from Walidah and Michaela during this process. Without the support of EE, many families simply did not have the capital and time to successfully navigate the selection process. Michaela explained, "You know we prepare them as much as possible, but some of these [affluent] kids are getting tutoring every day of the week. You know, how can our kids compare to that?" Although there are selective high schools that do a great job of preparing students in some academic areas, if they are outside of the student's region, the student cannot attend.

As the competition for elite, selective, and customized high schools increased, charter schools also began to proliferate in Dunbar. While Walidah and Michaela were often frustrated by the city's confusing choice process, Walidah and other staff members shared their skepticism about new charter schools in the area. On this day, Walidah was frustrated because the parent she spent the day on the phone with wanted to send her child to a charter school operated by a growing charter management organization. Over the course of my research with Educational Excellence, I learned that charter management organizations were becoming appealing to parents in Dunbar. However, staff members were very cautious and reluctant to encourage students to apply for these schools for a number of reasons that many educational researchers have highlighted in the last few years. Research evidence shows that students who attend charter schools are only slightly better off academically. Due to market-driven reforms to public education, the proliferation of charter schools has led to further segregation and stratification of students by race and class, which disproportionally affects Black and Latinx youth in poor communities. As Sanders, Stovall, and White describe, corporate charters are driven by financial gain and rely on competition as they embed themselves in Black and Latinx low-income neighborhoods, leading to the displacement of Black teachers and the loss of community control of schools.[2] Additionally, management networks that engage in corporate and militaristic approaches to pedagogy operate many of the new charter schools in the Dunbar neighborhood and were specifically designated for Black students. EE's directors and educators were very critical of the proliferation of these types of charter schools because many of them use draconian discipline practices and reflect cultural deprivation attitudes toward students and their families. As Walidah shared with me, many of these schools had "no track record" of success. Many were new schools started by people in the business sector with no experience in public education. These schools also relied heavily on teachers from alternative teacher certification programs like Teach for America that largely select white women as teachers, which a number of education researchers have shown to be culturally and pedagogically problematic.[3]

The context for the rise of charters in Dunbar reflected a trend in major cities across the country, including New Orleans and Chicago (and in states such as California), where traditional public high schools have closed, making way for charter schools that not all students have access to. Staff at Educational Excellence found themselves in the position of teaching families about the hidden danger of these schools (that were appealing because of their smaller enrollments and classroom size, perceived safety, and the myth that students were doing far better academically than other students not in charters). They also found themselves in competition with charter schools for funding and for students' time as some schools set up tutoring programs during after-school hours.

As the climate of public education began to shift in Dunbar, youth workers at EE began paying greater attention to the shifting landscape of public education and the impact it had on EE students and families as they tried to navigate schools in the area. Youth workers were cognizant of the shifts in public education throughout the city. As Walidah expressed during an interview,

> Even though the schools are "desegregated," they are more segregated than ever based on the way school[s] have been restructured. You know, the kind of small

schools initiative, and the ways in which that's been happening, has been really interesting and also political in nature too, you know the "failing schools" [signaled quotes], rather than really looking at the source of the issues they're just choosing to close them down, because they can forward the agenda of small schools initiative and really more specifically the charter school movement.

The closing of "failing" schools in the city and the influx of education management organizations (EMOs) had occurred in Dunbar at astonishing rates. Specifically, EMO-operated charter schools outpaced standalone charters in Dunbar: by 2013, there were forty-four charters in Dunbar, and approximately two-thirds of those charter schools were operated by EMOs; the same five EMOs monopolize the charter sector in the area. This process characterizes the current political landscape in which the privatization of public education is the dominant paradigm. This current context of schooling is situated within a broader macropolitical and economic context of market-based education reform.

Within this context, this chapter examines youth workers' critique of this current educational climate, particularly the development of charter schools and funding streams that are increasingly connected to neoliberal discourses and strategies for education reform. Given their unique position in the middle of a complex political terrain, youth workers placed their funding at risk by avoiding the deficit-based rhetoric that resonated with funders and that competing community-based after-school programs and privately run charter schools espoused. This chapter also explores the ways youth workers both resisted and succumbed to neoliberal ideologies including individualism and narrow measures of academic achievement such as test scores. Youth workers recognize that these approaches shape how they frame program youth, which in turn inform their programmatic decisions, pedagogical practices, and opportunities for funding. This chapter also examines how youth workers at Educational Excellence understood the ways that deficit language about Black youth was rewarded with public attention and financial support but also complemented neoliberal agendas and limited the pedagogical dimensions and possibilities within community-based youth spaces. I show how youth workers at EE were challenged by neoliberal agendas in their recruitment practices, fundraising, programming efforts, and their struggle to imagine Black youth beyond deficit narratives.

The Neoliberal Political Economy and Black Education

As a form of capitalism, neoliberalism is central to U.S. interests. Marked by individualism, market competition, and privatization, neoliberal ideology and its economic and educational practices have been widely criticized.[4] As David Harvey writes, "neoliberalism, has in short, become hegemonic as a mode of discourse. It has pervasive effects on ways of thought to the point where it has become incorporated into the common-sense way many of us interpret, live in, and understand the world."[5] As neoliberal ways of thought continue to pervade education reform, "public education" has taken on new meaning.

At the onset of neoliberal educational reforms in the 1980s, their impact on Black youth was uncertain. In an early analysis of neoliberalism, John Martin Rick foreshadowed the possible outcomes of such reforms on the education of Black youth. Rick cautioned against focusing solely on measurable outcomes via standardized testing and holding teachers more accountable for student learning on the basis of these measures. He warned that reliance on standardized tests would place Black youth at further disadvantage. While he considered the potential benefits of bringing businesses and schools closer together, he cautioned against the possibility of students being treated as merely objects "to be improved upon for the purpose of meeting national economic goals."[6] Rick suggested that if neoliberal politicians worked closely with educators, perhaps balance and cooperation would occur, leading to more equitable educational policies. Yet what has transpired is even greater inequity.

Under neoliberal ideology, public education has been replaced by new privatized forms of schooling and standardization—technical standards of what students should know, almost solely measured by high-stakes testing, and accountability, which advocates holding teachers accountable for their students' performance.[7] Although the push for greater accountability has helped to illuminate racial disparities in outcomes, the use of test scores as a solution has created a climate in which classrooms lack student-centered and critical approaches to learning and students' lived realities are neglected.[8]

The consequences of these reforms and restructuring have been well documented in the education literature.[9] Educational restructuring, including widespread public school closures and the mass production of privately run charter schools, has been a key feature of neoliberal education reform.[10] Under such reforms, hundreds of urban public schools have been closed around the country, creating opportunity for private companies to take over and create educational enterprises structured like businesses. Though not without community resistance, in cities such as Chicago and New Orleans, drastic school closings have ushered in charter school networks creating new "educational enterprises" in which private networks and businesses operate schools in low-income urban areas.[11] In 2014, New Orleans closed its last traditional public school, making it a city where schools are completely operated as charters.[12]

In a six-year study in Chicago with teachers, parents, union and education activists, community organizers, and youth, Pauline Lipman[13] found that neoliberalism is a social process enacted at the grassroots level via school administrators, teachers, and families that align themselves with education markets and privatization. Lipman argues that educational policy and reform in Chicago is a form of racialized restructuring of urban space. The privatization of education under neoliberal ideology is linked to a broader economic and political context. As Lipman and others have suggested, the manifestation of neoliberalization extends beyond education and is evident across urban landscapes. As Theodore and colleagues argue,

> The manifestations of destructively creative neoliberalization are evident across the urban landscape: the razing of lower income neighborhoods to make way for speculative development; the extension of market rents and housing vouchers; the increased reliance by municipalities on instruments of private finance; the privatization of schools; the administration of workfare programs; the mobilization of entrepreneurial discourses emphasizing reinvestment and rejuvenation; and so forth.[14]

The privatization of public education and the influx of the charter school movement flourished under the Obama administration, but the groundwork for neoliberal approaches to education crosses party lines. Supported by Republicans and Democrats alike, neoliberal ideals are reflected in efforts to increase "choice" and market-based competition. This was further demonstrated by past sanctions against schools, administrators, and educators under No Child Left Behind during the Bush administration, with disastrous consequences for students, teachers, and administrators as accountability rested solely on test scores.[15] Even more, under the Obama administration, the neoliberal ideal of increased competition surfaced again as the "Race to the Top" initiative allowed the public and private sector to come together in an attempt to increase educational outcomes for students. Now, under a Trump administration, market-based approaches to education will be a permanent practice in this nation. Though the resistance to Betsy DeVos's confirmation as secretary of education was important, her record in the state of Michigan for closing down public schools and increasing charter schools mirrors her predecessors' strategies. Under her leadership, Detroit became an exemplar of neoliberal privatization of public education.

Despite their wide appeal across political affiliations, charter school popularity coincides with core elements of neoliberal ideology.[16] Some charter schools are supported by corporate (private) donors and are controlled via business models by for-profit education management organizations.[17] Thus, the increased popularity and endorsement of charter schools have created a predicament for community-based organizations with regard to financial support.[18] This political and social context is important in shaping the framing of Black youth, their needs, and the construction of community-based spaces.

Situated in what Pauline Lipman would describe as a racialized urbanization of space,[19] Educational Excellence exists within a gentrifying neighborhood where there is a growing number of charter schools. As a community-based organization, EE is implicated in the current political economy and this privatization of education. EE youth participants hailed from a variety of contexts, mostly from Dunbar and surrounding neighborhoods, and the directors and youth workers at EE had an acute awareness of how the shifting landscape of education shaped their program and were often critical of how these processes manifested in their participants' schools. Despite the power and prevalence of neoliberalism in education, youth workers at Educational Excellence also found ways to resist and challenge reforms that threatened the mission of their program. The following sections in this chapter explore the compromises, challenges, and contradictions youth workers encountered as they sought to shift the framing of Black youth and provide opportunities for social, cultural, and political development despite the pressure to narrow their work to neoliberal definitions of academic success.

The Forgotten Middle

Prior to working at EE, youth workers held diverse employment backgrounds as former public school teachers and administrators, probation officers, nonprofit service providers, therapists, performance and visual artists, as well as youth workers at other organizations. Walidah Thomas was a former middle school teacher; Terry Niles went to law school and was a probation officer; and

Dr. Faith Davenport was a counseling psychologist. All Black and East Coast–born community-based educators, their experience as department directors at EE ranged from five to ten years during the first data collection period. Each of these youth workers described stories or "run-ins" with schools—either with teachers or administrators or with particular policies that directly affect students or EE's programming. They also discussed many concerns about the education of Black youth, particularly regarding the lack of meaningful engagement between classroom teachers and students, the absence of culturally relevant school curricula, and the rampant standardized testing in schools, all of which they believed stifled creativity and critical thinking.

EE staff took pride in serving the "forgotten middle"—students who were not the highest performing but who were not the lowest performing either.[20] Even with this espoused focus, requirements for program entry are based on the high grades and test scores of "high-performing" students. Although other factors such as student motivation, a strong desire to attend college, and familial support were also important to the organization, the program's success was measured by student attendance, acceptance into competitive high schools, and acceptance to and completion of four-year college degrees, so staff selected students with these outcomes in mind. This conflict between the desire to serve the middle and the pressure to serve high-achieving students highlights the complexity youth workers navigate in a climate that supports neoliberal notions of educational success through measurable outcomes like test scores. Youth workers negotiated this tension, while also advocating for other important features of their program and in many ways critiquing the consequences of neoliberalism that negatively affect their program.

As executive director, Leah Davis sometimes appeared on television and radio programs to discuss EE's mission and accomplishments. While speaking to reporters, she avoided labels like "at-risk" and "inner-city"—rather, she explained how the program targets students who are in the "forgotten middle." In other words, the program claimed not to actively seek students at the top of their classes. At the same time, they did not seek students who were performing at the bottom of the class either. Instead, EE claimed to target students who are in the middle, students who, without the proper resources or support, could slip through the school system's cracks. Often in program literature disseminated to donors, potential funders, or the larger community, EE framed students as "high potential" and in the "forgotten middle." High potential is indeed aligned with the idea of the "forgotten middle," yet "high-performing,"

another term used to describe EE students and prospective students in organizational literature, does not denote the same acceptance of those students
who are a part of the forgotten middle, as high-performing is largely defined
by high test scores.

Ms. Allan, the eldest member of the EE staff, directed the admissions and
recruitment process for youth participants. She began her work with EE as a
volunteer setting up opportunities for recruitment at schools, libraries, and local community meetings. For approximately six years, Ms. Allan was the lone
staff member coordinating admission into the program. Interested students
were allowed to apply between their fifth- and tenth-grade years. According
to the organization's interest form and application, students who apply to the
program must have "no less than an 80/B average in core subjects (Math,
English Language Arts, Science, and Social Studies, and History)" on report
cards. They must have a minimum of a "3 or 4 on the [standardized state] Exams," and students also must be committed to applying to competitive public
high schools.

Youth workers expressed great frustration with the ways in which school
curricula are designed to coincide with standardized testing. They described
youth taking only two subjects at a time because these subjects corresponded
with the material tested. Michaela, the assistant director for the High Achievers middle school program, had worked at EE for seven years at the time of the
study and was responsible for helping eighth graders apply to high schools. In
some cases, schools did not offer necessary courses that would make them eli-
gible for high school. As Michaela explained, "I also don't think our kids get
the services they always need or they don't get the support from their teachers. For example, we have a seventh grader who this whole year will not take
social studies, but she needs social studies in order to get into high schools."

The limited course offerings that EE students experienced were a common
occurrence and a result of the climate of hypertesting in public schools. Youth
workers like Michaela, who had considerable interaction with youth, were critical of high-stakes testing in schools. Their frustrations and critiques revolved
around the stifling impact of testing on students' critical inquiry. Yet EE's
eligibility requirements rested on these same practices, thus making their
opposition seem somewhat contradictory.

When asked about EE's eligibility requirements, virtually all youth workers sidestepped the issue and cited their desire to work with students, who are
motivated, have high potential, and want to attend college but may or may not

have the resources and tools to make it there. At the same time, prospective students were framed as high-performing in some of the organization's literature and in some public appearances. For example, in some settings, EE prided itself on serving a population of youth who were academically achieving "in the middle" (with regard to grades and test scores) in order to provide opportunities to a population staff felt were largely ignored but who indeed had potential to succeed. However, "high-performing" indicates that students are achieving high grades and test scores; and though EE provided more than academic opportunities for students, the language of "high-performing" was limiting and contradictory to the organization's other messages. Only two youth workers acknowledged this contradiction during interviews. While others casually mentioned the contradiction via informal conversations, there was never a concerted effort to change these eligibility requirements. "So sometimes it frustrates me when EE is living in a bubble," shared Janelle Campbell, an assistant to Leah. "I feel that every student has a lot of potential, and unfortunately, there are not enough programs. . . . I understand why EE focuses in on one group, and it makes sense because you can't serve everyone. But it is something that bothers me," Janelle offered. This tension in the program was apparent throughout some of my conversations with staff members, but relatively high scores on state exams remained among the criteria for student selection in the program, thus preventing EE from serving a wider range of students.

Janelle, a Black woman in her early twenties, moved near Dunbar after living in the Pacific Northwest. Her role was primarily administrative. Extremely bright and thoughtful, Janelle saw some of EE's practices as contradictory and sat in that zone of discomfort. As I noticed throughout my research, EE went to great lengths to protect its reputation as a community-based after-school program with a strong track record of helping students graduate from high school and enter college and complete college degrees. The board and the executive leadership of the organization had an interest in maintaining this reputation as the majority of their funding rested on being able to report program success through numbers-driven data like high school graduate rates, test scores, and college-going and college completion rates. The threat of these data being compromised was a real concern.

This concern became even more apparent toward the end of my fieldwork in 2012 as I sat with Terry and Faith. It was a common practice for department directors, coordinators, and youth workers to gather in offices to process their day, seek support in a difficult situation with a student or family, or to strategize about curricula or upcoming events. As I walked into the office during one visit, I noticed the mood was somber. Terry began expressing concern about the possibility of a high school student being held back a grade level. I watched Terry swivel in an extra office chair in Faith's office as he shared that a student being held back a grade could "mess up his numbers." While Terry and other youth workers were genuinely concerned about the emotional health of the student, the reality that the circumstances surrounding this student would jeopardize the reputation of the organization hit Terry hard.

This was a real tension that stemmed from pressure placed on EE staff by the Board of Directors, who defined success by high school graduation and college acceptance rates. This pressure experienced by staff echoes other research on how community-based youth workers and activists grapple with neoliberal education reform.[21] According to the executive leadership and department directors, the Board of Directors often communicated that the "results" of the program must be maintained. These results (student grades, test scores, college enrollment, and college completion) were defined by the board and helped garner financial support for EE. Despite Leah and youth workers' high regard for other dimensions of the program—namely, the political, sociocultural, and emotional support offered—many of these curricula challenged the board's conservative ideals set by the organization's founder, Richard Dunn. Still, the academic components of the program often overshadowed these other features of the program that youth workers and student participants found significant.

All About Academics

Increased standardization in education has created a hyperfocus on test scores. This climate incentivizes high scores on standardized exams, which leaves little room for classroom educators to emphasize critical thinking and creativity. Community-based youth organizations have been lauded by education and youth development scholars as spaces where youth can come, be supported academically, and learn vital social and cultural skills that help them navigate the world.[22] For example, these spaces often involve students in after-school courses that allow them to become more socially conscious, engage in politics and activism.[23] Although EE is both a college completion and youth development organization, there are often pressures to focus only on the college preparation and academic program components. On many occasions, youth workers in the Youth Lead department became frustrated by this narrow focus. Faith, the longtime Youth Lead director and psychologist, often asserted that "academics are not enough to make you successful in college and in life."

Youth Lead focuses on students' social development through social identity, media literacy, and youth development classes. These courses were valued highly by students in the program and tended to pique the attention of interested families and potential funders. Yet out of all the program areas, this was the least well-funded. During an interview in Monica's office, she captured the unique quality of this component of EE's programming:

> I still don't think that there is any program—college prep program—that addresses the socioemotional component in the way that EE has. . . . Leah was very specific about making it an education *and* youth development program, [and] that one never trumps the other. . . . We know that you could be super-duper smart, but if you were super-duper crazy, these issues were gonna derail you from your aspirations.

Monica said this humorously but was very serious and sincere about the importance of a comprehensive approach to working with young people. Monica's comment addresses the significance of how students understand and feel about themselves and the world around them and how this directly shapes their disposition toward schooling and academic outcomes.

Solomon, who worked with boys in the program in social identity, media literacy, and youth development classes, had been at EE for eight years and had close relationships with many of the young men. He, too, discussed the comprehensive approach to EE's work with youth and the significance of developing a wide range of skills, especially a commitment to others and the broader community. "Okay, you're gonna go to college," Solomon explained, "but what else are you doing? Something beyond the one-on-one academic advisement, seeing other people, not being in a class by yourself or not being this savant or genius who can't work in groups, but someone who can bring it home and educate other people and educate their peers and feel it's a commitment and a responsibility to have to educate their peers." As noted by Monica and Solomon, the Youth Lead department was adamant about nurturing critical thinking, social awareness, and personal reflection among students in the program— essential aspects of youth development often disregarded for narrow conceptions of academic success rooted in measurable outcomes like test scores. To illustrate, an important and powerful feature of Youth Lead was a high school course that helped youth explore identity and social issues. During this course, students were separated by gender[24] and had an opportunity to deconstruct and process personal explorations of various social identities and experiences with race, ethnicity, culture, spirituality, gender, social class, and sexuality. Upon walking into a social identity class for girls, you would find everyone in a circle. Facilitators would explain how and why race is a social construction, review racial hierarchies in the United States, and explore how ethnicity was tied to national origin. Students would often debate and deconstruct the role of race and ethnicity in their lives, what it meant to be Black and American or Black and Latinx. Students and staff worked through contradictions and processed the realities of living in a racialized society. Faith, the creator of this course, was able to share story after story of students' positive and powerful responses to the course content. The course became a key feature of the program and important to how the program articulated student success in college internally. I asked Faith to talk about how she came to develop the social identity curriculum for the Youth Lead department. She explained that she offered a few workshops for students around race, ethnicity, and identity and realized that students were confused:

> When I saw a lot of the confusion that the students had [about race], I said, "Are we actually doing the students a disservice by not talking about these constructs and then sending them off to these predominantly white colleges?" You know, we need to be able to send them off with a firm grounding and understanding of who they are. And, where they come from so that once they go into these settings, they can thrive.

The belief that Black students need a firm understanding of how race, class, and gender operate in this country and an opportunity to "read the world"[25] around them was widespread in the Youth Lead department. This element of EE's understanding of youth work stands in stark contrast to neoliberal approaches to education reform.

Virtually all the youth workers I interviewed expressed positive comments about the Youth Lead department. However, at times, Faith and her staff felt like outsiders within the organization, as their work was often overlooked and unsupported by funders. This point was revealed when EE's development team mentioned in a staff meeting that it is difficult to measure and write about "empowerment, maturity, or increased self-esteem." And yet, research shows that young people's feelings about themselves and their social worlds are central to their academic achievement.[26]

The sense of rejection expressed by Faith and Solomon was further heightened during the unveiling of a new promotional video for the organization. At the direction of EE's board members, EE partnered with a well-respected marketing company to make its promotional video more current and competitive with other well-marketed youth programs in the area. During a monthly late morning staff meeting, it was announced that the organization would be making a new promotional video. Leah and Patrick, EE's director of development, were excited about working with a new marketing firm. We were notified that we would all be interviewed at some point for the video, and we brainstormed a list of youths who would be great spokespersons for the program. Although most staff members were not keen on the idea of talking on camera or taking time out of their schedules to be interviewed, everyone knew that the current promotional video was extremely outdated and in desperate need of an update. Every staff member from every department was interviewed, including myself. We were asked to speak about our specific roles in the organization and what we believed to be special about the program.

About a month later, all staff members gathered in the lunchroom to watch the new promotional video for the first time. Excitement filled the room as we waited for the video premier. Those present were eager to have a video that reflected how the organization had grown over the decade that Leah had served as director. The new video was much more vibrant. Many of the directors and students discussed the academic enrichment and the innovative approaches to teaching core subjects like math, science, and English through courses like roller coaster construction and poetry. Longtime parents of students involved in the program were featured discussing how the organization helped not only their child but their family as well, by encouraging higher education and deeper connections in their families. The majority of the video highlighted the program's college preparatory curriculum and service learning trips, where students travel across the country or abroad to engage in cultural exchanges with other youth. Despite the visually pleasing features of the new video, there was one glaring aspect of the program missing. The new promotional video barely mentioned students' experiences in the youth development and leadership courses. Nor did it mention how high school students participate in action research projects or make presentations about the social construction of race at academic conferences at nearby universities. The video focused almost exclusively on how the academic programs help students get into four-year colleges.

Although Youth Lead staff were interviewed, the promotional video never fully addressed the range of the political, social, and cultural identity development youth participants gained through the program. Additionally, the video failed to mention the psychological counseling EE provided for young people who experienced personal hardship. The omission of Youth Lead's work with students was surprising given that those features of the program set EE apart from other organizations that are centered only on academic tutoring to improve test scores. After the viewing party ended, I spoke with Solomon and Faith. They were not nearly as surprised as I was. Faith, in particular, understood that the results-oriented college acceptances and academic opportunities resonated with potential funders more than hearing about sociocultural and political development. Faith noted her frustration with the fact that the social and emotional components of EE go unrecognized by funders and are therefore not financially supported:

> I think that the organization gets stuck. I mean this just came up two days ago when there's some proposal coming in from Citibank . . . and so Monica was like "oh youth development?" Leah was like, "no disrespect Faith, but they don't wanna do nothing with youth development. It has to be high school or middle school." It's all about academic, academic, academic, and once again I walk away with my tail between my legs not because the organization doesn't respect us, but the people outside the organization that only sees [sic] the academic component and only want to fund and appreciate that.

Although EE supported the political, social, and cultural work of the program, according to EE's leadership, including its development director, Patrick Denny, private donors and foundations want to support programs that are "saving Black youth" via academic success. Through my research, it became quite evident that the academic success of the program understates the important work the organization provided youth socially, culturally, and emotionally. This reality was difficult for Youth Lead staff to accept, as every youth worker interviewed stated in some way that the social and emotional development the organization provided was vital to the academic success of students. Consistent with youth development literature, community programs can be instrumental in providing opportunities for young people to develop all aspects of their identity.[27] Even more, social justice youth development scholars have noted the ways that social justice frameworks and critical consciousness building are essential for youth of color in urban settings.[28] Faith, addressing this tension, said, "I think the struggle is that when you move outside of that, people can't really see it, and so they cheer on the successes that we've had with the young people, but if you take away all of this that we do, will we still have the same successes?" Faith's question is an important one, as it points out the fact that comprehensive support speaks to the lived realities and full humanity of young people and influences their experiences in schools. Faith suggests that the social, emotional, and cultural work of EE is an essential component of the program that contributes to its academic success. Yet this part of what EE provided for youth often clashed with the influence of neoliberal ideals.

Benjamin Tucker, a white volunteer coordinator for EE during the initial study who became a program coordinator for the Step 2 College department later on, supported Faith's perspective. He discussed the impact of education policies that support this effort to improve and fund the "numbers":

> Funders and schools, and general people, you can't just legislate changes in methods and behaviors, even with No Child Left Behind, it's taken years and years for the school system to basically catch up to that. And so, to completely shift the inertia of the entire national system in another direction that's not focused on these observable, testable results, such as the youth development, that's really difficult. Especially when the results are kind of soft. It's now test scores.

Benjamin's remarks show how some of EE's work with youth was undermined by neoliberal policies that value testing as the sole measure of student learning and the basis to fund "successful" after-school programs. Although youth workers outside of the Youth Lead department claimed to understand the significance of the social and emotional development of youth, or "soft skills," I observed variation in practice among youth workers. For example, I noticed students being pulled out of YL classes by youth workers from the academic departments to practice taking standardized exams. Yet through my time in the program and during my research, I rarely observed students taken out of their academic classes. In theory, Youth Lead classes were considered to be essential and important to students' overall success. In practice, however, academic needs often trumped youth development needs. EE would provide practice exams for state tests often at the expense of nonacademic programming. YL classes were always the first to be sacrificed. At times, students would express frustration about having to take practice state exams or not having enough time to complete their homework prior to after-school courses beginning. Students also shared their epiphanies and growth as a result of their experiences in social identity and media literacy courses. Ultimately, most students spoke favorably about their Youth Lead courses above elective or academic classes. "I got a lot of my leadership skills from the Youth Lead office and the individuals that worked in those offices so they were the most impactful to me at my time at EE," wrote one student alum. Another alum writes, "[Youth Lead] makes a huge difference in the lives of young scholars finding their way through life and seeking the best education." Given alumni's appreciation for youth development during their time in the EE program, it is no surprise that many of them now work in youth development at schools and community-based organizations.

There is no question that the shrinking public sector and growing private control over education has shaped the practices of community-based nonprofit and social service programs.[29] As a consequence of the current neoliberal climate, the full range of EE's work gets lost in the quest to appease funders (and board members who are charged with raising money) who support programs that are helping to improve the test scores and grades of students. This study confirms that after-school community-based organizations with strong sociocultural and political components to their programs may not receive the same level of attention and funding as programs that are concentrated on numbers to measure academic success. Moreover, other constraints in gaining adequate funding, particularly for EE and programs with similar philosophies, are the competition with charter schools for a scarce pool of funding and these programs' refusal to define Black youth and the struggles they face in cultural and social pathological terms.

"Charter Schools Are the Hot Thing to Invest In"

As I learned from EE staff members, the current landscape of funding in the nonprofit world is defined by trends. According to EE's development team, the funding world is based on trends that are popular solutions for education reform—even if they are not deeply investigated for their impact on youths' academic achievement or social and emotional well-being. As Patrick, a Black male from the South who served as development director for EE and had been with the program for a year at the time of data collection, describes, "In the funding world, they really follow the leader . . . especially in education." I asked Patrick what following the leader looked like in the funding world, and he offered the example of Bill Gates's backing of small schools. "Wherever Gates is going, you would notice that everyone goes. Remember when everybody was chopping up schools and all of that? What good came out of that? What good came out of that? But everybody threw money at it." He went on to talk about alternative routes to teaching, like the Teach for America program: "Teach for America is another one. Why do they love Teach for America? I heard this over and over from funders—'It's so wonderful to see my sons or my daughters in an urban school. This is just so wonderful. So wonderful.'" Patrick explained how the current trend is characterized by immense public support for charter schools. Pointing to popular films such as *The Lottery* and *Waiting for Superman*, youth workers Michaela, Omari, and Alexandria shared during a focus group their thoughts on how charter schools are highly valued and often regarded as the solution to closing the "achievement gap" between Black and Latinx students, on the one hand, and white students or those with high family income, on the other. These youth workers were concerned about the popularity of charters without proper research. As Michaela passionately explains, "that's all they're seeing! So, this is my point, a lot of people who saw *Waiting for Superman* now think that they can speak about charter schools, but have you actually gone to any schools? Have you done research?"

Despite their historical emancipatory efforts to provide community control over education, the charter school movement today is deeply connected to privatization and is embedded in core neoliberal ideology.[30] Holding a doctorate in educational politics, Leah understood the political context in which after-school community-based organizations are operating and expressed fear regarding the current educational climate as a leader in the nonprofit youth development sector. Leah knew firsthand this challenge as she and the Board of Directors struggled to raise money for EE amid ever-fiercer competition with a growing number of charter schools for a limited pool of money. As she shared,

> There are a lot of funders who traditionally funded organizations like EE . . . that will not fund us to the degree that we would like so that we can build upon best practices and build capacity, because you know charter schools are the hot thing to invest in. . . . I've seen organizations that were, you know, from the outside at least, that seemed to be legendary youth development organizations over the last ten years, disappear from the landscape.

Patrick, EE's development director, echoed Leah's comments and discussed how prior to the growing trend to support charter schools, after-school programs competed with each other for funding. Now, with the popularity of charter schools, EE's development team and Leah viewed opportunities for funding as more competitive than ever. Several youth workers expressed disappointment over the current trend to favor charter schools or popular small independent schools and maintained that this attention was mostly undeserved praise. During an observation of a staff meeting, youth workers discussed the work of a popular small school serving Black and Latino boys in the area that recently received a large sum of money to move into a new building. Upon learning this information, some youth workers let out loud sighs and made critical remarks about the increase in charter schools in the city without proper examination of their effectiveness.

While observing staff meetings and monthly professional development in-services, there were often collective sighs reflecting deep concern among some staff members at the public recognition, praise, and financial support of certain charter schools and large community-based after-school centers. In one of my interviews with Monica, she directly addressed the competition for funding and publicity among charters, as well as the growing privatization of education:

> We're talking about public schools being taken over by charter programs. And interestingly enough that's been an interesting challenge for EE. . . . There [was] the extended-day movement within the public school[s] but a lot of the charter schools are now—they're doing their college prep thing—but they also have a lot more robust programming, and so it made it difficult for kids who are part of KIPP [Knowledge is Power Program][31] . . . to be a part of EE because they are doing their own programming.

Monica went on to say,

> Clearly the charter school movement within the education reform movement [is trending and] is frightening. . . . Why are charter and public schools fighting each other over the same population for space? I get this idea you want to create competition, but it's an unfair competition. I have all kinds of thoughts about why education is seen as a huge growth sector.

Monica's analysis of the education climate and the ways in which after-school programs are shaped by this current moment in education provides a frank perspective from the lens of youth workers rarely included within formal educational and educational policy discourse. The competition for resources encouraged and facilitated by a neoliberal climate positions community-based youth work on the periphery. In the eyes of youth workers at EE, charter schools are winning the competition for funding, and many after-school community-based programs are suffering.

Leah shared her disappointment and frustration with the massive attention the "zone" model receives as a result of the Harlem Children's Zone's comprehensive approach to education. In an interview, Leah explained that the growing support in the funding world for trends such as the zone model misses the root of the problem: "fundamental inequality and allocation of resources" across schools and neighborhoods. She argued that the playing field would not be leveled solely because more and more charter schools appear in the poorest communities with high concentrations of Black and Latinx students. Furthermore, failing to provide funding for after-school community-based youth programs that are not "trending" strips away possibilities for innovation and strategies needed to connect with young people.

Organizations like EE find themselves in the shadows of programs that adopt the zone model. These programs received federal support in President Obama's Race to the Top initiative, which encourages comprehensive approaches to improving schools and communities through partnerships with community-based organizations.[32] Competition for resources is also fueled by political agendas of standardization and "playing the numbers game," where schools and teachers are rewarded for their test scores. EE, like other programs, would be rewarded for presenting favorable measurable outcomes that highlight students' grades and testing history to board members and potential funders. EE's Board of Directors cared about the maintenance of these statistics, often at the expense of other features of the organization. Because funding was skewed toward measurable outcomes, EE often focused its annual reports in this way. For example, in EE's reports from 2006 to 2011, the organization leads with the academic courses, college acceptances, and college completions. Although there are testimonials from current students and alumni about the nonacademic dimensions of the program, like youth development and service learning, the report is largely numbers-driven in order to attract individual donors and foundations to contribute financially to the program. Marketing for the organization mostly focused on programming geared toward improving academic achievement. The criteria used in admissions frequently parallel criteria emphasized when EE seeks funding opportunities, both of which highlight academic statistics. There is also pressure to define youth in the program in deficit ways to potential funders. Youth workers at EE sought to protect the framing of Black youth in their program but often were challenged by their board and funders' requests.

Although Educational Excellence valued the components of its program that centered on the lived realities of its youth participants, as an organization, it was held accountable for measurable outcomes reflected in grades, test scores, college acceptances, and college completions. This created tension in how EE wanted to report its "success" in the program versus how the Board of Directors or even the development team needed to report their success in order to acquire and maintain funding.

"How We Describe Our Kids Is Important"

EE youth workers sought to refrain from defining Black youth via deficit labels, particularly in the Youth Lead department. Obtaining money for nonprofit community-based programs is challenging, particularly for programs serving low-income Black youth.[33] Small, Pope, and Norton's study[34] suggests that charitable giving to community programs serving Black youth decreases as youth move beyond their elementary years because of negative racial stereotypes associated with Black adolescents. According to the study, once Black youth enter their preteen and teenage years, they are no longer perceived as adorable children and thus become more threatening and undeserving to donors—echoing what Ferguson describes as the "adultification" of Black children.[35] Aware of this, youth workers at EE hold expectations for student behavior largely rooted in white middle-class cultural standards to ensure that students look and act a certain way in EE brochures, in photographs of students sent to donors, and during site visits by current and potential funders.[36] Fully aware of the underlying cultural and racial messages communicated to students and the potential consequences of this kind of performance (though critiqued by some youth workers more than others), youth workers at EE felt that donors and board members heard the progress of EE students in youth development courses only through tropes of paternalism, pathology, and deficiency. For example, in my interview with Monica about funding obstacles, particularly for the Youth Lead department, she explained the difficulty in getting funders in the youth development world to see low-income Black youth from an asset-rich perspective:

> I think that we've really struggled with articulating youth development in a way that resonates with funders, because they want to know how many kids didn't get pregnant or [are] not on drugs. There's a lot of deficit language in the

youth development world. . . . Funders want to know how many people did you save. And guess what? We're not saving anybody; people save themselves. I believe that.

This rhetoric of saving or fixing Black youth is a common narrative in literature about youth and traces back to a long history of "benevolence" and "charity" in American culture.[37] At EE, the framing of Black young people was crucial to how the organization presented itself in media appearances, to potential funders, and to youth participants and their families. The framing of youth within EE sought to reflect asset-rich language. The words "scholars" and "college-bound" could be heard throughout the space when youth workers were talking to or about students. Additionally, "high expectations" was an EE mantra heard frequently throughout the space and written in the classrooms and hallways. College flags and college acceptance letters from former student participants covered walls around the space. Imagining students from an asset-rich perspective and setting high expectations were intentional facets of the program's philosophy and practice. According to youth workers, this language acknowledges and honors the talents, gifts, and strengths that young people already possess. From EE's perspective, these attributes were only enhanced by the organization. All potential staff, instructors, and volunteers were expected to share this same imagining of young people. As I witnessed on a number of occasions, youth workers pushed back on the board by changing deficit labels of Black youth in organizational literature and challenged prospective staff members to reframe their understanding of Black youth, to consider and celebrate their assets and strengths.

Leah and the department directors went to great lengths to protect the framing of students in the program. Leah, for example, often described during staff meal times and in our interviews how different the organization was prior to her arrival ten years prior. As I shared in the previous chapter, Leah was hard-pressed to find anything she liked about Educational Excellence upon her arrival. Literature espousing perspectives that youth of color would be jailed or killed without support from the organization reflected a pejorative and paternalistic tone all too common within community-based youth work. Deficit-oriented framing of youth was once paramount for EE. But now, in the hiring of other staff members, within recruitment literature, and during media appearances, EE had become very careful not to fall into the trap of racially and class-coded language like "inner city" or "at risk" to describe youth participants.

According to Leah, it had always been a challenge getting Richard Dunn, the founder, and the majority of the Board of Directors to understand this perspective. In one conversation, Leah shared with me an interaction with board members that crystalizes this tension between the competing frames youth workers have with board members and funders:

> So even yesterday, we're planning an event with some of our board members and they wanted to write something about inner-city kids. It's like, we don't use that anymore [laughter]. It has nothing to do with inner city. This is like underresourced, underserved. It's not them, it's something that we're not doing . . . but it's interesting, I was talking to a wealthy person one time and she said, "just think about it this way. Certain words that are triggers for you, that are negative triggers to you, are a call of action for other people, who have money.

Although the struggle to have the organization's founder, board members, and funders use less pejorative language was an uphill battle, youth workers did expect every adult who taught at EE to use language that reflected a positive, affirming, and asset-rich imagining of minoritized youth. EE youth workers sought instructors who had passion for working with the population EE serves, but their passion could not be about "saving" youth. As Leah expresses, "how we describe our kids is important," and "using less pejorative language" to describe Black students was essential for youth workers at EE. Or, as Monica describes, "what I look for in language is possibility, is hope, is high expectations and support."

Youth workers' attempts to reframe how Black youth were imagined in society or, as Leah put it, to "create value for our kids and to leverage this work to change perceptions of who our kids are" is ever present. The effort to reframe how Black youth are imagined was apparent throughout EE's work, from how staff engaged youth in after-school classes to how they built curricula anchored in high expectations to pedagogical practices that center youth voice and social awareness. EE was successful in hiring youth workers who brought an asset-based approach to working with youth. These youth workers framed Black youth as talented and capable scholars who are in need of nurturing and support, not of "saving" or "fixing." I see these acts by youth workers as strategies of resistance against discourses of deficiency operating within a larger social and political context that shapes the ways Black youth are educated and engaged. Although youth workers were indeed challenged by policies and funding obstacles that obstructed aspects of their mission, EE exhibited a high level of control over its hiring process, curricula development, and pedagogical approaches when staff did not share their full intentions with Richard and the rest of the board. In other words, although EE did perpetuate some neoliberal approaches in documenting and overemphasizing its academic work, staff were also subversive in the ways they established curricula and hired people with a specific imagining of minoritized youth. Their collective imagining of Black youth was reflective in their everyday cultural practices and pedagogy. They did so by not divulging all of their practices with youth to the board. As a result, Educational Excellence was able to reimagine Black youth beyond deficient and culturally pathologizing discourses to create a humanizing experience and affirming space for them.

[handwritten margin note: also contributes to delegitimizing of certain aspects?]

Putting the Deficit in Its Proper Place

Though not without deep tension, complexity, and contradiction, Educational Excellence was unwavering in its desire to reframe Black youth in more positive and humanizing ways in public and in its desire to relocate the deficit unfairly placed on Black youth and the communities from which they come. While youth workers were aware of and strived to reject deficit framing rampant within the after-school youth development world, when funding pressures arose, youth workers often found themselves challenged and defeated. Yet EE's public image as an asset-based program was well known, making it stand out from other programs. The organization's framing and imagining of students fueled its curriculum development, pedagogical practices, and engagement with students. Nevertheless, EE sometimes succumbed to the pressures of neoliberal education reforms as "academic rigor" and "accountability" measured by test scores overshadowed these other powerful features of its program.

Due to increased privatization of education fueled by neoliberal agendas, community-based spaces like EE must cater to private funders who value test scores as a primary marker of achievement. Like many other programs, EE had multiple dimensions that tap into a broader understanding of youth development. Yet because of these economic pressures, EE staff members sometimes felt forced to feature the academic component of the program at the expense of other powerful elements of its work. These other areas—the social, cultural, and political dimensions of the program—were overshadowed by the focus on academic preparation for college. Because of the available options for funding,

EE's recruitment and selection process favored students who fit neoliberal definitions of success (that is, high test scores). Many after-school community-based spaces are being forced to ground their success in their numbers, thus reducing the flexibility that traditionally is experienced and valued in these spaces.[38]

Youth workers and EE as an organization attempted to reframe and reimagine Black youths as whole beings who need to be nurtured and supported. They understood the importance of the negotiation of race in language and sought or tried to frame Black youth in their program in more humanizing ways. Their efforts, and that of others, work to reject the pathology that is often attributed to Black youth in educational research. As they see it, deficient rhetoric and "needing to be fixed" framing of Black and poor youth denies their agency. This rhetoric and framing diminishes the strengths and competencies that Black youth already possess and carry with them through their school and neighborhood contexts.

In today's educational climate, all educators—whether they are traditional classroom teachers or youth workers—face particular challenges in the face of neoliberal reforms. As evidenced by the experiences of youth workers at EE, a shift toward neoliberal policies can constrain and narrow community-based youth work within after-school spaces. Rather than providing asset-based approaches to education and development that explore youth identity and social awareness, the persistence of neoliberal ideology pushes community organizations like EE toward narrow measures of success and deficit-oriented framing. Narrowing the focus of after-school programs to just tutoring and test prep sites diminishes the crucial social, emotional, and cultural needs that after-school spaces are capable of meeting. A rethinking of the possibilities of community-based youth work is essential if we are to create comprehensive educational opportunities that consider the totality of young people's social, cultural, and emotional needs.

Given that social contexts of education shape, sustain, and complicate formal schooling experiences, it is important to consider how community-based educational spaces contribute to and challenge neoliberal ideology and pedagogies within traditional school contexts. Neoliberal education reforms pose a tangible risk to what makes community-based youth work unique and worthwhile for young people. Through the experiences of youth workers at EE, this chapter provides a glimpse into the pedagogical richness and political contribution community-based programs provide to educational discourse and the very real threat of education reforms that jeopardize the pedagogical richness and flexibility of these spaces.[39] Numerous scholars have researched the ways that youth and staff alike consider these programs instrumental in helping youth mediate difficult school, family, and life circumstances.[40] Although the research presented in this book draws much needed attention to the complex ways youth workers are engaged in community-based youth programs, research on the dilemmas and triumphs experienced by youth workers in other geographic, political, and policy contexts is needed to uncover the myriad ways youth workers navigate complex political and educational climates in order to engage youth in after-school spaces. As after-school spaces are set apart from schools in order to supplement, augment, and complement what schools may not be able to provide, these programs have the opportunity to foster sociopolitical development, cultural awareness, and emotional wellness for youth. Reforms that make it difficult for community-based programs to do this work cause more harm than good. Education policy makers and funders of after-school programs need to recognize young people as whole beings who require more than academic tutoring. To uphold this holism and integrity of youth work, youth workers need the flexibility and resources to carry out the full range of their work with young people.

While this chapter examined the multiple ways community-based programs can support the complex and multiple needs of youth, it also emphasizes the strong impact of deficit rhetoric and labeling of Black youth and the implications these have on community-based, school-driven, or policy-driven initiatives. Discourses of deficiency often become embedded in programs designed to support marginalized youth.[41] If Black youth are imagined from narrow and deficit perspectives, then the strategies and organizations designed to support them will also be narrow and limited. I argue that a strong relationship exists between how youth are framed and imagined and how they are engaged in educational contexts.

Considering the current broader political and educational climate, it is imperative that researchers challenge the persistent narrative and trend toward "damage-centered" and deficit framing to include more humanizing methods to capture the experiences and voices of youth and youth workers within marginalized communities.[42] This chapter illustrates the need for deeper reflection and commitment from educational leaders to reflect on the ways in which deficit-oriented rhetoric ascribed to Black youth shapes not only how youth are framed and imagined but also the ways in which they are engaged in a variety of educational contexts. Examples within this chapter can be instructive for education practitioners, policy makers, and leaders to consider the critical relationship between imagining, funding, and pedagogical practices.

A deficit does exist, but it is not inherent within Black youth. Rather, structural deficits exist within a school system that enacts and reproduces harm on Black youth. The perpetuation of deficient labeling of Black youth in after-school community-based contexts removes the focus from the systemic inequality that shapes their opportunities for educational and social mobility. Black youth must be reimagined and affirmed as capable and gifted agents of change coming from communities of strength. Despite neoliberal forces that stifle flexibility and critical thinking in schools, it would be deeply unfortunate to force community-based educational spaces into diminishing their much-needed comprehensive approach to working with youth. Youth workers must be given the opportunity to fulfill the range of their educational promise through innovative academic, social, cultural, and political development that engage youth in vital and meaningful ways.

Although youth workers at Educational Excellence worked hard to ensure that asset-based framing was central in their program philosophy, curriculum construction, pedagogical practices, and engagement with youth, they operated within a macropolitical context that values quantifying academic success, thus downplaying other essential aspects of development for youth. Further, the organizational structure of EE—which had a twelve-member Board of Directors with varying expectations and understanding of Black youth and their educational experiences, and with funding pressures that often do not align with the organization's core values—created a certain level of tension and frustration among EE staff members. Despite the pressure EE felt to downplay the youth development components of its program in order to highlight the academic development and college-going success of its students, the methods of resistance youth workers displayed in their direct engagement with youth through media appearances, after-school courses, retreats, and professional development with staff members is notable and cannot be taken lightly; these acts—some subtle, others more overt—document the methods of resistance employed by individual actors within a larger organizational and political context.

• • •

Part I of this book has captured the history and purpose of Educational Excellence. The first three chapters have highlighted the pedagogical tools and significant relationship building between adults and youths in a way that supports affirming rhetoric despite the attempts to use deficit language to describe youth experiences. The present chapter notes the challenges, contradictions, and tensions youth workers faced in their quest to please their Board of Directors and funders under the current political and economic context of education. Neoliberalism, the ideology that society functions best when all institutions adhere to the principles of the market, has had perilous effects on Black life, especially within public education. Yet little scholarship has documented the challenges faced by community-based youth work and the professional lives of youth workers. Although many youth workers featured in this book were keenly aware of growing privatization of public education that shaped the framing of educational success and of Black youth, they were often challenged and made to compromise some of their values and elements of their practices with youth in order to maintain certain levels of funding. Despite these challenges and compromises, youth workers were adept at subtle forms of resistance and acts of refusal in the face of pressure to define Black youth in deficit terms and requests to diminish the cultural and political dimensions of their work with youth. Whether it was correcting terminology used to describe young people in media appearances, finding ways to quantify and measure the sociopolitical and cultural work of the program, or making it clear that while applying for certain pots of money they would succumb to the rhetoric to receive funding, EE staff tried to push back in other ways via reports, presentations, or media appearances. Even though youth workers at Educational Excellence have varying dispositions about the world, as a staff, their camaraderie and commitment to youth participants under the direction of Leah and Monica made Educational Excellence a strong force in the Dunbar neighborhood and in the city. Perhaps the relationships and camaraderie established between staff coupled with the inherent belief that Black youth were brilliant and capable allowed EE to flourish.

In Part II, I discuss the major shifts in personnel that took place between one and three years after the initial study. The original study began in 2011 and continued until 2012. Follow-up interviews began in 2013 and continued until early 2015. Protecting the framing of Black youth was a critical feature undergirding the work of EE and was severely jeopardized amid rapid turnover of key positions in the organization. In the following chapters, I tell a different story of Educational Excellence, one reflecting staff transition and reduced levels of resistance by program directors and youth workers. Along with new leadership came a culture no longer rooted in a shared imagining of youth of color, structural explanations for inequality, or deep connections and camaraderie among staff members. Educational Excellence would come to be synonymous with neoliberal definitions of success: expansion, increase, and capitalizing on tropes of poverty rooted in notions of racial deficiency and anti-Blackness. Along with the very noticeable change in the racial makeup of the staff, the focus of the program and philosophy of students began to change as well. In the final chapters of the book, I call for a reimagining of the capacity of community-based youth work and the importance of fostering new language for how we discuss the possibilities of these spaces under the threat of neoliberal control.

PART II
THINGS FALL APART

4 "Expanding EE's Footprint"

Navigating Organizational Change

It seemed very corporate-like. I was very nostalgic [for] the homey-feeling
and the warm vibes the old structure of "the Floor" gave off.
—*Former Youth Participant*

MANDATORY MORNING ALL-STAFF meetings were rare at Educational Excellence. Although department directors and program coordinators were often required to meet in the mornings, part-time staff members were not expected to attend. Typically, an all-staff meeting in the morning signaled that something important was to be shared. In May of 2012, a mandatory all-staff member meeting was called. As I walked into the meeting room, I could sense the anticipation and nervousness. Despite the apprehension, youth workers and other staff members appeared to be in their usual playful and jovial mood. We all sat in anticipation at several tables that had been arranged in a large square in the room where we always ate lunch. People nervously made small talk and speculated on the purpose of the gathering.

Shortly after I arrived, Leah entered the room alongside Carl Washington, the current chair of EE's Board of Directors, and Felicia Johnson, a former board member and mentor to Leah. Felicia and Carl were prominent Black board members who understood the academic *and* youth development components of the program. Leah's arrival with two board members indicated that whatever would be shared during this meeting was critical to the future of the organization. Leah began by thanking the staff for attending the meeting on such short notice and took a moment to introduce Carl and Felicia as board members. After their introductions, we went around the table to introduce ourselves. Following introductions, Leah announced that she was resigning as executive director and announced her new role as the executive director for a national youth organization supporting young women of color. Monica interjected and added that Leah would be the first Black woman to serve as executive director in this organization's history. This announcement prompted staff members to applaud Leah for her achievement. Felicia, Carl, and staff members began to praise Leah for her service to EE, to young people, and to families. Despite the excitement for Leah's new leadership opportunity, the staff also expressed disappointment for the impending change to EE and the void that her departure would create. Leah shared how her journey as executive director was not without its challenges, though her ability to lead with a blank slate and mold EE into something remarkable had occurred only because of the support of competent staff members. "EE should continue because of everyone around this room making it what it is," said Leah. During the discussion, some people expressed that change could be a good thing. Carl noted that "ten years is a long time for anyone," referencing the length of time that Leah had served EE as executive director. For this reason, department directors like Walidah and Terry were not surprised by the announcement.

Following Leah's announcement and questions from staff about the nature of her new role, Leah introduced Felicia as a dear friend, mentor, and former board member who would be serving as interim executive director as the organization searched for a new director. Felicia reassured staff that programming would function as normal, and she would be available for support during the transition period. Carl began talking about the transition and hiring process, explaining how important staff feedback would be to selecting a new director for the organization. To this end, Carl announced that the board had selected Faith as the staff member who would serve as a liaison between the board's search process and the rest of the staff. As staff members asked more specific questions about the search process, Carl explained that board members would present a short list of candidates, and staff members would have an opportunity to talk with those candidates and then make their recommendations to the board. Both Carl and Felicia stated that the staff's expertise and understanding of young people would be critical during the search process for a new executive director.

At this point in the conversation, Carl asked staff members to think of anyone in the world of nonprofit youth work and education who could be targeted during the search for a new executive director and encouraged to apply. After a few staff members made suggestions, the meeting ended. Staff members appeared comfortable with the hiring plans shared by Carl and Felicia. As the meeting ended, the energy in the room felt hopeful but also uncertain. In that moment, I knew that Leah's departure would be a great loss. But I understood why, after ten years of service, she wanted a new opportunity. I would soon learn that there were deeper layers to Leah's decision to leave connected to her relationship with the organization's founder, Richard Dunn.

Although it was difficult to imagine EE without the leadership and direction of Leah, I was confident, as were others, in the staff's ability to maintain the integrity of the program and ensure the success of youth participants. Given that other members of the executive leadership team and longtime program staff members would remain at EE, there was an expectation that things would function close to normally. And, for a while, they did. As Faith explained, "I would say the first six months were still what I call kind of stable," due to the presence of longtime directors, youth workers, and administrative staff still working for the organization. Felicia, the interim executive director, was someone Faith and other directors believed understood the mission of the organization as an academic and youth development program and was generally supportive of what youth workers aimed to accomplish at EE. But about six months after Leah's departure, other members of the executive leadership staff began to leave, including Monica Matthews, the head of programming, and Cynthia Gladys, who was in charge of the organization's finances. As Faith shared during a follow-up interview in 2014, "So, for the first six months, stuff ran fairly smoothly like we didn't even notice really that [Leah] wasn't here necessarily, at least not on my level. Once the director of programs and the administrative and finance left . . . it all happened kind of at the same [time]. And, then we hired a new ED. Things changed dramatically."

The youth workers most often characterized the changes that occurred at EE at this time as "dramatic," "quick," and "constant." Often surprised with how fast these changes occurred, youth workers expressed various explanations as to why people fled the organization after Leah's departure. At a minimum, there were clearly three major factors that contributed to the rapid turnover and change at Educational Excellence over a short time frame. First, changes to the organization's leadership, coupled with new styles of leadership, proved to be incompatible with the community of practice and organizational culture established under Leah's tenure and prompted youth workers with deep ties to the organization to leave. Second, the ripple effects of the privatization of public education began to reconstruct EE, its programming, the scope of its work, and the narrative about the youth and families served. And, last, linked to the second factor, the narratives about youth in the program changed in ways that severed relationships and camaraderie between staff members.

Rapid Turnover and Swift Change

Educational Excellence was characterized by a distinct culture and identity, set with routines and rituals shared by staff and students. Organizational members' shared meanings are important to the culture of the organization; how they define themselves; and the ways they interpret and make sense of their roles, responses to organizational problems, and outcomes. The organizational routines established at EE were central to its functioning—both the ostensive (the perception of what the routine is) and the performative (specific actions; routines that actually occur) aspects.[1] Although routines can feel impenetrable and inflexible, they can also breed change, particularly in a time of crisis, deep ambiguity, or uncertainty.[2] The uncertainty of what EE would look and feel like amid continuous staff turnover and new leadership proved to be difficult for longtime staff members.

As described in Part I of the book, the "Golden Era" of EE was characterized by a culture of camaraderie and relationships between staff members where race and political education was important to the professional development of the staff and youth participants. Though not without contradiction, the leadership of Educational Excellence and youth workers during this time strived for a shared imagining of Black youth, cultivating high academic expectations and political and critical consciousness. Those working within community-based youth programs might argue that the culture created in the program is not only what sustains it but also what draws youth participants and staff members to the program. After my departure from Dunbar and Educational Excellence, I would occasionally touch base with youth workers throughout the various stages of transition to new leadership. During the transition and interim phase, staff seemed to be functioning as usual considering the absence of an executive director. Roughly six months after Leah's resignation, Monica (director of programs) resigned and joined the leadership team at the new organization where Leah now worked. Roughly six months later, Cynthia Gladys, the director of finance, also resigned and joined Leah and Monica. Faith Davenport served as interim director for approximately six months. Once Monica left, Faith and Terry shared the responsibilities of her position as co-directors of programs. Michaela Delgado left in the spring of 2012 (at the same time as Leah) to pursue a master's degree out of state. Michaela had been a part of EE as an assistant director of the High Achievers department for six years at the time of her departure, was beloved by students, and was an integral member of staff.

Six months later, after the hire and arrival of the new executive director, things quickly began to change. Staff members shared that the hiring process of the new executive director had created deep tension between staff members as well as and between staff members and the Board of Directors. Additionally, it seemed like once every month or so, I would receive a message from a staff member sharing that another person had left the organization. Rapid turnover and swift change seemed to now characterize the organization. Almost everyone I interviewed discussed their surprise and disappointment with just how quickly the program had changed. Camille Kent, the coordinator of counseling services, explained, "I mean it was—I don't even know how to describe it . . . like it was actually kind of appalling how quickly I felt the culture and the climate change."

The rapid turnover of staff members and rapid change in the culture of EE created an unstable environment, one that was constantly fluctuating as long-time youth workers began to leave and new youth workers were hired and quickly departed.

Returning to Educational Excellence

In 2013, a year and a half after completing my initial study at EE, I returned to see for myself how the organization felt without the presence of key staff members. Prior to my arrival, I scheduled interviews with staff members who were still present at the organization and those who were still in the area despite having new jobs. As I exited the subway and began my walk to Educational Excellence, I was comforted as I recalled the things I had missed about traveling down major streets in the Dunbar neighborhood. I was pleased to still see street vendors selling politically charged t-shirts, incense and oils, books, and music. I felt a sense of joy watching a diverse group of Black folks moving about Dunbar. I also could not help but notice more white faces than I remembered. The new presence of large chain restaurants next to iconic cultural spaces and the destruction of world-renowned Black cultural spaces to make room for luxury apartment buildings and a Whole Foods Market were jarring.

As I exited the elevator and stepped onto "the Floor," I immediately noticed the fresh coat of new paint on the walls. Next, I saw the key-code box and immediately reached for it, forgetting that I no longer had access to the building (and that the code had likely been changed several times within the year and a half since I had left). I rang the bell and was buzzed in by a young Black woman I did not recognize. I introduced myself and explained that I was there to visit with Faith and Walidah. She smiled as though she knew who I was and led me to Walidah's office. As I walked through the high school lounge and into the main hallway where staff members' offices were located, I observed changes in the floor tile, new paint on the walls, and new carpeting. Outside of those changes, everything else appeared the same. Students' college acceptance letters still lined the walls of the high school lounge you had to walk through in order to get to staff members' offices.

As I walked the halls in search of Faith, Terry, and Walidah, I noticed a subtle energy shift among the staff who I came across and talked with. They all communicated that things were not the same. During the week of my visit, two additional staff members would depart EE for other job opportunities, something that would lead to a sense of panic and defeat among staff who were already coping with the loss of so many longtime staff members who were integral to the culture of the program. Faith, after almost twelve years of service, was leaving EE to work with Leah at her new organization. Her departure scared a lot of people. With her background in psychology, racial justice, and social identity development, Faith almost single-handedly created the Youth Lead department. Alongside Leah and Monica, Faith had helped to build a strong, comprehensive program that valued both academics and the social, political, and cultural development of young people. Faith's departure was a huge loss, and finding another person with her expertise would be difficult. In addition to Faith's departure, it was Daniel Morris's final week as well. A lead grant writer, Daniel had joined EE as a temporary member of the development team, and after a year, he was hired as a full-time staff member. Daniel was white and was originally from the South. He moved to the East Coast with his wife in pursuit of jobs that would complement his passion for writing and social justice. Daniel's excellent grant writing skills proved to be invaluable to the organization.

Upon my arrival during the week of Faith's and Daniel's departures, I learned that three other new staff members, who had been hired within only the last year, had also resigned shortly before my visit. At this point, EE had become a revolving door of youth workers, something that changed the dynamic and mood within the organization. So many staff members, old and new, began transitioning out of the program and into other jobs. Prior to Gina Roy's hire as executive director, for six months Terry and Faith shared the duties of director of programs while Felicia (the former board member) served as interim executive director. After the new executive director arrived, Terry was promoted to director of programs. I spoke with Terry during the week of Faith's and Daniel's departures. His sense of frustration about the exodus of core staff members and the reality that he would need to hire more staff heightened the pressure he was already under. "No, I mean it's gonna be on me to manage the absences and it's tiring. I just hired a director [for the Step 2 College department]. Now I have to hire a new director of [Youth Lead] and counseling. Benjamin [Tucker, program coordinator for Step 2 College] already mentioned that he's gonna move on to grad school and he wants to be out by the fall. That position has to be filled," explained Terry, exasperated.

Terry went on to mention the possibility of hiring a staff member named Kamau for the position. At this point, Kamau had recently been hired as the second replacement in two years for Alexandria Jimenez, the former director of alumni programming. But, Terry said, "Kamau's only been here three months. He barely knows anything," then added, almost to himself, "I suspect Walidah is gonna be out soon." The climate of fear and uncertainty was palpable on the floor among youth workers and was reflected in Terry's comments. Terry's anxiety regarding fleeing staff members and training new ones was shared by other staff members. According to Terry, Walidah, and others, "the revolving door of youth workers" was also fueled by changing and uncertain leadership and growing interference from the organization's founder, Richard Dunn, via his active role on the Board of Directors. This was surprising to learn, but I would later find out that Richard's control and attempts to interfere with Leah's leadership had a major impact on her work and health.

A Line in the Sand

Immediately following Leah's announcement of her pending departure, many of us gathered to discuss the impending changes to the organization. A few people shared their lack of surprise about Leah's resignation considering her contentious relationship with Richard Dunn, the organization's founder and biggest financier. Throughout my time at Educational Excellence, I would occasionally hear a director allude to the tension in Leah's relationship with Richard. I was curious and eager to find out what their relationship was like. Almost three years after her transition from EE and into her new position, I spoke with Leah about her departure in an interview. As the interview went on, she described incident after incident with Richard. Leah described the moment where she felt her relationship shift with Dunn during her first year as executive director. She explained that a writer at a local newspaper "wrote an incredibly flattering article" about her personal and educational background and vision for EE as one of the few Black women chief executive officers in the city. After the article was published, Leah claimed that her relationship with Richard Dunn was "never the same." Despite the article's flattering coverage of EE, Leah felt slighted by Richard in a few instances as a result of the interview. Richard started brokering relationships and establishing a direction for the organization that did not include her as executive director. For example, according to Leah, Richard sought the help of a "$200,000 public relations firm to build an identity for the organization that did not include [her]." Angered by his actions, Leah said that she confronted Richard to highlight what she had accomplished for the organization in her first year: "So I decided to take it upon myself to kind of confront him, and you know I had sent him a memo basically saying this is what I did for your organization, from the logo, and the tagline, to the colors to—I mean everything about the brand I had put in place." Leah continued to speak about her tense relationship with Richard and how she understood his perspective and expectations of her as a Black woman:

> So, EE had already been around for ten years before I got there, with little movement basically because my predecessor spent ten years being bullied by him. And I think that one of the reasons I got this opportunity was because I was young, because I had the right pedigree, and I think he had planned to continue that kind of controlling bullying relationship and I just ended up not being the person. I think I stayed as long as I did because even though I had to put up with a lot on that side, I knew that we were having a tremendous impact for families and kids and I felt good about that.

The "bullying relationship" described by Leah seemed to be a consistent narrative about Richard often shared by other staff members. As an Ivy League–educated scholar, Leah suggested that Richard valued her pedigree and validated her formal educational training, yet he underestimated her strength and fierce advocacy for youth of color. Throughout our interview, Leah shared a number of unpleasant experiences with Richard during her ten years as director. From the very beginning of her tenure, Leah said that Richard was dissatisfied with her leadership. For instance, she hired Monica and Walidah, who he did not believe were appropriate hires because they wore their hair locked. He also expressed disappointment with programming choices, such as music or art lessons as students prepared for cultural exchanges with youths in West Africa or the Caribbean. Monica once shared with me that Richard would regularly withhold money from EE if he became upset with Leah. Because of this, at times much-needed repairs to the physical space went unaddressed and some events and programs were in jeopardy of being cut.

Richard's writings and speeches often reflected a postracial and bootstraps discourse that drew on neoliberal notions of color blindness as he often quoted Martin Luther King Jr. incorrectly in an attempt to "reduce hostility" toward America among Black communities. Espousing that "racial pride" is a "misguided concept," Richard often made claims about the struggles facing Black and Latinx communities being rooted in their cultures. While sometimes acknowledging racial discrimination and poverty as barriers, Richard preached, "What one group can achieve, others can, too." During a time when the organization was being publicly lauded as a result of Leah's efforts to shift the narrative about youth and establish a culture of high expectations and holistic programming for youth at EE, according to Leah, Richard began a series of speaking tours about the state of Black America.

In 2011, Leah's fighting with Richard reached a boiling point during one of his speaking engagements where Leah was present. Leah shares,

> He felt it was time for him as an eighty-year-old white male to weigh in on the Black community and what needed to happen in the Black community so you can tell this conversation probably wasn't going to go [laughter] go that well. But, yeah, so he went into this whole thing about Daniel Patrick Moynihan was one of his very good friends and at some point in the conversation he looked at me—and this is a direct quote. He said, "the problem with—do you want to know what the problem of Black America is right now?" And I didn't answer because I was like whatever is about to come out of his mouth is probably not going to be good. This is November 2011, and he said, "The problem with Black America is that fourteen-year-old black girls don't know how to keep their legs

closed." So, I wanted to talk about the amazing things that our kids were accomplishing, and he wanted more information about pregnancy rates. So, I went back to my office and I called the board chair and I said, I really—I appreciate what you've felt comfortable doing, but if this had been a law partner at [firm], where we have board members . . . there would be a major lawsuit going on right now. So why don't we just agree to separate amicably, and you know I know that I can count on the board for stellar recommendations. Because I used to be a fourteen-year-old black girl and I was the parent of a fifteen-year-old Black girl at the time and I said, you know, everybody—you have to have a line in the sand.

Following Richard's comments on Black women and girls, Leah believed "signs [were] everywhere" pushing her away from EE:

> There was also a cost to me in terms of my stress level, the emotional impact of always having to balance—do this balancing act. So that was really the beginning of the end. And so, you know by the following [year] I was in several searches. What was interesting was that I had also started working with an executive coach who felt like the personal costs to me at the point had exceeded what I should be willing to put up with. And I got a phone call from a search firm that I had worked with previously and . . . I hadn't talked to him in years. . . . [It] was a Black guy at a search firm [who] had just had lunch with [Richard], and he said, "the conversation on race was so toxic," he decided to see if I still worked [at EE] and decided to make it his personal responsibility to help me get out.

Once she informed the board of her resignation, Leah says Richard refused to contribute to her parting gift and would not attend her going-away party. Despite the board's effort to provide a counteroffer for Leah, she remained firm in her stance not to continue as executive director if Richard persisted as an active board member.

The dynamic relationship between race, gender, and power was reflected in Leah's tense relationship with Richard. The power here lies in the capital Richard wielded around the city and his deep investment in whiteness reflected in his control over the program and his expectations of what he felt Black youth "needed." Leah and Monica often talked about Richard's lack of understanding of his white privilege, racism, and patriarchy and the way they functioned in his paternalistic relationship to Educational Excellence and through his relationship with Leah. As Leah, Monica, and other directors have shared, Richard often criticized Black and Latinx communities for not possessing the same kind of work ethic as Asian or Jewish Americans, who, in his eyes, had overcome great adversity but who were able to obtain mobility. The paternalistic relationship Richard had with EE was reflected in his demands of Leah.

Less than a year after Leah's departure, Monica Matthews and Cynthia Gladys, EE's finance director, joined Leah at her new organization. This move infuriated Richard and was also difficult for staff members to accept. Leah was forwarded a recording from an executive meeting with Richard and other board members where Richard responded to her hiring Monica and Cynthia by saying that "he's going to erase [Leah] from the EE history books and destroy [Leah's] reputation in the philanthropic community." Richard certainly held power in the philanthropic world, but Leah's reputation as a strong organizational leader was solidified and proven by her transformation of EE into a highly regarded and respected youth organization in Dunbar and the city.

As the founder and main financier of EE, Richard held a seat on the board and sought to be involved in all aspects of the program; his level of control over the organization was unusual to many staff members. Throughout my conversations with Leah in 2011 and in 2014, I learned that she was not always transparent about programming decisions with Richard or the board. This was a form of control that Leah took and saw as being necessary to protect students and staff. Once Leah left EE, remaining staff members felt the board gained much more control over the day-to-day decisions of the organization, including programming structure, after-school course offerings, and events for youth participants and their families. When Leah was executive director, she saw herself "standing in the gap" and being a buffer between Richard and the board on one side and the program staff on the other. Program staff were shielded from board requests that were not aligned with the asset-based ideology and standards they held. Once the board hired a new executive director, the staff began to see how much they were shielded from under Leah's tenure.

New Leadership and Board Interference

After Leah's announcement of her resignation, the board chair at the time, Carl Washington, told the staff that they would be involved in the hiring of the organization's next director. However, according to staff members, the board's claim that staff would be represented in the search process for a new executive director felt empty. Faith was told that she would be the staff member involved in the search process; however, she was never included in reading applications or in initial interviews with the finalists. "We were able to sit down and have a conversation with various candidates. We couldn't really interview them. They were more interviewing us," explained Faith. Each of the department directors (Walidah, Faith, and Terry) and Monica were allowed to see candidates' résumés, but during their meetings they were allowed only to respond to questions and not ask any.

After the directors met with candidates to answer their questions about the program, Faith was asked to share the staff's feedback about each candidate and make a recommendation to the board. The staff adamantly requested that one particular candidate not be hired. Unfortunately, those requests fell on deaf ears. "We actually wanted a different candidate than was chosen. We felt that the candidate that we wanted had a lot more to offer EE and could take it in a whole other direction. Um . . . but the board chose someone else," shared Faith. Disappointed by the board's decision to go against the staff's recommendation, youth workers felt defeated by the search process. When I interviewed Monica about her perspectives on the transition to new leadership, she called the entire process "crappy" and "messy":

> I say that the search process was crappy because, while they engaged a search firm to do this, there were very specific instructions about how the staff could be involved, and so they provided a token voice of staff on that committee with board members that was supposed to represent [staff members]. And then, there was the setup of interviews that occurred with candidates and programs staff in particular . . . actually, program, finance, and development staff in which I specifically was told that I couldn't ask the candidates questions. I could only answer their questions.

"Even you? Or just the program staff?" I asked. Monica replied, "The programs staff was . . . in the meeting I was in. I was told we could only answer questions, not . . ." Confused by her comments, I interjected, "At the executive level?" She responded, "There's nothing to be confused about. I said what I said, is what I said [laughter]. Yes. We were told that you could not ask questions, but that you could answer questions. So, I spent my meeting time answering questions."

Knowing that Monica did not trust the search process to include the voices of staff members signaled that future decisions regarding the program might not include their voices either. The board conducted the entire search process without any representation from EE staff. In all of my conversations with the program directors, Monica, Walidah, Faith, and Terry, they each described how the four finalists selected by the board had various levels of experience. As Monica explained, she along with the program directors were invited to meetings with each of the candidates to answer questions about the organization. They were explicitly told that they were not interviewing the candidates and should not treat the meetings this way by asking interview-like questions. Frustrated by this process, according to Monica, "some staff members decided not to follow along with that, but it was code to me and let me know that there was a shadow, parallel experience going on. . . . We met with a number of candidates, we made recommendations. The individual hired was not the first choice of the staff." As Walidah shared,

> There were four people chosen, and they were two men and two women: one African American man, one Latino man, one African American woman, and one white Jewish woman. So instantly just off the demographics, which were identifiable via the names, one of these kids is doing their own thing. I immediately saw a flag in that there would be such a distinct difference, I guess, in the range. The range, but I think that if you have three candidates of color and one who's not, it stood out to me initially.

Both Walidah and Faith shared during their interviews that each candidate had strengths and weaknesses. The candidate who was eventually chosen to take over the organization, Gina Roy, caused great concern for the staff for two simple reasons: she held no background in education, and she had no background in educational youth programming. Gina held a background in social work, and all of her experience in the field of nonprofits comes from a national organization—a program that operates very differently from EE.

Gina was also the only white candidate. From my observations of the space and my analysis of the follow-up conversations with staff members, the other major challenge in Gina's leadership was her lack of awareness and acknowledgment of the role race and social class played in the lives of students and in her own life as a white woman from a wealthy background. Although Monica and other staff members always wanted to ensure that students saw themselves reflected in the staff hired, Monica ultimately believed that liberated thinking was more important than race. When asked if race came up at all during the hiring process, Monica explained, "some of the worries and some of the tension

I think obviously, with the new ED being a white woman, that has its own, you know, built-in concerns, barriers, and challenges." When I asked if race was ever discussed during the hiring meetings and if it was a factor in the decision made, Monica answered, "I think that race came up to the extent that . . . yeah, I probably wouldn't go on record as to what was discussed. But, to some degree, yes it was." As I probed a bit more about how people felt about the decision, Monica responded,

> I think the reservation is always around what are you getting. You need liberated people in this space. Black, white, Asian, and otherwise. There had to be a level of liberated thinking and process that people had gone through that wasn't evident in any of the [people of color] that walked through the door either. . . . I don't really care what's on the outside of you. That doesn't tell me anything. It's sort of how you understand. But, for me, because I wasn't allowed to ask questions, I could only answer questions, I didn't really get into that piece.

As mentioned earlier, conversations about race and all of its intersecting forces were integral to how staff members were trained and oriented to the program. Even more, youth participants unpacked race and how it informed their lives in their schools and communities. From the perspectives of staff members, the board followed Richard's lead. In the eyes of staff members like Walidah and Faith, Gina appeared to be Richard's choice.

Feeling defeated by the hiring process but still wanting to be optimistic about new leadership, staff members Terry and Camille, a program coordinator who oversaw the counseling program, initially thought that changes in leadership could be good for the organization. Camille explains,

> I think that a lot of us were like, a change in leadership could be good. It's gonna suck, but it could be good. Bring in some new energy, some new life, some new ideas, but that's not what happened. It's like, it was just a—everything came crashing. And maybe not everyone feels that way, like I want to say that it could just be my observation, but I think once that change—it was like a trickle-down effect. Once people stopped feeling supported, once people started feeling like there was no real leadership and there was no vision for the organization. It just went crazy! And people started getting unhappy. People started realizing they didn't want to be in that type of organization where they felt like there was no leadership, no vision, and yeah. It just happened very quickly. Quicker than I thought it would.

As an organization, EE is not a stranger to turnover. Youth workers come and go for a variety of reasons, including new job offers and transitions to graduate or professional programs. Because program directors and the executive leadership valued personal and professional development, they often encouraged leaving the program to pursue opportunities to encourage growth. Once Gina began her tenure as executive director, longtime staff members began to see the organization unravel rather swiftly with more influence from Richard and the Board of Directors. During my follow-up conversations, youth workers pointed to several major contributions to the rapid changes in the program, including lack of leadership and a lack of understanding by the new executive director of how EE's mission and values were anchored in an acknowledgment of the ways in which social structures operate against Black youth, as well as Richard's (and the board's) interference in programming. The resulting changes in the program stemming from these issues would leave EE feeling unrecognizable to longtime staff members and youth participants.

Expansion and Growth

As discussed in the previous chapter, neoliberalism has created a dynamic whereby privatization and corporatization of public institutions have been unrelenting and pervasive. The privatization of public education has encouraged models of education reform that rely on corporate sponsors and neoliberal notions of success and academic progress. As has been well documented in literature on education reform throughout major American cities, such as New Orleans, New York City, Chicago, and Philadelphia, the corporate model of education has ushered in a new wave of educational leaders trained in business, not in education; and teachers trained by fast-paced alternative route programs often devoid of political, social, and cultural contextual understandings of the forces that shape the lives of young people and their educational experiences.[3] The logic behind reform efforts under neoliberal agendas has brought about the closure of hundreds of public schools across major cities in the country and fostered the development of charter school networks that function like corporate businesses—from using rhetoric that mirrors corporate language to instituting militaristic pedagogical practices that target poor, Black, and Latinx youth.[4]

As I noted in the previous chapter, neoliberalism shaped some of the decisions directors at EE made with regard to funding and their programming. Although they sometimes succumbed to the pressures to frame their organization in a way that foregrounded their academic programming (rather than their social, political, and cultural work with youth because of funding constraints), they resisted pressures to take up neoliberal rhetoric of expansion or to frame the "achievement gap" in ways that neglected the influence of systemic racism and capitalism. Yet with the departure of Leah, the arrival of new leadership, and the development of more control by Richard, EE began to shift its focus from intimate, comprehensive programming to a corporate model of "serving more students" and "expanding the footprint" of the organization throughout Dunbar and the rest of the city.

During interviews and informal conversations with youth workers, two sentiments kept surfacing: first, that the organizational priorities were different and, second, that "things [were] noticeably whiter." The racial dynamics of the staff were in flux, and there was no clear vision on this issue from the new director. It was also visibly apparent to the staff, almost immediately, how differently Gina managed the Board of Directors compared with Leah. Staff members began to notice that Gina allowed the board to shape programming and the organizational culture in ways that were not previously aligned with the mission of the program and that would prove to be damaging to the program's culture by shifting organizational focus to the goals of development, expansion, and serving more students. Under this new leadership, EE began taking up the language familiar to business models of academic success, focusing on efficiency and celebrating business-like practices.[5] This corporatizing language began to be used to define the work of the organization, helping drive the program's fast expansion into new neighborhoods.

Once Gina Roy had been selected by the board to lead EE, Terry Niles, who formerly served as the director of the Step 2 College department, was promoted to the director of programs. Rounding out the executive leadership of the program are Patrick Denny, the development director; and Cynthia Gladys, the financial director. Howerver, six months following Leah's departure, Cynthia joined her, leaving her position vacant at EE. These cultural shifts within the program had an impact on the work of staff members. They caused tension between departments and breakdowns of communication between those departments (communication that was crucial in shaping how youth participants engaged in the program). They also undermined the staff's struggle to maintain race-conscious comprehensive approaches to working with youth.

Development-Driven, Not Program-Driven

During the beginning of my tenure as a youth worker and researcher at EE, the Development department never consisted of more than four people, including a director, an assistant to the director, and one to two grant writers who were often short-term employees. "Programs"—which includes directors and youth workers in the High Achievers, Step 2 College, and Youth Lead departments—designed curricula, taught youths, and engaged with families. It was the core of the organization. All other areas, such as development and finance, did their jobs so that Programs could carry out the mission of the organization. For example, staff members from the development team would often come into Programs staff's offices to engage in conversations about their work and to discuss the curriculum and its impact on youth. The development team would literally sit at the feet of program staff to understand what was special about EE and why so many young people and families stayed connected for so many years. Soon after Gina's transition to executive director, and as Richard began to have more influence, this dynamic changed. First, the number of staff members in Development began to increase dramatically while Programs staff decreased. This caused concern among Programs staff who worked directly with students, as they felt the increase in staff working in Development communicated that the work actually done with youth and families was less important. In a focus group I conducted with youth workers across all programs (High Achievers, Youth Lead, and Step 2 College), staff made clear their frustration with the apparent shift in emphasis on Development. They described how prior to the leadership transition, Programs drove the organization. In other words, a focus on programmatic efforts including the curriculum and services provided to young people was always at the center of discussion. While conversations about money and fund-raising were always important, the program culture and opportunities provided for youth were shaped by Programs and not by Development.

Frank Robertson (Youth Lead), Samira Montes (Step 2 College), and Dana Baldon (High Achievers), three of the program coordinators, made their frustration clear in a conversation about the direction of the program and how it was being led by the whims of the Board of Directors. Frank described how Programs, as a result of the increased focus on development, now felt like "the lone wolf" in the organization. The program coordinators also described how the organization's focus on expansion and serving more students had begun to drive the organization and was now the primary topic of conversation in meetings. The Development department, which used to be a small team of two, had expanded so much that Programs staff were now outnumbered.

During a focus group conversation, Samira pointed out how the increased number of students was not being matched by an increased number of Programs staff. "Now, we're expected to serve a lot more students with the same number of staff," she said. Dana agreed with Samira and felt that "they should hire more." Similarly, Walidah shared with me:

> I'm super frustrated because it's still very unclear, like the vision for the organization is very vague, if you wanna call it a vision. I asked repeatedly as the transition was settling in if we're talking about expansion or just in general. We added a gang of different job positions. . . . My program is still bare-bones, but Development has blown itself out in terms of people on staff.

According to staff, this push toward focusing EE's efforts on development and fund-raising stems from Richard and Gina's desire to expand the organization into other neighborhoods in the city. Although the elaborate vision staff members were expecting was never articulated, Gina did explain that expanding the organization and increasing funding were her priorities. Yet staff members were not sure if these messages were coming from Gina herself or if she was simply passing on directives from Richard via the board. What became really apparent after my interviews is that the only vision that was articulated was the importance of expanding and growing the organization.

The tension between Development and Programs quickly escalated under new leadership because of orders from the Board of Directors, delivered by Gina. In a conversation I had with Daniel, one of EE's lead grant writers, he revealed that Gina began asking that he and Patrick, as part of the Development staff, create a career pipeline program for students. This request was confusing to Patrick and Daniel as they were responsible for seeking funding for EE's programs, not creating and running them. Initially, Daniel and Patrick felt that their hands were tied and suspected, rightly so, that Programs staff would feel undermined.

DANIEL: CEO says you have to do it, you have to do it.

INTERVIEWER: And then what was the conversation with the Step 2 College . . . ?

DANIEL: There was no conversation. They were shut out. I mean to my knowledge [Gina] felt like that was not something Terry would be interested in working on, so, you know?

INTERVIEWER: But he . . . wow . . . isn't he supposed to be like the . . .

DANIEL: The Director of Programs? Yes.

INTERVIEWER: You know . . .

DANIEL: Second in charge?

INTERVIEWER: Yeah. So, what's the latest on that?

DANIEL: Well, I mean there is a proposal and I'm happy to share that with you . . . we've pitched it to [a] foundation. We almost got in there, but it was ultimately declined. It's still a proposal that we might shop around. I don't know. It's not that it's a bad idea; it's just a principle of trying to get something done at any means, at the risk of isolating your lead programming person.

INTERVIEWER: Have you had a conversation with Terry about it?

DANIEL: Terry? No, I shared the proposal with him, but I felt that, and that's another thing, I think that [Gina] unwittingly exacerbates tensions between Programs and Development by . . . making those kinds of choices. So, there is this idea that, for example, that Development is the favorite child, and I can understand why [Terry] would feel that way. But it wasn't quite reflective of our position either. I mean, we don't want this. We're not here because we want to be doing your job . . . That's not what we want. We were told to do it, and now, to his credit Patrick has asserted himself and said, "Gina we're not creating programs anymore. Programs are going to come from programming. And we're gonna get the ideas from them. And we're going to propose funding around their ideas. The way it should be."

These types of requests from Gina and the board heightened tension and anxiety between departments and between staff members. In the voices of frustrated and unhappy staff members, it appeared that new leadership was not communicating to or listening to staff. To many staff members who remained at EE after mass turnover, new leadership acted according to their understanding of what they "thought" a community-based organization engaging mostly Black youth entailed without understanding how EE had previously operated. Put another way, the organizational culture—established with a very specific set of practices and routines—was threatened under change.

Benjamin Tucker, a program coordinator working in the Step 2 College program, began working with EE as a volunteer coordinator. The rapport he was able to build with students and staff during his short time as a volunteer made a huge impression on the executive leadership and directors. Benjamin was the only white youth worker directly working with students in the three

years I had been researching the organization. EE often hired course instructors from diverse racial/ethnic and cultural backgrounds to teach academic
after-school classes, yet there were rarely white youth workers as part of the
Programs staff that provided direct service to youth in either permanent full-
time or part-time positions. Benjamin explained how expansion into a new
neighborhood, serving more students, and expanding EE's "footprint" in the
neighborhood were all suggestions from the board by way of Richard. Confused about whether this was something Leah resisted, staff members felt that
goals of expansion and growth were unrealistic and that the organization was
not equipped with staff members to carry out the kind of growth expected by
the board and Gina. Benjamin stated,

> The goal that Gina has set for us, although which was apparently set by board
> members, is that EE is going to service 600 students in the course of the 2013–
> 2014 school year . . . and so the goals of growth I think were set unrealistically
> high and that puts a lot of pressure onto certain staff members. One of them
> definitely being our admissions person who is Lucia . . . And it's unfair that the
> growth—the goal of growth falls like inordinately on one person . . . so she's
> just under a lot of stress to meet the goals that have been handed down when
> we all think it's unrealistic.

When I asked about other expectations Benjamin or other youth workers felt
were unrealistic, he quickly shared that Gina's "mantra has been growth, growth,
growth. And growth in terms of more visibility in Dunbar." Curious about
what "more visibility in Dunbar" entailed, I asked Benjamin to interpret
what he thought Gina and the board meant by this. He laughed and said,

> I don't know. Yeah, like more visibility. Serve more students this year. We found
> out at a staff retreat that the board's vision for EE is that we serve like five thou-
> sand students per calendar school year in five years, which, like, do the math
> and it's like the organization that serves five thousand students in one school
> year has very little resemblance to the model that EE has had.

Benjamin's point is an important one. In his accounts, the board's goals for the
organization completely ignore the purpose and culture of EE, which is to
holistically engage young people through academic, social, cultural, and leadership programming. The depth of relationships that youth workers are able
to forge and sustain with students from the time they enter the program in the
sixth grade until, hopefully, their completion from high school and college is

a critical feature of the organization. If the board's goals prevail, serving five thousand students per year would likely transform EE into a drop-in program for students, providing little depth to their experience and lessening the connection between students and staff members. Further, having too many students would require more from staff members who work intimately with students, their families, and in many cases their schools to ensure they are supported. Or, alternatively, it would require surface-level work, which would mean that youth workers would have less contact with youth and their families. In effect, this could push staff members into a "helicopter"-like mold where they are working with students in a fashion that replicates managing cases. Fundamentally, this pushes EE away from its strengths in social justice youth development.[6] Much of the work and progress that EE made was in building intimate and authentic relationships with youths, which positioned youth workers uniquely to support youths' academic efforts and personal development. Thus, changing EE into a "drop-in" center could have a deleterious impact in *how* youths are engaged in EE—and, possibly, could diminish *why* youths might engage with the organization. A few significant appeals to students' experiences are that they developed a strong sense of belonging within EE, they felt family-like bonds in the relationships they established with EE staff and youth workers, and it was a space that spoke to their whole selves. With the announcement of expanding into a new neighborhood, Bayside, about an hour away from Dunbar, some youth alumni were happy that the organization's reach would go further in another neighborhood and highlighted things like "convenience," as many students commuted from Bayside to Dunbar to attend EE. Yet other alumni questioned how the organization would feel. "I think it would be good if done properly," wrote one alum. Another former participant wrote several important questions including, "How would that affect the students? Has the [Bayside] site proven to be effective/help? Are there enough resources? Would EE lose that small feel?"

In addition to the new leadership requesting that more students be served in the program, the board's influence also began seeping into programming for students. This was unusual considering the range of professions board members represent. There are no active board members who have backgrounds in education or youth organizations. There were a few college professors, one of whom Leah and other staff members appreciated and another who was celebrated by Richard, but loathed by EE staff. But in general, as Leah once said to me, "education is not their industry," suggesting that they understand very little about education, teaching and learning, and youth work. Yet Terry, the former director of Step 2 College now serving as the director of programming during the second phase of study, Walidah, and Faith all stated that after Gina took over as executive director, the board began making suggestions (however off base the staff found these) to which Gina would be amenable, often then passing the suggestions down to Terry, who was responsible for communicating them to Faith and Walidah. Confused by many of the requests asked of them, youth workers felt frustrated by the board's influence on how youth would be engaged in the program. Directors felt as though their power was being stripped from them. Educators who had years of experience in teaching were now being asked to do things that were distant from the purpose of the organization. Faith shared how the lack of vision coupled with interference by Richard and the board shifted the work of the organization:

> So . . . [laughs] it's just not, it's not being pulled together by like this common vision of let's do this because this is ultimately what we want or how we should do it. You know, there are requests that "we should do this" and then that request is being honored. Or "how about try this? Oh, yeah, alright, let's try this." And then that request is being honored. And whatever comes down of "let's try this, let's try this," even if one program doesn't marry to the next program . . . everything feels willy-nilly.

The orders coming from Richard via the board, delivered to Gina, given to Terry to communicate to the staff, were often half-baked ideas without any real thought about how they would be implemented. And, as a result, these orders often struck a racial, class, and cultural nerve among the staff. In two separate conversations, Camille and Walidah described an incident that insulted and disturbed many staff members. Richard suggested that the vocabulary skills of EE students were subpar and demanded that a reading club be implemented into the program. Richard's suggestion did not stem from assessment data. His beliefs were rooted in his own ideas about the inferiority of Black youth. "So, a long-term gripe of this gentleman has been our kids are ill spoken. They don't speak well. They need to be trained to speak," shared Walidah during an interview. Because of Richard's frustration with the language spoken by Black youth, the board requested that a board member's son facilitate a reading club. This particular board member's son was white and in the eighth grade, the same age or younger than many EE students. The racial and class implications, as well as the power dynamics of this suggestion, were apparent to staff members.

However, Gina was adamant about following through with Richard's request because it was a request that came from Richard and the board, and she insisted that Terry hold a meeting with the eighth grader. Camille explains:

> Well, there's like random programs that they would want to do . . . They suggested some reading group, which could be great, but they wanted to have one of the board members' kids, like an eighth grader, do the reading group! And it was like, is this a joke?! Our [Program Director] has to meet with like an eighth grader and a tenth grader who are like the board's children about their ideas for EE. It was just like, what is happening?

The racial, class, and power implications of entertaining this suggestion did not sit well with many staff members. Partly due to the tone set by the leadership prior to Gina, staff members' attention to race, class, and other social forces was encouraged and expected. In my conversation with Walidah about this incident, she explicitly discussed how Richard, Gina, and board members never considered the racial and power dynamics in this decision. Under Leah's leadership, it is likely that these implications would have been considered and discussed at length, and the decision most likely rejected because of the message it sent to youth workers and, most important, the message it sent to students. The assumption that Black youth were so deficient that they had trouble reading because of their use of slang or various versions of Black English is off base and highly offensive. Further, even if students at EE struggled with reading, suggesting that a white male of the same age as youth participants was in a better position to teach EE students over other students at EE or staff members or class instructors, was insulting professionally and personally to youth workers. The entire assertion was rooted in white supremacist and classist notions of the perceived inferiority of Black youth. This was one of many incidents that seemed bizarre and out of context for EE.

Expansion to Bayside

One of the main goals for Gina's first year at EE, which was driven by the board, was a new expansion project into the neighborhood of Bayside. Thought to be ill-conceived from the beginning by many staff members, this expansion project ultimately compromised the culture of EE, its reputation, and its relationship with other organizations. Walidah, the director of High Achievers, was chosen to oversee this project. She had arrived at EE in 2007 and had been with EE for four years at the time of my initial study. At the time of our follow-up

interviews, Walidah had been with EE for six years. As the director of High
Achievers, Walidah's primary role was to oversee the academic development
of middle school students in the program. Alongside a program coordinator,
Walidah developed thematic curricula and hired and coached after-school
teachers to design academic and elective courses for students. Additionally,
Walidah had the huge responsibility of running EE's summer program, "Summer Experience," for middle school students. Further, Walidah and her team
supported students through their application process to the city's competitive
high schools. This required constant communication with young people's families and took up an enormous amount of time.

The expansion process frustrated Walidah. Walidah, Benjamin, and other
staff members had major qualms with how Gina and the board callously
wanted to expand the program under personnel distress with the disruption
of numerous departures and without providing the proper support for staff
members to carry out such a large task successfully and in a manner aligned
with the mission and values of the organization. Walidah was promoted after
completing her doctorate in educational leadership to the director of expansion in addition to the director of the High Achievers department. Although
the new responsibility came with a "pay increase," it did not change her "authority" within the organization. "I think really the title was essentially to
symbolize and justify giving me a pay raise and more responsibility," shared
Walidah. The concern from Walidah and other directors was that she was set
up for failure because of the way Gina and the board had hastily decided to
expand into a new neighborhood. Even more, Gina, coming from a national
organization, wanted to mirror that model:

> WALIDAH: If we're talking about expansion, one of the visions for the organ-
> ization is to make it a national nonprofit organization. If that's the case, given
> that we are still extremely small, what's the vision for what the structure will
> look like? I don't believe we have created anything new in the way of an orga-
> nizational chart.
>
> INTERVIEWER: How do you feel about that expansion as a national organ-
> ization, what do you think about that?
>
> WALIDAH: I think it's a reach. I think it's a reach. Like I said, there's no vision
> around how that process would work, and so I think it's a nice aspiration to
> have, but if you don't have a plan or a vision to realize that aspiration, then
> you're just gonna fly by the seat of your pants, and I feel like that's what we've

been doing. There are certain directives that are unrealistic for the organization right now, so in addition to saying that we're gonna be a national organization, one of the things is this expansion that I'm leading. I've essentially had two to three months really to make it happen. I was told that rain or shine, we needed to launch the program and the expansion site in January.

The language of "expansion," "expanding EE's footprint in the community," and "serving more students" is rhetoric that began to surface once Gina settled into her role as executive director. Since the beginning of my time at EE, there had always been murmurings of expanding into other areas of the city. Every few years it appeared that money and finding the right time to expand were major roadblocks. I later learned that the funding challenges were in part due to Richard's dissatisfaction with Leah; he had a history of withholding money from the organization when he was upset with Leah (according to Leah, Monica, and Walidah). Monica informed me that prior to Leah's departure, Richard said that he was not willing to provide funding for the Summer Experience program—the summer enrichment program for middle school students. "Despite our telling him that without this we're going to have to cancel our Summer Experience program," said Monica, "the minute [Leah] walked out the door, the check rolled in." This kind of "manipulation" occurred often, according to Monica, and would affect programming efforts as well as any future plans for the organization that required financial support—from expanding to other neighborhoods or completing simple repairs to the physical space.

Because the expansion project was happening so quickly, longtime staff members were apprehensive about it. Despite being cautious about the expansion process, Walidah was placed at the forefront of the effort. Not only did Walidah need to sustain the High Achievers program in Dunbar; at the same time, she was responsible for building a version of Educational Excellence in Bayside, another neighborhood about an hour away from Dunbar. Walidah often expressed her concerns to Terry, who was now her supervisor, and to Gina, yet tension continued to rise as Walidah felt unsupported. Other staff members also knew how unsupported Walidah felt and were just as confused about what expansion meant. Terry was apprehensive because "expansion" was not well defined. As he stated, "we're in our own backyard. And in the event of failure, how do you chalk that up? People are going to say you're in the same city. Even though we know it's very different, neighborhoods are different." Terry's frustration was high as he complained that Gina was always "responsive" to Richard's demands. And, as Terry recalled, because "Mr. Dunn [Richard] once said, we should be serving ten thousand people," that became Gina's goal, which threatened the culture of the program.

Despite Walidah's efforts to get the new EE off the ground, there was little time to enroll students and hire staff members. To make matters even more complicated, the new EE site in Bayside would operate on Saturday mornings and afternoons at a school. "The work that we do, I think, is not done best as a school-based program," offered Walidah. She went on to tell me the following:

> So, schools essentially build their own cultures to either good or bad. Those cultures can either hurt or support students. If you as a separate, independent organization go into a site, you essentially are going to be inheriting whatever culture exists in that site. It becomes extremely difficult to establish and develop your own culture in the place that already kind of has one. Secondly, you are kind of at whim to the politics of that space. You have to deal with the politics of the principal and all of the managing staff. You have to deal with the relationships of sharing that space, so you can't really keep a fixed presence of what your organization is when you are site-based because at the end of the day, the priority is always going to be the school and what the school needs and not who you as someone coming in from the outside may need or want for the kids. And then relative to that are competing interests, too, depending on how it is you come to that space . . . but you don't have control over how the physical space is structured to a great degree. So you can't even have the resources and the materials that you would like all the time because the space is not yours.

The heterogeneity of community-based youth spaces provides options to young people and their families. Whereas grassroots community-based programs may have the freedom to control their space in the way they see fit, programs that operate on school grounds have a greater challenge of negotiating the culture of the school that already exists, as Walidah explained. Further, as offered by many scholars of community-based youth work, out-of-school time spaces have a history of providing a unique kind of support to students specifically because they are not school.[7] Schools are not centered in the culture or the process by which students are engaged within community-based programs, something that allows for more flexibility than schools traditionally provide.[8] Educational Excellence, like many other after-school community-based programs, is supposed to be a departure from the culture of schooling.

I visited Walidah at the new EE site in Bayside. The feeling of the site stood in stark contrast to the Dunbar site. Upon entering the school, I was approached by a uniformed armed police officer. This was unsettling, as the presence of armed officers reinforces the ways in which Black and Latinx youth are surveilled by police officers across many contexts of their lives;[9] moreover, it is in complete contradiction to the ways that a community-based youth program typically feels. The school felt extremely large (I later learned that it served both elementary and middle school students) and was similar in size to other average midsized to large public schools. There were long intimidating hallways lined with lockers, classrooms full of desks and tables, and multiple administrative offices. The presence of security and other traditional school features was a complete contradiction to the culture EE had created in Dunbar. Saturday programming in Bayside would take place in a school classroom. In addition to the academic and elective courses, Walidah needed to manage the youth development course as well. Walidah struggled to enroll students at the new site; the program almost existed as a drop-in center for students, thus weakening the comprehensive approach EE had been celebrated for. Drop-in centers are useful in providing fast or short-term services to students and can engage many students at one time.

During my initial work with EE, the board usually requested reports and updates on the outcomes and impact of specific programs. The board would also sometimes encourage innovation to an already existing program, but never did it shape programming or curricula in any real way. Leah was up-front with the board about board members' lack of understanding about education and therefore encouraged them to rely on the qualified staff members she hired. The success of the program was captured through perfect high school graduation rates and college acceptances. Nearly every youth worker I talked with pointed to a lack of leadership from Gina as the primary reason why the board began to hold too much power in programming efforts. From my interviews, however, it feels more accurate to say that with Leah out of the way, Richard Dunn now exercised a strong level of control and was able to interfere with the organization in ways he saw fit. Terry provided his explanation of why the board influence became strong once Leah departed:

TERRY: But, again, lack of leadership. No one wants to fight Mr. Dunn [Richard]. Whatever Mr. Dunn says. Whatever board member John says. Whatever board member Mary says.

INTERVIEWER: How was that different under Leah?

TERRY: 'Cause she fought. She fought the board. She fought the board. Which is why Mr. Dunn never liked her, 'cause she's an educator. She was like, "No, that's an antiquated notion. No, that's not gonna work. No, no." She said "no" a lot. And you know, Mr. Dunn . . . I think Mr. Dunn is well intentioned, but I also recognize that he is old and rich, so he is out of touch. I'm not gonna use the white part 'cause I don't know, you know? Apparently he's been doing work . . . he's been doing this type of work for a long time. Even when he was young, he was doing charitable work. So, but I'm saying he's old and rich. He's out of touch.

Terry's understanding and speculation of Richard's intentions are fascinating in a few ways. First, he makes a critical point about Leah's background as an educator and as a fighter unafraid to speak back to Richard and other board members when the interests and well-being of students were in jeopardy. Second, Terry draws on Richard's identities as a person of wealth and his age but refuses to consider how Richard's identity as a white man functions in his philanthropic work. Further, he pulls apart all four of these identities—race/ethnicity, class, gender, and age—as a factor in Richard's understanding (and lack thereof) and gives less credence to the social context of education and the work of EE under Leah's direction.

Terry's reluctance to discuss Richard's past racist and sexist remarks is perplexing. Questions often surface regarding how it is possible that those who are providing support (financial or otherwise) to minoritized groups can be racist or hold racial biases about the communities they are supporting. Indeed, they can. White people can provide financial support to organizations supporting people of color while still holding racist and cultural pathological perspectives. Simplistic ways of understanding racism as only overt slights and harms against people of color dismiss the nuanced and subtle ways in which white supremacy functions. This thinking ignores the pervasive reality of structural racial and cultural violence inflicted on people of color in a society in which whiteness is deeply embedded.[10] Other staff members including Monica, Faith, Walidah, Solomon, and Leah were always equipped to discuss and analyze Richard's views not only about Black women but about Black youth and families as well. Richard's financial contributions to and creation of the program do not absolve his anti-Black, racist, and sexist views about Black communities, reflected in his paternalism toward EE, in his public speeches, and through his attempts to control Leah. Once Leah resigned, Richard made more frequent appearances to EE. "Now all of a sudden, he's bringing people up to visit. He's smiling. The man is smiling. The man is smiling . . . I've never seen a picture of this man's smile. I never see him!" shouted Solomon during a follow-up interview. Youth workers surmised that, now that Leah was gone, Richard had free reign to control the executive director in ways he saw fit.

Race exerts an important function here, particularly, in philanthropy and education.[11] Jackman in her analysis of the relationship between philanthropy and the intersections between race, class, gender, and power strongly suggests that these identities are inherently present in the relationships established in philanthropic giving, as conflict and struggle for control and power are almost always present, whether on or beneath the surface.[12] Leah, Monica, Faith, and Walidah understood this dynamic at its core and had witnessed very similar relationships in their experiences with other programs. Terry's refusal to discuss Richard's whiteness as a function in his relationship to the program and in his interactions with Leah was puzzling. As a staff member for over a decade, Terry was privy to many of the racist remarks Richard had directed at Leah, Monica, and the young people served in the organization. Throughout a twenty-year relationship with EE, Richard's enactment of race, class, and gender-based power surfaced at various moments throughout Leah's tenure as director. Coming to terms with and acknowledging the fractured and mismatched ideology between Richard and the board on one side and the directors and youth workers directly engaged with youth on the other side was fascinating yet not all that unique in youth work.

Nonprofit organizations' relationship to their board of directors and to their funders is complicated—especially if that nonprofit functions in the service of social justice for marginalized groups. There is a long-documented history of the State and funding sources quelling social justice efforts and undermining grassroots organizations in what is known as the nonprofit industrial complex.[13] Organizations funded by outside forces—federal funds, corporate foundations, or philanthropic donors—can control how the money should be spent. This relationship and power dynamic mean that the ideals and expectations for the program are often mismatched. Just as EE youth workers did, many community-based educators develop subversive tactics to meet the needs of the youth participants while also appeasing donors.

Growing Frustration   Young staff members including Dana, Frank, and Samira shared their frustration with Gina's lack of leadership and protection of the integrity of the program. Dana, Frank, and Samira each participated in

EE as middle or high school students. Samira began participating in the program in middle school, while Frank and Dana both started at EE in high school. Frank and Dana were recent college graduates, while Samira was nearing the end of a master's degree. When I approached them about speaking with me in a focus group, they were more than eager to accept. With fear, pain, and utter frustration, they jumped at the opportunity to share their growing concerns with the direction of EE.

During our conversation, each of them expressed their initial enthusiasm about returning to EE as staff members. Finally, they were able to be a part of the staff they had all admired greatly. They understood firsthand the impact of the program and how painful it was to see a program culture they once knew so well dissipate so quickly. In describing the current climate, with Gina saying "yes" to the board for everything, Frank discusses Leah and Monica, their personalities, strong leadership, and their ability to hear the concerns of staff members:

> Under normal circumstances, like if Leah and Monica were here, I'd be like "what's going on because I don't like this, this, and this!? . . . And you know how can we do whatever?" And even if they felt disrespected by that comment, they would still hear it out. They would still be like alright, you're feeling some type of way, but this is why it's happening. There's no "why" factor [under Gina's leadership]. You know, the whole why we do things. And you know, that's part of the EE culture that I—you know just thinking in retrospect—that's what it really was. Everything is so intentional and there is a [reason for everything]. And there's not just this mysterious [reason of why things are done]. It's like you know why! . . . You know why people are leaving. You know why these changes are happening. And you know why we can't do retreats this year. [Now], it's empty. It's just real empty. Real empty.

In the past, EE, composed of a group of educators, strongly believed in having a purpose for all of its programming and events. Every pedagogical practice, every event organized in the program, and every piece of curricula had a purpose. The playful culture and rapport cultivated between students and staff were intentional. Difficult financial decisions that caused cuts in programming had an explanation, and every effort was made to create the same outcome with fewer resources. But in the new leadership era, directives coming from Richard and the board via Gina with little to no explanation were jarring for many youth workers struggling to make sense of the new climate and culture of the organization. Terry, Walidah, and Camille believed that Gina was driven to appease the board without consideration of the impact it would have on the rest of the staff and youth participants, thus creating obstacles for staff members to do their jobs. Terry describes Gina as a "yes person," saying yes to anything the board asks of her. "Any board member, a potential funder, 'yes, yes, yes we can make that happen. Yes, we can do that. Yes, we can make it happen. Yes, we can do that.' When the problem is, no we can't. Or, we can but why should we? I do feel a little bit like I'm selling my soul to the devil," Terry said, sounding utterly defeated.

The *why* question is critical as it connects deeply to the culture of the organization and its stated mission. Saying "yes" to everything, as Terry put it, runs the risk of taking EE off its selected path to appease those who are not embedded in the organization in the same way as youth, families, and staff.

Under the new leadership and greater influence from Richard, Terry began to feel immense pressure and a sense that he and his colleagues were working for a board of people and not the youth and families they had previously served. Camille, who had worked with EE for four years, also shared that Gina's leadership style created a dangerous situation that allowed more board influence, which ultimately began eroding the purpose of the program and the culture that had been established over the course of the prior ten years. Here, she describes how, from her viewpoint, this process began to happen:

> It was almost like there were more board-fueled ideas coming in, and so it would just be like, the board says we're going to do this, the board wants to do this, and it was like, umm what? I think a lot of the directors [are] like "okay, the board wants us to do this, [but they would turn and] like say something to the president [like] this is not feasible." But it was just like Gina was like we're going to make happen what the board wants. People were just like, what is going on!? [laughter]. Like, I think Leah used to do a lot of filtering and . . . not all her ideas were going to make it to us if they were not feasible. But I think like when Gina came in, I think that was different. She was more like, let's make what the board requests happen rather than let's really think about if this is a good fit.

Frank's, Terry's, and Camille's comments capture what was once a strong feature of EE's culture: intentionality. Intentionality was imperative in the leadership through coaching of staff and through teaching and engaging students and families. I am not suggesting that things were always egalitarian; there were many situations I observed, usually related to financial cuts, where an order would come from Leah and Monica. Their decision might not have required input from youth workers, but they explained why something happened even if the answer was about money or if their hands were tied because of the board. However, these moments were few and far between because Leah pushed back against Richard and the board. Reflecting on her time as executive director and digesting the complaints she received from staff members once she transitioned to her new role at a different organization, Leah talked very candidly about staff not being aware or "fully appreciating" until after her departure just how much she provided a buffer between program staff and Richard and the board. "You know I did have staff say they did not understand the extent to which I stood in the gap until I was not there to stand in the gap. And the dam broke and the floodgates—and it was like wow, is that what you were putting up with for ten years? Hell fucking yeah!" exclaimed Leah. Solomon echoes Leah's experiences as he described her relationship with Richard as an abusive and racially hostile one. Once Leah resigned, Solomon shared that Richard's attitudes and beliefs about Black people and "what he thought of the children" became really clear.

Physically and emotionally exhausted by her relationship with Richard, Leah simply could not take what she described as abuse any longer. Proud of what she had accomplished in her ten years as executive director, especially considering her contentious relationship with Richard, Leah explained that she was saddened by how quickly the program changed:

> I can't put my fingers on it because it just seemed like it fell apart—from my standard—it fell apart so quickly! I think they had really sold it as even if we hire someone who is not as skilled, it's been institutionalized enough to run on its own steam because I didn't manage the transition in a way to sabotage anybody's opportunities for future success.

Prior to Leah's arrival as director, EE did not hold any distinct cultural philosophy per se, low standards were set for students and staff, and it was one-dimensional—focusing only on academic achievement and not supporting the multiple identities and needs of young people. In the ten years Leah served as the director for the organization, she was able to hire highly qualified directors and youth workers (with backgrounds in both education and youth development), who held high standards and had a desire and passion for working in service to youth of color. Finally, after her departure and under new leadership, what she and the staff she hired had created quickly began to unravel. I contend that a combination of factors contributed to the stark changes within the organization. Leadership is certainly a major factor. More specifically, a failure of leadership to have a deep and nuanced understanding of the dynamics of race and education and a lack of intention about the well-being of Black youth provided the impetus for a breakdown in the organization, creating distrust and eroding years of camaraderie that had been central to the success of the organization. The stark difference in the framing of youth in the program was another key factor that contributed to the change EE endured. As shown in Chapter 3, one of the strengths of Leah as a leader was her understanding of how the framing of Black youth and their educational experiences mattered. After she departed, the framing, tone, and, as a result, the culture of the program began to shift in ways that were uncomfortable to longtime youth workers.

Shifts in the Framing of Race and Class   In 2013, I returned to the program to visit staff and conduct interviews while also hoping to see some of my former students. Right away, I noticed subtle changes in the appearance of the space. All of the flooring had been remodeled, and some of the offices had been painted. In many ways these were needed upgrades, though I later learned that staff members had no input in what needed to be upgraded in the space, despite the need for better technology and other pieces of equipment that would assist programming with youth. However, the physical differences in the space were not the only change noticeable. The tone of the organization had also changed, and it was reflected in the appearance of the space. In particular, the way the organization framed itself and its work shifted dramatically and was expressed throughout the space in a variety of ways. Typically, the hallways are reserved for student awards, student work, college acceptance letters, and honors the organization receives. Instead, on a bulletin board right outside of the High Achievers office, I immediately noticed an oversized poster of a news article about the program. I could not help but notice the image of Gina, standing over two Black middle school girls in a manner that would lead viewers to believe that Gina was assisting the students with homework or a project. The picture was clearly staged as most brochures are; but I was taken aback by the image's focus on Gina. Similar images are common in philanthropy and especially in development, where images are presented alongside narratives that position those being "helped" as being broken or troubled and who are now redeemed or saved by those who have come to help them.[14] As I took a photo of the flyer, I asked Walidah about it and she simply stated, "yeah, it says a lot about where the organization is right now." Under Leah's leadership, EE was very careful not to depict images or reports that positioned youth workers as saviors to youth in the program, so this came as a surprise to me and to longtime staff members like Walidah. Since Leah's departure and the exodus of other longtime staff members, Educational Excellence had begun to frame itself in ways that were aligned with mainstream deficit rhetoric about poor communities of color.

Camille, a coordinator for Youth Lead in charge of counseling, reflected on her last few years with the program and shared how the board and new leadership not only changed the framing of the program, but they initiated a practice that misled who the organization actually served:

> I think that when, you know, [Gina] came in, it became this vision of "let's help these underprivileged children" [laughter], and it's like, that's not what this organization is . . . And I think there became this tone of like, let's like help these little black kids. It's just this weird tone and I think a lot of staff reacted negatively to that. The organization was then starting to market itself as this, "we're helping poor kids." . . . So it was just like this weird dynamic emerged when she came in. And I don't know if that was coming from her thinking of what the organization is or if the board wanted to revamp things, but the tone changed very much though.

Camille also shared that students began to pick up the change of tone in the organization:

> But even one of the students started getting that vibe when they went to a— you know they always have our kids going to speaking events. So, you know just being like, "is she trying to save the little poor black children?" Actually, I do remember what student said it. She was one of our tenth or eleventh graders at the time and was like, "people think that we're here because we need it. Or like we're here because we can't get to college without this organization, and it was just really weird." So here, the first sentence of the mission now is *EE changes the lives of underprivileged young people*—I just don't think that's what we—I'm sorry—when I signed on that's not what—that's not how we were marketing ourselves. It wasn't about them being underserved or needing a savior organization. . . . We wanted to give them more opportunities that maybe would be harder for them to have access to because of, you know, them being in this middle.

Although the organization was certainly established by Richard Dunn with these ideas in mind, as Camille knew the organization under Leah's leadership, it was far from an organization that "helped poor Black kids." The organization had evolved over time. From the outside, Educational Excellence was viewed as a program where students are generally doing really well academically. "Serving the forgotten middle" was a widespread phrase used by staff and as a marketing strategy to bring awareness to the fact that there are programs throughout the country that target students who are at the top of their class and those who are at the bottom, yet rarely are there programs and services set up for those who are in the middle—students who may just be getting by but who may need additional resources, a push, or better opportunities. As a former youth worker and researcher at EE, I saw how the organization served students from diverse financial backgrounds and at various academic levels. Although some students' families were solidly middle class, most were far from middle class (at the time of the initial study in 2011–2012, EE did not collect financial information from families). Some students came to the program with high grades, while others barely got by. Multiple staff members had varying perspectives on the type of students served in the organization. Overall, most might agree that the majority of students were usually somewhat successful academically when they entered the program yet were still in need of tools and resources to attend college. Despite EE's mixed income and diverse levels of achievement among youth participants, Gina and the board began capitalizing on framing Black youth as poor, helpless, and in need of saving. As scholars Kathryn Moeller, Amy Brown, and others have argued, organizations serving youth of color living in poverty have the tendency to present "poverty as spectacle"—placing their hardships front and center, either by parading youths around to discuss their "personal obstacles" or by plastering their photographs on marketing materials that position their obstacles on display for the world to see.[15] As poor children of color all over the world are paraded around to speak about the hardships they have endured to donors, organizations begin leading with the spectacle and ignore the structural inequality that led to poverty. In a sharp critique of the program's racial lens today, a student alum wrote, "I think it's been robbed of its essence and the things that made it great. It feels more like a factory exploiting young black excellence with no real sense of community or care."

Given Gina's new leadership, a staff experiencing rapid turnover, and the board now fully under the control of Richard Dunn, there was no one

the capital of narratives of poverty

asserting the importance of framing students in more affirming ways. As a result, organizational literature and media appearances by the new director began to reflect the racist and deficit language the organization had previously tried to avoid. Faith's and Walidah's frustration with the hiring of Gina over the other three candidates of color reflects their desire not simply for an executive director of color but for a leader who held ideas about Black youth that were not rooted in racist, pathological, and deficit perspectives. The board's decision to hire Gina dramatically changed one of the most powerful features of the organization. Staff members discussed Gina's whiteness as the elephant in the room, when, as an organization, EE had never shied away from conversations about race and privilege. Camille described it to me:

> And so, I think race in that way played a part and also I think she wasn't—you know, our staff is predominantly people of color and I don't think that she was really understanding the dynamic in that way. Nor did she try to get it or, like, try to connect. And there were also no conversations about race, which hello, if you're coming into an organization that predominantly serves people of color I think we should have a conversation. Or there should be a space to talk about the climate, the culture, how does this shape your role? How people might be responding to you as a person who is not a person of color and like how our families might be responding? And how can we have that conversation with them and talk about these differences. It was just like an elephant in the room. It was, like, hello you're white, like let's talk about it. It's okay. So, it was just all these issues, but we didn't have the conversations.

As Camille and other staff members suggested, Gina's whiteness did not mean that she could not run an organization that engages students of color. However, it should mean that she understands the ways in which race functions in her life and in the lives of the youths and families served by the organization. Gina lacked the tools to talk about her own racial and class privilege. For instance, Daniel, a lead grant writer and white male, shared that during an exercise with board members about memories from their applications to college, Gina shared that her parents hired someone to write her personal statements. According to Daniel, Gina shared this memory without any analysis of privilege and the advantages that her class background and race afforded her.

According to directors Faith, Walidah, and Terry, those who had been working for EE for a long time understood the importance of framing Black youth in affirming ways and continued doing so through their coaching of instructors and engagement with youth, despite the shift from the top of the organization. Though the work with youth during after-school courses remained relatively the same because of the commitment of youth workers, EE as an organization was presenting itself in direct opposition to all that it had stood for prior. Daniel became concerned with Gina's leadership and the "mentality" of the board because of the racial and cultural pathological undertones they reflected in their language when discussing students in the program and the families from which they came. As Daniel began attending board meetings, he further understood the gap between Gina and the board from the rest of the staff committed to affirming Black youth through their work. Daniel shares,

> Because you know from the get-go the board is . . . you know . . . they have a completely different conception of the population that we serve . . . I had some concerns about the way we were framing the need . . . It seemed when Gina came along the ways in which we spoke about the youth that we serve changed a little bit. And it changed in a way that reflected the board's mentality.

Daniel began attending board meetings with Patrick and Felicia (interim director after Leah's departure) after Leah's exit as part of a new restructuring of the Development team. Careful with his words and somewhat apprehensive, Daniel described the majority of board members as "tone-deaf," unaware and uninterested in affirming asset-based language. Daniel was struck by several board members who espoused what he regarded as "warped views of people of color." As Leah, Monica, and Faith shared in separate interviews, the Board of Directors' racial framing of youth in the program was a problem Leah often buffered. For example, Cynthia Gladys, EE's director of finance during the initial phase of study, shared her views on the board and says,

> Even though nobody has said it, I got a little feeling that it's like "you wanna help these poor black kids." As a matter of fact, now that I think about it, someone on the board wrote a letter or something. There was some document being sent out and which I—there was a derogatory statement in it, at least in my opinion. But it was something like—these little poor black kids. That's not exact, but it was something that was indicating that these kids were needy or, gosh I can't remember what the word was, but I remember when I read it, I was offended because they don't just have to be black to need EE.

The standards for defining youth in Educational Excellence in humanizing and affirming ways were set very high—yet what is most important about the framing of youth is that it served as an anchor for the ways in which youth workers engaged, taught, and facilitated programming. As shown in Cynthia's comments, staff members who might not have engaged directly with youth understood the importance of framing youth in non-deficit ways. Affirming and humanizing framing was also a guiding principle shared by all staff members—from executive leadership to part-time staff members.

Typically, most boards operate as "an objective entity comprised primarily of fiduciary and legal considerations";[16] however, their role should not be separate from the shared meanings held by organizational members who serve on the board. For staff members who attended board meetings, like Leah, Cynthia, Patrick, Daniel, and later on Walidah, Faith, and Terry, it became clear that the Board of Directors did not fully understand the work of the organization. To the leadership in the Golden Era, an understanding of fundamental racial and class oppression was the reason EE existed, not because something was inherently wrong with Black youth. Despite this conflict, under Leah's leadership, the day-to-day practices and the cultural practices in the program sustained affirming language to support youth and their work. Once this was threatened, racist undertones and cultural pathological explanations for youth behavior began to surface throughout the program.

As I have shared in previous chapters, the board's understanding of the youths and families served by Educational Excellence was often at odds with that of the programming staff. Once Leah left the organization, Richard and the board began to push the framing of youth participants in a direction that Leah and Monica strived so desperately to circumvent. Aligned with Camille's analysis, Daniel claims that the board began talking about youth as being in "dire straits." As Daniel expressed during an interview, "Patrick and I both know that's not the population that we serve. Not necessarily." Daniel noted the ways that both Patrick and Leah describe how Richard, the board, and other donors frame EE youth: "Patrick has kind of a lighthearted shorthand whenever he refers to the board's mental model of our youth, he always refers to the youth jumping over trashcans dodging bullets, because that's how, honestly, the board sees our youth." The positioning of all EE youths as being in dire straits is common in deficit framings of Black youth in urban contexts. During our interview, Daniel appeared distressed and expressed disappointment as he shared his feelings about the board's "mentality" and how they saw the youth participants in the program and their families:

> I think the board has to do with this kind of savior mentality of needing to be the "thing," the solution to this population's problems, and it really messes with their narrative to say anything to the contrary. Or to say, "Well, actually no.

Our parents are really smart. They come to EE on a regular basis to talk with Walidah, and they're really looking out for their kid." And maybe they didn't get a bachelor's degree and maybe they don't hold an associate's degree or what have you, but they're very smart. They're very intelligent. They're fun to talk to, they're clever, and I think that gets missed at the board level.

Daniel's comments reflect a disconnect in the board's beliefs about Black youth versus the beliefs of youth workers at EE. Perceiving Black youth as all coming from low-income contexts, from single-parent homes, and escaping daily violence is a gross assumption rooted in racial stereotypes and is fundamentally anti-Black. As Daniel stated, presenting youth to the contrary of these racial stereotypes caused great disagreement and conflict. The narrow imagining of Black youth is sustained through stereotypes that are embedded and shaped by mainstream discourses that continue to frame individuals and communities that are disenfranchised as intellectually, culturally, and morally deficient.[17] It not only "messes with the narrative to say anything to the contrary" about youth of color; it fundamentally reorients the deep-seated logics of whiteness within which board members operate. In a society where whiteness is elevated as superior, benevolent, and savior, the thought of communities of color possessing agency and succeeding without the support of white people challenges those operating within a framework of whiteness. Sadly, one does not have to identify as white to operate from this framework—as such, schools, programs, and curricula get created where communities of color need to be "saved" and "redeemed" through the goodness of whiteness or a savior of any background.[18]

One of the most challenging aspects of running Educational Excellence was finding funding to maintain the long list of programs for students. Financial worry and stress is understood by directors and youth workers in nonprofit organizations that rely on financial support from foundations and philanthropists, as well as government grants, to support their work. The Development team, including Daniel, often found themselves in tense situations when grants desired the kind of language and labels to define youth that were at odds with how the organization labeled the youth and communities they served. Daniel shared that he was often placed in compromising situations where framing the organization in deficit ways was necessary in order to obtain certain funding. These situations made him uncomfortable considering the training or, as he described, "the education" he had received from staff members about race, the social context of education, and the importance of reimagining Black youth.

My interview with Daniel happened to occur on his last day working for EE. Daniel frankly stated that he could not continue working under leadership that did not reflect his values. A critical moment for Daniel came one day as he and Gina walked down a busy Dunbar street to the train station to attend a meeting with a donor. As they walked through the streets of Dunbar, past vibrant street vendors and a sea of majority Black faces, Gina told him that "Dunbar wasn't a safe place for us white people." Daniel told me that he was furious and taken aback by her comment, but he did not respond. In recalling this moment, Daniel expressed disgust and disappointment and could not reconcile how Gina would be able to lead an educational organization for youth in Dunbar with such an attitude. Sincere and reflective, Daniel expressed gratitude for the education he had received during his time at EE. Because of the changes in leadership coupled with a strong shift to becoming a development-driven program, Daniel decided he could not work alongside someone who was not thoughtful about the dynamics of race, class, and power and the deep impact these forces had on Dunbar and social and educational opportunities for minoritized youth.

The comment from Patrick that I quoted earlier about the board's unwillingness to imagine Black youth from a place of wholeness and agency because "it messes with their narrative" perfectly captures the conflict and disconnect that occurs between community-based organizations, their board of directors, and primary donors. As I argue throughout this chapter, race is a central organizing factor in EE's relationship to its board and funders. Race and class together are also central features in the drastic changes that occurred at EE as it adopted neoliberal tactics of growth and change under new leadership.

• • •

In addition to the shift in the framing of youth, EE began to take up neoliberal rhetoric, focusing on expansion and serving more students in order to remain competitive. The structure set by youth workers under Leah's leadership helped to nurture youth from a holistic perspective—focusing on their academic, socioemotional, and cultural needs. Expanding the program without the proper infrastructure shifted the organization in an entirely different direction—one that would lead to damaged relationships and altered the reputation of the organization. Leah's departure from Educational Excellence was not expected to prompt such a radical shift in the scope of EE's work nor in the culture of the program. It is important to add that the drastic changes at Educational Excellence do not rest merely on Leah's departure nor does they rest on Gina's arrival.

Rather, the combination of departures and arrivals of new ideologies, rhetoric, and styles of leadership transformed EE into a different organization. Although it was not Leah's departure itself that sparked such dramatic change within the organization, her ability to refuse demands from Richard, the board, and outside political pressures and her ability to assert the brilliance and potential of young people in the program proved to be the difference.

Also key to understanding the micro-level shifts that occurred within the changes in leadership and new cultural practices in the organization are the macro-level logics of education rooted in neoliberal notions of success and how they translate to the world of youth work. EE began to rely on the work of its development team and not the work of the departments that labored with and on behalf of youths and families. Rapid growth and increase in the number of youths "served" by Educational Excellence became the new language and mode of operation for the organization. Under these new logics, racial and economic discourse about Black youth and educational opportunity within the organization began to drastically disrupt life at Educational Excellence. These cultural shifts in the organizational dynamics, including the relationships between youth workers, students' attention to the new ways they were being talked about, and a hyperfocus on serving more students and expanding the organization's footprint in Dunbar and the city at large altered the relationships and the ways in which EE functioned. A breakdown in relationships and gross mistrust flourished at the onset of these larger organizational shifts. Anchored by the narratives and experiences of youth workers, the next chapter seeks to analyze these breakdowns in further detail in order to understand how altered relationships between youth workers led to subtle forms of resistance to challenge leadership in order to reassert the types of agency that flourished once before.

5 "The Family Is Dead"

Corporatizing After-School

The staff was great and treated me as if I was their own. We were all accountable for another. I remember them involving my mother in so many things that used to go on as well. I appreciate them showing me that there are successful Black people out there who are committed to the greater good of youth. I wish they could come back to take over EE again.

—*Former EE youth participant*

Now, it's more like everybody does their own thing. So, it's become really kind of traditional business-like versus sort of this collective family-like atmosphere where we all are working towards the best interest of the young person.

—*Dr. Faith Davenport, Youth Lead Director, 2002–2015*

While the new renovations make the seventh floor look fancy, I feel like it is to attract a new demographic of students. I believe EE is being whitened for the sake of a business transaction.

—*Former Youth Participant*

UNDER LEAH'S TENURE, those who walked into Educational Excellence while programming with students was under way would notice the vibrant engagement between youth workers and students. They would also notice the close relationships between youth workers. The executive leadership, department directors, and part-time instructors were all well-trained pedagogues with years of experience engaging youth in school and community-based spaces, and they knew how to build an infectious rapport and camaraderie to anchor the organization. Staff members like Monica, Faith, and Leah had professional and personal friendships with each other prior to working at EE. Faith, Leah, and Terry had all worked together for nine to ten years; their working relationships were rooted in respect for the work they did and a compassion for each other. As with any professional and personal relationship, there were indeed disagreements and frustrations, yet staff at EE generally liked each other as people or, at the very least, respected each other's commitment to youth and competence as community-based educators and leaders. I suggest that the respect and camaraderie shared by youth workers was also rooted in a shared ideology about Black youth and their demand for setting high expectations because they truly believed in the agency of Black youth. The culture, climate, and camaraderie at Educational Excellence were always palpable and noticed by everyone who entered the space. "The Floor," as EE was affectionately called, was often filled with laughter and lively conversations, and the creative curricula sought to nurture the academic, sociocultural, and emotional needs of youth. The community of practice—a sustained identity formed around a shared domain of interests where members of the community share a set of experiences, tools, ways of being, and addressing problems[1]—established at Educational Excellence was essential to its success in the "Golden Era."

The professional and personal relationships between staff members, the shared affirming and asset-based language used to describe youth participants, and the setting of high academic and social expectations are essential components to the community of practice at Educational Excellence. Most youth workers described EE as a fun place to work alongside others who genuinely cared about young people and who were committed to the mission of the program. The commitment to the mission of Educational Excellence was secured by a shared ideology among staff members. Understanding and embodying asset-rich language and pedagogical practices were imperatives for all staff members. Youth workers were intentional about the language they used to describe youth participants and educational achievement. This shared language helped develop cohesiveness between staff members that permeated through the entire program. The culture and climate of Educational Excellence was sustained by the strength of the professional relationships established between executive leadership, department directors, and youth workers. Although there is no such thing as a perfect organization free of conflict, the shared ideology and language among staff members, accountability, and commitment to youth work anchored Educational Excellence.

Literature on youth experiences in community-based after-school spaces has shown that authentic relationship building, role modeling, and meaningful mentorship between adult and youth participants are primary benefits of the engagement in these spaces.[2] Although this finding in the research has been extremely important to understanding youth experiences, little research has explored the relationships between youth workers themselves. As educators within community-based settings, youth workers experience a tremendous amount of pressure as they are centered in the middle of young people's schooling and familial experiences. Additionally, because of the deep work they engage in on behalf of youth, youth workers must be coordinated and in constant communication in order to provide comprehensive support to students. At Educational Excellence, I observed staff members in seamless coordination with one another as they worked to seek solutions to challenges young people or families faced. They also pushed back on the Board of Directors and the founder, Richard Dunn, as they attempted to frame youth from deficit perspectives. Once the transition to new leadership occurred, the coordination between youth workers, communication, and camaraderie was jeopardized, leading to distrust, hurt feelings, and deep frustration. This chapter explores how relationships at Educational Excellence began to break down as a result of broader ideological shifts in the organization due to interference from the Board of Directors and the founder, the program's expansion and subsequent reliance on racialized neoliberal rhetoric and patterns of success via growth models, as well as the more corporate-style culture of youth work. Even more, the demise of important relationships between department directors and new leadership resulted in a lack of resistance against the external political pressures coming from the board and Richard.

Culture and Camaraderie

I held follow-up interviews with remaining staff members at the Educational Excellence site. The vibrant energy of the space indeed felt different as described by remaining youth workers I spoke with. There also seemed to be tension present—a tension that spoke to the stress of the transition, the uncertainty in the future of the organization under new leadership, and, most palpably, a sense of conflict between staff members. As explained in Chapter 2, student participants and staff members alike often described EE as a family. There was always a sense of fun and joy among staff despite the serious nature of the work. In my follow-up interviews with Camille, she described the balance that people tried to find at EE between being serious about the work and enjoying the work by creating a fun work environment:

Everyone has to feel it out, but I feel like there's a real family here amongst the staff. And people joke and they have fun with each other, but everyone's also really serious about the work that we're doing here, which I really value. Because, it's like in the same breath you could be having fun, and joking [laughter], but you're also like—everyone's about the same purpose and I think that's so important.

Although conflict and tension emerged on many occasions at EE during Leah's tenure, relationships that were established and nurtured throughout the program via professional development opportunities generally remained strong. Monica discussed the importance of relationship building for accountability between staff members and to the youth participants in the program:

A relationship is built on your ability to say something and do what you say. As my grandfather would say, "Say what you mean and mean what you say." That's where relationship is built. . . . Relationship is the ability to make real, to manifest, you know, your care, your connection, your, you know, desire to create something with other people, and to be accountable for that. Relationship is everything. To be honest, to be loyal, you know, to, to be willing to admit you're wrong, you know, to be willing to say, "Is what I'm about to say, right now, does that make me right or does that build or preserve the relationship?" And there are times when I know I'm right and I have to stop and ask myself that question because I have to build for another day. So . . . learning that relationship and the power of relationship affords you the opportunity, obviously to genuinely celebrate and to have difficult conversation[s] when it's necessary.

Monica's comments about the strength of relationships at EE included the relationships between staff members and also between staff and youth. Despite frustrations between staff members who worked closely together, throughout my interviews it became clear that there was a widespread belief that everyone working in the program cared about the students and the families in the program.

Under new leadership and with the hiring and departures of staff members over a short year-and-a-half period, trusting the intentions of staff members—and believing they were present because of their love of Black youth—was difficult for some. The "family-like" atmosphere at EE began to deteriorate rapidly after Leah's departure and the growing interference from board members and from Richard. Tension within the program was high as distrust and resentment began to surface between youth workers. Many staff members were shocked by the tension in working relationships between staff who had worked together for several years prior to the changes. "Seriously, it was shocking to me to see ten-year working relationships just fall apart," shared Camille:

> Or people not feeling supported . . . [that] surprised me the most and also saddened me the most. Because of the changes people just weren't, like, in the work together anymore. It became people, like, feeling really independent—I found it really isolating. Yeah, I think that surprised me the most. And also, like, the staff turnover. It just got crazy, how many people were leaving and realizing that they'd rather do other things really. I mean, I don't think it was about the kids. I mean, everybody loves working with the kids, but at the end people knew they needed, that that wasn't the type of work environment they wanted to be in.

After Leah's departure, youth workers who stayed shared that they were "hanging on" in hopes that things would get better for them so that they could be present for students they had worked with for so many years. Many feared that leaving the organization abruptly might cause harm to students. As the organization began having problems stemming from Richard's demands and Gina's acceptance of them, staff members experienced immense stress. Working with youth became the only reason staff remained. This reality for EE youth workers speaks to the tensions inherent in youth work. Staff members must balance their relationship and position in the organization with their engagement and relationships with youth. These are sometimes difficult for educators to reconcile, while they experience continued slights, underappreciation, and tense work environments.

Staff members who remained after Leah and Monica's departure, like Terry and Walidah, felt the culture and climate of the program shift away from the family-like atmosphere created under Leah's leadership. Terry attributes the new climate and culture of the organization to staff members no longer being aligned with and connected to the mission of the organization. As a result, Terry explains how "EE is not a family":

> Because we're here because of the mission, you know? And that's what it is. Um, I think that's how you continue. It's not family. I think, you know, we got lucky here at EE having a family. With all the people like-minded similarly, you know? . . . I mean similarly in passion. I don't think it's about family. I think it's about commitment to the mission. It's not even about commitment to the young people; it's about commitment to the mission. And that's why we have them; that should direct all the things we do.

Here, Terry emphasizes that all he and others can do is work toward the mission of the organization now that EE feels less like a family. "The family is dead; the family is dead," said Terry. He went on to add, "My focus now is on getting students through college. I'm mission focused. I'm not thinking about the individual students. I am mission focused." When I asked Terry to explain what he meant by "mission focused," he shared, "I'm here for each student that I see by name . . . I'm here to make sure students are qualified and prepared and equipped to get through college successfully . . . that their minds are [pause] broadened, so that they're not limited in their thinking in their scope of what's possible." Terry went on to describe his ideal world where an EE alum is a success story in the mainstream: "where is our success story?" He continued by saying that the lack of a mainstream success story was "why we can't get any money." He added, "and they keep wanting to tell the story of kids jumping over trash cans."

I understood two things from Terry's comments. First, he was interested in seeing the mission of EE come to fruition, where youth complete college and go on to create social change and have fulfilling careers that make an impact on society, as per the mission of the organization. Second, I understood his frustration with the leadership and the Board of Directors focusing on deficit framing of youth in the organization, instead of spotlighting alumni who are considered to be "successful" based on their completion of college, career paths, or their contributions to the communities to which they are connected. I also recognized the exhaustion, frustration, and fear in Terry's voice and body language. His frustration was profound as he and other longtime staff members mourned what EE had been.

Once so special to the organization, the personal and professional relationships between departments and staff members anchored by shared ideology of youth work and the overall community of practice began to wither under a new organizational culture and climate. The new leadership and the interference by Richard Dunn and the board facilitated and exacerbated conflict and tension between segments of the organization and department directors. They added cultural dimensions to the day-to-day operations of the program that were incongruent with the culture previously established where relationships were central and where affirming language and high expectations were vital to all relationships between adults and young people in the space. Under the weight of these cultural and programmatic shifts, relationships began to suffer and many dissolved altogether. Camille explained:

Oh yeah, there was a lot of tension, really crazy. Because these were, like, friendships and relationships and working relationships that have been going on for years and had been great strong relationships that really fueled the organization and they were, like, falling apart. I mean, I wasn't surprised, because there was this dynamic created where there was, like, you know, there were these expectations being passed down, but I don't think were reasonable. And I think a lot of people were feeling unsupported in that. And so, even when I think of some exec leadership not really advocating or some of the directors in the way that they were hoping, or the way that it had been—in this previous camaraderie that wasn't really, it's not really holding . . . it's weird. I felt like some people were aligning with the new leadership and some of the directors who weren't feeling, like, what the new leadership was passing down was reasonable weren't being supported. So their needs weren't being considered, what they're able to do wasn't really being considered. Because you know it's not a huge organization, there's like two or three people in some departments. It's not feasible for certain things to be done, and I don't think those needs were being considered, and I think that caused a lot of tensions and lack of support that some of the directors were experiencing when all these recommended changes were passed down from the board. A lot of the things that weren't consistent with the mission or the work we had been doing were not like feasible.

As Camille described how friendships and working relationships that had lasted many years were breaking down, the pain and disappointment in her voice was clear. Nevertheless, because of the dynamic that had been created by the new leadership of the organization and by the board, she was not surprised that relationships between youth workers would begin to fragment. The new dynamic and climate of the program had quickly changed after the six-month interim period. Most probably believed that the relationships established at EE would be protected against any larger political shifts in the organization. Unfortunately, this was not the case. As working relationships began to change, the culture of the organization changed dramatically in ways that became unrecognizable to youth, families, and longtime EE staff members.

Hearing Terry say, "the family is dead," was difficult to digest. During my early days working in the organization and to the moment I began researching the organization, the familial atmosphere is something that all agreed on. To say that the familial nature of staff and youth relationships was a source of strength would be an understatement. The familial nature of the program was an intentional design in the culture of the organization under Leah's direction that was supported by all youth workers and accepted by youth participants. I do not mean to romanticize the program in any way. Like all families, there is usually tension and conflict, but love is present. A culture of critical thought and reflection, love, accountability, and strong relationships once anchored EE.

"You Create the Culture, or the Culture Will Create Itself"

For roughly ten years, staff members at EE worked diligently to establish a strong culture and community of practice. With the leadership transition and subsequent turnover, longtime staff members feared that EE would transform into an entirely different program as Gina and the board began to move the culture of the program further away from the mission. Indeed, once the transition of leadership occurred, Gina and the board began changing how the program operated, which created conflict between the departments, as the board had its sights set on expansion, "serving more students," and "expanding EE's footprint." After receiving direction from Gina, Daniel and Patrick began to notice that Gina was trying to market the organization in ways that did not speak to the mission of the program. As Daniel reflects in the comments below, Gina tried to shift EE to more of a mentoring program, which was much more familiar to her previous work. Although there are a variety of programs that engage youth in community spaces, they are not all the same, nor should they be. As the exchange with Daniel below reflects, the focus of the organization began to shift under new leadership:

INTERVIEWER: Is there funding for mentoring programs?

DANIEL: I think there is, but I think this is a reflection of her ignorance in fundraising, because, yes, there's funding for mentor programs that are [national mentorship organization]. It's a national organization, they have name recognition. If EE were to do that? No. EE should stick to what EE does. I don't think that she's pursued a smart conversation about how to replicate EE elsewhere. Again, keeping in mind that she is always divided. Whoever sits in front of her has the most influence.

INTERVIEWER: Is there a conversation between staff members about where it's all coming from?

DANIEL: I think Gina is trying to make her experience, her background is in [national organization], where she served as the mentor coordinator of sorts and that was her job for fifteen years there. Pretty sure that's what she has in mind to do, to turn EE into more of a mentor program than supplemental education or youth development or anything like that.

INTERVIEWER: What do you think about that?

DANIEL: I'm horrified by it. That's literally when I decided to start looking [for another job], there are always numbers of reasons why you leave an organization that you love, but that was scary. To think about how she's not communicated about that in any way. I remember Patrick and I were talking to Terry at one point, and Patrick was asking all these terse questions about are we doing this with the students, are we doing that, who's going to be taking charge of this, can we get something. It was clear Terry was visibly upset by that conversation. And we left his office and I said, "Patrick, what was that, you railroaded him. What was going on?" And he himself had been rattled by Gina, who was like, "They hired me for my social worker experience and my only experience is in mentoring programs, so obviously they want me to turn this into a mentor program." That's what he shared with me. And I said, "Really?" She's not being straightforward if this is indeed what she's planning to do. It's not coming through. I think she's trying to be delicate and subtle in how she does things but that's not helpful because we're still thinking she wants EE to be EE and it turns out she may not after all want it to be EE, she might want it to be [national organization].

My conversation with Daniel illuminated a serious conflict facing EE. As a relatively small community-based after-school organization, youth workers at EE were intentional about establishing long-lasting relationships with youths and their families through their continuum. The "EE continuum," as it was sometimes called, included nurturing students from the sixth grade through completion of college and into advanced degrees or their careers. The organization's framework for teaching, learning, and engagement with youth would not be supported by a structure built for large organizations where hundreds of students occasionally "drop in" for programming. Daniel's belief that Gina intended to transform Educational Excellence into a large-scale drop-in mentoring program prompted him to look for another job. Her lack of transparency and clarity with the staff also rubbed Daniel the wrong way and made his departure from EE imminent.

Let me make clear that there are hundreds of organizations and agencies that engage young people of many different age groups. The heterogeneity of community-based youth organizations makes them beloved. At the same time, many assume that they all function similarly. But they do not. So much is dependent on funding sources, leadership, program structure, communities of practices, relationships, how the program is marketed, and the context in which it exists. There are many mentoring-based programs or "drop-in" centers where youths come in to receive support for a particular academic, emotional, or social issue from adults or their peers. Indeed, there is room for a diverse set of youth organizations. However, Educational Excellence, for over a decade, was known as a comprehensive program that sought to work with youth beyond academic support. Fostering critical consciousness, sociocultural development, and leadership for social change were essential to the organization. Transforming EE into a "drop-in" center where students who could "afford" to pay for services in order to generate some revenue while targeting "underprivileged poor" youth would position EE squarely in the market and into the hands of neoliberal reformers who believe that competition is always good for academic and organizational success. According to the youth workers at EE, Gina and the Board of Directors were leading EE into competition with other organizations for more students—aligned with larger political trends rooted in neoliberal competition. Many felt that there was more focus on quantity instead of quality, while the intimacy of relationship building between youths and youth workers was threatened. Discussion of the board's plan to transition EE into a drop-in model reflected a neoliberal consumer efficiency model detached from deep connection and engagement with youths and communities. Creating a more transactional model would fundamentally erode the comprehensive nature of EE as an organization that recognized that minoritized youth needed support fighting against external political and social forces that shaped their academic and social lives. Even more, these plans, as staff members feared, would create transactional relationships between adults and youth participants instead of the deep relationships they worked so hard to build over the years. These ideas, passed down from Richard and the board to Gina and then to Terry, led to a tense working environment that began to mirror a corporate work environment.

"Too Much Laughter"

There were specific cultural practices established at EE that helped to create a sense of family and accountability between staff members. Staff members constantly reflected upon their commitment to young people; an authentic caring for youth and their educational experiences was the core and strength of the program. Some staff members felt disappointed by how quickly this focus on youth shifted under new leadership. According to Benjamin, the program coordinator working in the Step 2 College program, "the message that they're all our kids is not stated or repeated" throughout the organization. During my research, I observed a sense of ownership of students in a non-pejorative way. The message that students were cared for by staff members was communicated throughout the program in a number of ways, including after-school courses, personal conversations, and large-scale events attended by youths and their families. Benjamin continued to discuss how the purpose and "big picture" of working with youth was lost as the culture of the organization started shifting:

> I think that the culture has changed . . . we're more—I guess I remember when, like, when the organization was still fairly established, feeling more static. There was, I felt like there were more opportunities as staff to discuss and deliberate on the big picture and that's one thing that I think has been lost. Or just like fallen by the wayside as leadership has changed. And, Felicia was our interim [executive director] and she was wonderful. Gina has come on and everyone just brings their own priorities I think.

The priorities of the organization shifted dramatically as many youth workers expressed concern that the program began to lose sight of its purpose and mission. As suggested by Terry, Walidah, Benjamin, Camille, and Daniel, Gina was concerned with making her mark by pleasing the board by expanding the organization into new territory. I repeatedly heard from staff that neither Gina nor the board really understood the mission, purpose, and culture of EE. The story of EE shows the complicated dynamics of organizational leadership and the fragility of organizational culture. Having studied organizational and nonprofit leadership, Walidah was fascinated by the story of leadership change within EE. Since EE had such a strong and vibrant culture, many were surprised just how quickly things changed once new leadership arrived. Reflections on leadership by youth workers revealed important insights to organizational change and the ways in which individual actors shape and reshape organizations.[3] Terry explained:

I'm quoting Monica, who said, "You create the culture, or the culture will create itself." Right? And so, I think the family component can stem from anything. It can stem from a strong leader. It can stem from an organizational structure, or a committed team. The challenge is, you know, there's . . . I think . . . on the line, on the line level, like the line staff level, direct service providers, there can be . . . I think what's essential is to make sure there isn't a catalyst. Like there is not culture barrier. At the leadership level you're screwed. Because one thing that has been said to me is, you know, by a board member before Gina started, and I was negotiating salary in the interim [director of programs] position and they were like, "look, we have to give her the freedom to create what she wants, otherwise why come?" You know? When I hired Kamau I said look, I told Ben, I said look, he is the director of this program, he may come in and say, "I want to rearrange this office," and even though you sat at that desk, in that corner for three years, it doesn't matter. I have to give him that freedom.

Although staff members who remained after all three executives departed (Leah Davis, Monica Matthews, and Cynthia Gladys) knew that the incoming executive director would make some changes to the organization to ensure the program could receive funding and maintain its reputation in the nonprofit world, staff members did not expect major changes to the culture of the program or significant changes in their interactions with each other. In conversation with me, Faith talked about her role in the program as being rooted and "immersed in the old culture" of the organization. She went on to describe the formal cultural practices through which staff engaged with students:

Well, there are different pieces—there is a formal piece and an informal piece. The formal piece is sort of the ways we interact with young people. The ways in which we place young people in the forefront, that we talk to them, we ask them what do they want because we are working for them. Um, the culture was more, like, inclusive and not, we know what is best and we are going to tell you want to do, but also just more of . . . just kind of the ways we move around the space with the young people. I feel like in the past it was much more hands-on involvement, everybody that worked here with the young people. Right now it feels like people just kind of stay in their space and they do their job. And it's not a lot of coming out and interacting with the young people and helping to just informally teach and educate the young people. Like there was this synergy that would go between high school and middle school and youth development. And it was just kind of . . . I'm an artist so I think of arrhythmic dance, right? Now it's more like everybody does their own thing. So, it's become really kind of traditional business-like versus sort of this collective family-like atmosphere where we all are working towards the best interest of the young person.

Faith's concern about the lack of engagement with students struck me. As a participant observer, I witnessed staff members operate in the program with the belief that everyone was responsible for students regardless of their role in the organization. The synergy between High Achievers, Step 2 College, and Youth Lead was an intentional facet of the organization to ensure that students received all of the support they needed. The Youth Lead department communicated often with the middle and high school programs if a student had a particular social or emotional challenge or if a student needed additional support academically. If a student's parents were divorcing or if there was a death of a relative, staff members would communicate with each other in order to make sure the student was supported while at the program and also in their school. It was typical of department directors to contact school administrators and teachers if there was a serious incident that occurred in a student's life. On any day of the week during after-school programming, youth workers could be seen flowing in and out of each other's offices. Youth participants would be flowing in and out of staff members' offices and back and forth between student lounges, where their peers ate snacks, did homework, or played games while waiting for after-school courses to begin. When students would find staff members in their offices or in the hallway, they would ask questions about a wide range of things—about challenges at school, with family, or with their peers. A student could seek out Terry for a solution and end up with several more staff members extending advice. In the fall of 2011, the senior class was deep into submitting applications to college. Sofia, a high school senior, had applied to several colleges and was waiting on her school guidance counselor to submit transcripts and letters of recommendation. She came into the Youth Lead office to share that her counselor was poorly handling students' records. All present, including Solomon, Camille, and myself, offered strategies. Leah happened to be walking by the office. She stopped in the office and spoke to Sofia to say hello. Sofia shared what was going on and Leah promptly began offering additional strategies. Before she left, she told Sofia to keep everyone posted and let Belinda (the coordinator for senior programming at that time) know if she needed to intervene. This kind of support from multiple people at one time was an important practice in the program that highlights the comfort students felt with staff members and that staff members felt with each other. The constant communication between staff members helped them support students in more robust and dynamic ways.

As influence from Dunn and the board began to seep into the organization's programming under new leadership, everyone began doing "their own thing," said Faith. People operating on their own seemed to be the new culture instead of constant communication, collaboration, and relationship building. I asked Faith to explain what she meant by "traditional business-like" instead of a "collective family-like atmosphere" and also to elaborate on why she felt things had changed in that way. She explained:

> That everybody is in their own space doing their own thing. Before the culture of the organization was one where we all kind of laughed. We'd come together, we would laugh. We would joke. But we would all still get our work done. It's been told to us [since Gina became the executive director] that this is a work setting. And that people should not be making a lot of noise. And as a result there have been, um . . . people in leadership positions that go around "shushing" people when they are in a meeting and something is funny. If someone laughs kind of loud, then you know, now we are being "shushed." . . . You don't see people moving in and out of each other's office because that was shut down as well. That everybody should, you know, don't gather in people's offices.

Curious as to how these messages were communicated to staff, I asked how they were told not to laugh or gather in others' offices. Faith explained that there was an e-mail sent out by executive leadership, though she did not mention a specific name. She shared that the e-mail mentioned that there is "too much laughing and um . . . there's too much gathering in offices and . . . so people kind of heeded to that . . . everybody has just been doing their own thing."

The declaration that there was "too much laughter and gathering in each other's offices" bothered many staff members, and it became one of the most discussed issues during my follow-up interviews. This was shocking to me and, of course, to longtime staff members. Laughter, joking, and familiarity were definitely a part of the culture of the program. This extended to interaction with students and was tempered by stern expectations around academics and behavior. The directive to end laughter in the office seemed to be antithetical to how a youth organization that centered on the experiences and needs of youth would operate. It signaled that new leadership did not understand the culture of EE, the culture(s) of young people, and, of course, the culture of community-based youth work. Often lauded for the ways they stand far apart from schools or stiff corporate environments, community-based youth organizations tend to be more relaxed spaces where youths and staff members can build, connect, and thrive in a space that is less hostile than traditional school or work spaces.[4]

The suggestion that there was "too much gathering in offices" was not only disturbing but quite opposite of the already established culture at EE. Gathering in each other's offices occurred usually so that staff could seek and receive professional support or check in about students. Solomon, for example, described the former culture of the program, where some staff members relied on each other for professional and personal guidance:

> So, we had this thing—we always had this thing where you go in somebody's office, you close the door. You go in somebody's office, you close the door because you got to share something very personal. Some personal shit happening in your life or some shit happening on the floor that you're not feeling. Or you're about to surprise the hell out of somebody and you're trying to get other people in cahoots with you to do this thing that you're trying to do. Right? So we had this kind of culture where that's just what you do. There's a lot of laughter. And I guess that's what I was trying to get at earlier, a little bit earlier, about the spirit and the emptiness. . . . But we always had a way of collapsing that just for dealing with one another on a personal level. . . . Or the way you did this wasn't cool or whatever. But that began to be unraveled a little bit. And there was a lot of tension.

Staff members were baffled and angered by these new policies and the dynamic they created between staff members. Business and corporate models of working are often considered to be stoic and serious. A corporate business model seems to be antithetical to a community-based youth organization, where staff need to be energetic and joyful to connect with young people. The comment from Solomon captures the rapport between youth workers as they utilized each other for both professional and personal support. As the psychologist on the floor, Faith would support colleagues on occasion. Though the environment was often vibrant, light, and fun, there was indeed a time and place for everything. I would argue that the relationship building between staff members and the sense of vibrancy throughout the program were a function of the relationships between youth workers. Relationship building was formally encouraged through yearly overnight staff retreats and monthly staff professional development and team-building activities. The relationships fostered within the organization created a professional courtesy among staff members. As Solomon explained, if there was a major challenge facing the organization, supervisors would give their youth workers a heads-up if appropriate and depending on the circumstances.

Demands from Richard and the board were given to Gina, and she left them to be communicated to the rest of the staff by Terry, which often led to tension. Relationships became strained between staff members. Many of the staff members, including Faith, Solomon, and Camille, and even Leah, expected that the culture that had been established at EE would remain in place, at least on some level, despite changes from the top. Understanding that changes to the program were inevitable, some staff expected that new leadership would take into account existing social and cultural dynamics among the staff and inform how particular changes were carried out. Rather, when the board and Gina gave orders to Terry as Director Programs or to Patrick as the head of Development, according to some, they would just implement them without acknowledging the impact it would have on relationships between departments or between staff members. For example, as discussed in Chapter 4, the tension between Development and Programs staff increased as the Development team continued to hire more staff and began designing programs for students without the input of Programs staff. The conflict that emerged between Programs and Development continued to heighten as Gina settled into her new role as executive director.

I was struck by the shifts in organizational culture and how quickly staff members acquiesced to them in a manner that jeopardized strong professional and personal relationships. During all of my follow-up interviews, the change in organizational culture and the strain between departments and professional relationships were the main topics of conversation. I asked staff members what they felt was the cause to the breakdown in relationships. Solomon suggested that dominant personalities like Monica fostered the kind of environment where relationships mattered. He also offered that directors like Faith were always interested in supporting colleagues and maintaining a healthy work environment, so the mission of the program could be carried out in a way that helped students succeed. Gina's transition to EE and more influence from Richard and the board created a panic where staff members had different approaches to managing the stress that came along with the changes imposed on the organization. As Solomon explained,

I think Faith might have been stepping up as an older sib, in a manner of speaking, but Terry wasn't really willing to go all the way because of his own anxiety and angst around the changes and what that could mean. And I think Faith and Terry were very concerned about two different things from the beginning. I think Faith was mainly interested in generally the social, emotional piece for everybody involved—and her own. She was concerned about her own personal, social, emotional stuff. And Terry was concerned about, okay, what does this mean? What else needs to be done? What do I need to be doing? What kind of work do I need to be doing? What kind of things do I need to be setting in motion? People are gonna be looking at me and expecting me—these higher-ups might be looking at me. So, he's kind of looking at himself for himself, and he's not looking at the social piece at all, to the point where I think he might have even said something like, I got to do what I got to do . . . And he kind of just followed his suit, which is [to] be very logical and removed, superobjective, and almost painfully objective. Like, really? Because I think there might have been a situation, I remember Faith telling me, where she kind of opened up to Terry, and Terry was like, "I can't help you." You know what I'm saying? Like, I can't help you. And I think he articulated his stress load was something different than what she was experiencing . . . it wasn't about the kids for him necessarily. In terms of what his—not to say he don't care about the kids or ever cared about the kids, but his priority was about what he was supposed to be doing for the organization, the new organization.

Solomon's perspective here is an important one. As discussed in Chapter 4, employees respond differently under the pressure of changes to organizational culture. As I observed strained relationships between youth workers, EE appeared to be a different organization entirely. Youth workers were isolated and in their own silos as they did their jobs. Solomon's point about priorities is a critical piece to the failure of the organization to maintain its foundation of connections. At the heart of the work with youth at Educational Excellence are relationships—relationships between staff and students and relationships between staff members. Solomon was the only staff member to directly speak to this point. Two major concerns for youth workers at this time were (1) that they might lose their jobs (as the new director had the ability to fire anyone from the previous staff in order to build the organization in the way she saw fit the way Leah had in 2002) and (2) that they might end up working for an organization that no longer put youth at the center if EE's approach to learning through sociocultural and political education was jeopardized. Some youth workers retreated inward and tried to stay afloat by completing the tasks given to them, while others questioned the motives of the new leadership and relied on previously established relationships for support as youth workers needed to process the changes occurring rapidly to the program so beloved by all of them. Using Terry and Faith as examples, Solomon explained to me how since Terry had been promoted to a leadership role in the organization, there was new pressure to get the work done, whereas Faith's response to the changes was to make sure that there was a sense of stability for youth and to ensure that her colleagues were supported. "Faith was thinking about the old culture of the organization that is gonna be good for, at the very least, the students that are involved and that we can help each other out in this thing . . . The difference . . . to some degree, can be looked at as a hierarchy of priorities between Faith and Terry," shared Solomon. The difference in priorities noted by Solomon can't be defined simplistically as right or wrong; rather, it is indicative of how people respond differently to external pressures.

"Help each other out in this thing" is a comment I was desperately seeking to hear throughout my follow-up conversations. Longtime youth workers who were still present understood that Gina, Richard, and the Board of Directors were taking EE in a different direction that would drastically shift the role of the organization in Dunbar. There was, however, an awareness of what was happening to the organization, and instead of directing attention toward strengthening relationships to sustain the type of programming they knew was beneficial to their youth participants, a bunker mentality ensued as the actions taken created a deep sense of distrust between youth workers. Though some youth workers, like Solomon and Walidah, suggested that Terry in his new role as director of programs chose to isolate himself from the rest of the Programs staff and appeared to support the changes from the board and Gina, throughout my conversations with him it appeared that he felt his hands were tied and that he needed to support the organization in a way that kept the organization's programs going. As he shared with me, he often pushed back on some of Gina's requests given to her by the board. Unfortunately, this resistance was never communicated to the rest of the staff, which created further distrust and isolation for him. "So there's been a lack of leadership," shared Terry, with deep irritation reflected in his voice and body language. "So what's happening is all these directives are falling on me . . . I've just been holding it. I'm trying to balance the shit."

I witnessed Terry's frustration as well as the disappointment of other staff members. Terry shared with me that Gina was hired while he was on a sabbatical. When he returned to EE as director of Programs, he felt pressure to perform and do his job well. From his point of view, Gina's hire indicated that Faith and Walidah were satisfied with the board's choice—even though Walidah and Faith explained to him that the board hired Gina against their wishes. In the end, Terry's approach was to give Gina a chance to do her job. Ultimately, this created tension that was exacerbated by Terry delivering orders from Gina, Richard, and the board to department directors.

Youth workers who remained close talked to each other, and there were different perspectives among them as to why Terry felt isolated. According to Camille, Walidah, and Solomon, Terry isolated himself and created boundaries between them as he adjusted to his new role as their supervisor. Conversely, Terry offered that "no one talks to me." Each youth worker coped with organizational changes and in some cases, new roles, in the best way she or he knew how. I would argue that Solomon's analysis was correct—that mismatched priorities and perceived priorities, along with miscommunication and misunderstandings, fueled the tension mounting in the organization. Terry was most definitely in a difficult position as he once was a director at the same professional level as Walidah and Faith (being promoted to director of programs made him their supervisor). It is difficult for anyone to transition into position supervising those with whom they have shared professional and personal challenges. However, as Monica offered, there was an expectation that relationships would remain intact as a result of the strength of the culture that had been established and maintained during the prior ten years. Additionally, Monica also suggested that she had hoped that given the strength of these relationships, youth workers would collectively and individually push back on directives from the new director that were not aligned with the mission and culture of the program. As I sat with Monica in her office at her new organization, I listened as she discussed the critical nature of relationship building between the organization's leadership, youth workers, and students:

> I thought in getting someone with a social work degree that there would be a level of emotional intelligence that would speak to really understand how the culture was built there and building on and maintaining some of those practices that would make the [executive director] accessible to young people in a

way that uplifted their aspirations and certainly their connections. Really powerful. You're not always there in their face, but to be able to gain access to the executive leadership I think was important for modeling, for relationship building, for building social capital and the like. As far as the staff goes, my assumption was that the staff would maintain the status quo of the core of what EE was and think intelligently through the process of expansion, push back when necessary, push themselves and each other when it was being resistant versus a legitimate claim. I thought that the staff was more sophisticated in their ability to do that, and certainly in the leadership of the three directors I thought that there would be more sophistication in that. And when I say sophistication, I mean being able to kind of work through some of the tension that would come with one person being promoted . . . that situation and the changing dynamics of reporting, working through the nuances of building your own relationships with the new executive director and how important that is. And I didn't really hear about that happening at really any level, with anyone, that people sort of understood that that was part of the work, building relationships.

For an organization like Educational Excellence, relationship building and the importance of connection were vital to its success. As numerous staff and students alike have claimed, EE is an "experience"—it is a continuum whereby youth maintain a relationship with the organization and youth workers, from middle school until their completion of college. EE is not designed to be a drop-in program, with loose connections between youth and staff. The intentionality of relationship building within Educational Excellence was indeed the anchor of the organization. The failure of the staff to collectively push back and resist, while maintaining and nurturing important relationships, presented major consequences under the imposition of neoliberal expansion.

In addition to the relationship breakdowns, race was once fundamental to the discourse within the organization. A core feature of the program was to engage youth in critical conversations about race as a socially constructed and politically informed social identity that shaped their experiences in the world. Race, social class, gender, and sexual identity were constantly explored by youth and facilitated by staff members. Even more, staff members—from executive leadership to part-time volunteers—had to confront race and other social identities as part of their function in the organization. Through professional development, hiring interviews, and teaching, race and racism were always discussed as a permanent factor of American life. Personal reflections on the role and function of race in the lives of all at EE, and how it shaped the educational opportunity and experiences of Black youth, were no longer central to the culture of the organization after the transition of leadership.

"So, You're White. Let's Talk About It."

From the beginning of the hiring process, youth workers were skeptical about Gina's ability to understand the organization's purpose and adopt an affirming ideology of Black and other minoritized youth. From the perspective of youth workers, any executive director of EE, regardless of their racial background, should understand or be willing to learn how the political and social context of education and youth work informs the experiences of young people—mainly the ways in which race, class, power, and the politics of education shape the academic and social experiences of Black and Latinx youth. Some youth workers reserved judgment about Gina's level of racial awareness and her comfort working for a youth program serving primarily Black youth and facilitated by a highly educated, predominantly Black staff. Others felt confident that Richard's desire to place a white woman in the role of executive director was deliberate and would prevent the kind of contentious relationship he held with Leah.

Under Leah's tenure, Educational Excellence's leadership strongly believed in the importance of hiring talented and competent Black and Latinx staff so that young people could see a reflection of themselves and understand what is possible for their lives. At the same time, they believed that hiring competent staff members of any racial background who held high expectations for Black students and had an understanding or willingness to work through their privilege was important as well. Deeply concerned by the four candidates the board selected for executive director, Monica shared how critical it was for staff members and the leaders of EE to be "liberated" regardless of racial identity. Having liberated critical thinkers was essential to the community of practice established at EE. There was an expectation that staff members were able to reflect on their own socially constructed identities and unconscious biases and that they understood the ways in which structural obstacles affected their work and the lives of the youths and families they engaged. The imagining and framing of Black youth, as I discussed earlier, was a critical function of the organization. How youth workers thought about Black youth directly shaped how they built curricula and how they engaged with students. There was a pressing fear among staff members that this particular framing of youth would be compromised under new leadership. Monica shared that on the surface, including on the website and printed literature about the program, the imagining of Black youth had not changed significantly. But, as Daniel, Camille, and Patrick shared, the organization had begun to shift the framing of its program as one that helped "poor kids."

Monica's reflection is based on the six months she remained at EE following her departure to join Leah at her new organization, as well as her own observations and relationships with staff members who remained. Walidah and Camille, who both remained for a longer period of time (Camille for a year and Walidah for two and a half years), had different perspectives. They witnessed both subtle and more obvious changes to the way youth were framed in the program under Gina's leadership and as the board continued to have more influence. Walidah, in particular, felt a deep sense of sorrow and frustration at the thought that everything the organization had built with youths and families in Dunbar was now in the hands of leadership who understood very little about the experiences of youth of color in Dunbar. Walidah feared that EE would be "destroyed":

WALIDAH: But destroyed in the sense of quality, the quality of what has been created over the last twelve years. I'm worried about that just being destroyed. I worry that in light of the fact that we serve Black and Brown children, they're gonna be shortchanged and that their narrative is going to be defined by someone who has no clue about their experience. I was thinking about this very thing the other day, and really the word "co-opting" just kept coming back to me. The work that we've done is going to be co-opted.

INTERVIEWER: How so, how do you see that?

WALIDAH: This might sound like really an extreme analogy, but in the same way that revolutionary messages are often co-opted for the dominant ends. I feel like a lot of the work that we did with the kids, the explicit conversations around race and their existence in the world, just the work on helping them build themselves up and understanding who they are and supporting their self-esteem, all of those things I felt were very revolutionary because they live in a world that would tell them that they're worth very little. So all of this work that we have done to serve that legitimate purpose I feel like is now going to be taken and shifted in a way where the message they receive is not gonna be the same anymore. So, we can't even as a staff, as adults, have—we used to have conversations about race.

INTERVIEWER: At the lunchtime, you mean?

WALIDAH: At lunchtime. We can't even bring it up. It's just like there's a discomfort when it's an obvious elephant in the room, an obvious elephant in the room. We can't have those conversations, so if we can't have them as a staff, especially in the spaces that we created for those conversations to happen for the kids explicitly, if no one is there to keep that legacy, is it really gonna happen? If it doesn't, what does that mean for the persistence of the kids that we serve when all the kids we serve are Black and Brown? That's what I mean by co-opting, like you're gonna be leading kids to believe that all they need to do is follow whatever little yellow brick road you're painting, and you don't even have a real sense of their lived experience, so how is your road gonna be the one to follow? You think they're the problem.

This exchange with Walidah captures how the new culture of the organization threatened a vital feature of the program that is so central to Black and Latinx youth. Prior to the transition of leadership, department directors, youth workers, and leadership who ate lunch together often held conversations analyzing racial incidents that shaped the program, their personal lives, or their previous professional roles. Significant political and cultural news topics surfaced during lunchtime conversations. The 2009 police shooting of Oscar Grant in Oakland, the execution of Troy Davis in Georgia in 2011, and incidents that occurred in students' schools are examples of the kind of issues that would be discussed. These issues would often later be worked into programming for students in their after-school courses. These conversations about police brutality, the prison industrial complex, and the death penalty carried over into the classroom with middle school and high school students and on buses to and from field trips and retreats. The lunchroom became a space for staff members to process and deconstruct social issues that shaped their lives and the lives of youth participants in the program. By no means did everyone agree on every issue. There was clear dissent between staff members across age, social class upbringing, and, most often, gender. Programs staff—High Achievers, Step 2 College, and Youth Lead—had more members who identified as women (in these departments, only two to four staff members identified as men at any given time). With over half of the staff being women, at times there was conflict about how male privilege operated within marginalized communities of color. Again, conversations about gender and its intersections with race were normal. If something came up casually in a discussion over lunch, it would sometimes be included in staff professional development at a later time.

EE staff also discussed the dynamics of race, class, and power between the leadership, Richard, and the Board of Directors. I learned after my first year as a youth worker that EE was functioning with a very particular understanding about the world and about education—an understanding of structural barriers related to race and class—and one very distinct from that of the founder and the board. The climate created and nurtured by the leadership and program staff helped to establish an environment in which staff and students alike felt supported personally and professionally and also challenged. Professional and personal growth and relationship building were important elements of the organization. Staff members were pushed to think critically and to push beyond previously held notions about minoritized youth and educational attainment. Researchers from nearby universities, who were often personal friends of staff members, would sometimes be invited to speak with staff members during retreats or professional development sessions. EE was a place where all students, with the proper support and resources in an environment sustained by affirming and dignity-based frameworks for engaging youth, were viewed as capable of achieving.[5] The affirming, asset-rich, and racially aware climate created at EE shifted once Leah and others left the organization, causing immense stress and frustration for staff members. Camille described this challenge:

> I think what most frustrated me was the climate. I mean the mission went from, like, this, you know, let's help these kids in the middle to hey, let's help these poor black children who can't help themselves. I was like, who are you even talking about?! It's crazy. It really irked me. Just thinking about it—it's like that's not who this organization is . . . Are you going to continue to serve our kids or now are you just going to push them out so you can bring in the population you're really trying to serve or are you just going to market our kids who aren't that, as these little poor black children who need you to save them? It's really crazy. Anyways, I'm having strong reactions to that [laughter].

Under new leadership and more influence from the board, the climate at EE shifted in tone and direction. As the organization expanded, so did the message that EE served the "underprivileged." The critique of deficit racist and cultural pathological language and narratives came to the surface and frustrated staff members who were committed to using only affirming language. Although the website and printed literature about the organization continued to reflect previous affirming language for a time, the culture of the organization began to shift.

Leah and department directors were always intentional about translating the work of the organization in ways that affirmed Black youth identities in ways that were not deficit oriented or pathological. I was curious if the board understood this major shift in the tone of the organization. According to Walidah, "boards are not typically in touch with what's really happening in organizations in general." Walidah's understanding of the shift in tone with regard to race was that it reflected Richard's racist and paternalistic attitudes toward Black and Latinx communities:

> In my personal opinion, I think it's about the founder of the organization. He has his own views for what is going to "work" for our children. This is a man who in his infinite wisdom thought he was the foremost authority on the Black narrative as an older Jewish man, so he has his own ideas as to what he believes is effective for doing this work, but he has no education background. He's a philanthropist and that's it. His education background is as deep as his involvement with this organization and the work that he did prior to founding the organization and giving money to schools. So, his ideas now are being thrust upon the organization with an executive director who, I think, feels like she's good as long as she jumps when he says jump. He's the one that's saying we need to have cultural programming infused, so we're trying to figure out how to infuse cultural programming.

The cultural programming Walidah refers to included experiences like going to the opera or classical music concerts and other things typically associated and celebrated by white middle-class values as dominant forms of cultural capital.[6] Again, here we see Richard and the board positioning whiteness as the standard that EE students and staff were expected to conform to. Unsurprisingly, these cultural programs suggestions never sat well with Leah, and therefore they did not occur. Leah told me that she dismissed many suggestions that came from Richard and the board because they might have been racist or very far from the mission of the organization and were not important to the needs of Black and Latinx youth in her view. Under Gina's leadership, conversations among staff members about race stopped altogether.

As the narrative about the youth served at EE and the culture of the program began to shift, many youth workers became unhappy and started to look for positions outside of the organization. Making the decision to leave was difficult, as many youth workers were connected to youths and their families for several years. The new patterns and practices in the program that changed the nature of relationships between staff members resulted in tension, conflict, and discontent among youth workers.

. . .

This chapter captures aggressive change in the culture and practices of EE under new leadership and as staff members attempted to adjust to leadership changes. An organization, once anchored by familial-like relationships between youth workers and between staff and students, became reflective of a traditional business-like environment and corporate attitudes about serving more students, expanding, and establishing protocols that prevented staff members from communicating in the way they had for years. Listening to the stories of youth workers who, day after day, stayed in an organization changing right before their eyes showed the power of relationships between youth and youth workers. The relationships fostered between 2002 and 2012 among youth workers and between youth workers and students anchored the organization. The strength of the curricula, the competence of youth workers, and the intentionality of pedagogical practices rooted in providing culturally relevant academics, socioemotional learning, and sociopolitical awareness catapulted the organization into a highly regarded program for students of color in Dunbar. The vibrancy and enthusiasm I felt during my first visit to the program were no longer present. The relationships and camaraderie between youth workers— something that provided a trust that helped foster accountability and risk taking in the student programming—had begun to erode.

The new era of organizational leadership at EE established goals rooted in neoliberal ideas and corporate styles of functioning, without an understanding of education, pedagogy, or how race functioned in the lives of youth and in Dunbar. After the transition, the "EE family" was no longer a family. Relationships were disrupted by the imposition of neoliberal expansion that shifted the goals and culture of the organization. This new era of EE is marked by misaligned expectations and mismatched ideology about the purpose of youth work and about the community being served. Youth work occurs in many spaces, including community-based nonprofits, schools, parks, and other places. However, community-based youth work stands apart from other spaces, as these organizations have the autonomy to establish culture in the way that the context demands. Yet, with the onslaught of neoliberal ideologies and practices rooted in efficiency models that seek to serve more and do more, the comprehensive and intimate approach to youth work is threatened. As shown throughout this chapter, the culture of EE shifted under new leadership and as Richard exerted more control over programming after Leah's resignation. The cultural shifts within the organization disrupted professional and personal relationships between youth workers and caused many staff members to question their future at EE. The following chapter explores the external and internal factors that pushed and pulled youth workers away from Educational Excellence.

6 "It Was Never Ours"

Race and the Politics of Control

I think it helped having almost the same staff members at EE almost all
7 years I was there, because it made it easy to be open and honest. We built
relationships with [staff] that are memorable.
 —*Former Youth Participant*

I think [EE has] been robbed of its essence and the things that made it
great. It feels more like a factory exploiting young Black excellence with no
real sense of community or care. The high turnover and experience I've had
with young folks coming out of EE now is saddening.
 —*Former Youth Participant*

We ruled EE. We ruled that thing, but it was never ours . . . It was never
Dunbar's. It was never the children's.
 —*Solomon, Youth Lead Coordinator/Instructor, 2005–2013*

MAKING THE DECISION TO LEAVE youth work can be a difficult and painful process. The connection and rapport established between youth workers and young people within community-based spaces can be deeply powerful and meaningful for both. Similar to the experiences of school-based educators, youth workers enter the field for a variety of reasons that are typically centered on the desire to support youth and the communities from which they come. Youth workers at Educational Excellence did not take the decision to leave the organization lightly. As illuminated in this chapter, external and internal factors contributed to youth workers' departure from Educational Excellence. Considering the broader political and social context of education, youth workers seeking to shape the academic and social experiences of youth are also affected by larger educational politics. As argued throughout this book, the current climate of public education, marked by neoliberal approaches and strategies for reform that include privatization and the complete restructuring of public education, often via public school closures with takeover by charter management organizations and a hyper–audit culture based on high-stakes testing, has devastating consequences on the educational experiences for Black, Latinx, and low-income students across the country.[1]

The dangers of education privatization resulting in market-based school reforms, such as the proliferation of charter school networks and alternative teacher entry routes, have contributed to the commodification of education in which minoritized youth are hurt the most. As a result, messiah-like narratives surface whereby community-based spaces targeting youth of color in low-income contexts are positioned as spaces of containment.[2] The transformation of Educational Excellence described in this book captures some of the core dimensions of neoliberal control over public education. Neoliberalism pushes for quantifying success through expansion, racialized framing of youth of color emphasizing individual and cultural explanations for failure, and a downplaying of structural explanations for inequality. Within this context, EE was transformed into an organization that focused on expansion and serving the "underprivileged"—a direction far from Leah's vision and even further away from the community of practice and norms established under her leadership. This chapter takes a deep dive into the external and internal pressures that pulled and pushed youth workers away from Educational Excellence.

Leadership, External Pressures, and Organizational Change

As I walked the familiar hallways of EE, two years after my initial study, the grim mood was palpable. The language used to define the work of EE and youth participants had changed dramatically. After the transition of leadership and the exodus of longtime staff members, the focus of the organization shifted to rhetoric aligned with neoliberal frames of success. Growth, expansion, and broadening the organization's footprint were now EE's central focus and a desire stated in the organization's mission. Despite the disagreements and challenges that came from department directors and other youth workers, Gina (with backing from the Board of Directors) was steadfast in her quest to "serve more students" at any cost. The board's push to expand the program once Leah departed the organization was swift—much too swift for longtime youth workers who understood that the strength of EE was in part due to the deep connections they had established with young people and their families over a long period of time.

Educational Excellence was once a vibrant, energetic, and unapologetically Black organization—committed to providing young people with opportunities to expand their talents and understand and respond to the world around them. With subtle and more overt methods of resistance, Leah and her staff were able to define their work in ways they saw fit. In other words, they had the ability to determine how young people would be framed and engaged within the organization. Leah blocked some external political pressures and interference from Richard Dunn and the Board of Directors if she felt they jeopardized the goals of the organization, and especially if they did not reflect the agency and humanity of youth in the program. The "Golden Era" of EE as described by participants who had been connected to the program for almost ten years or more was not without contradictions or conflicts. Although, much to the chagrin of students and some staff, there were definitely moments where respectability discourse surfaced in response to certain cultural styles and expressions of youth (as mentioned in Chapter 2), the core of EE's work with youth was love, admiration, and hope for possibilities in their futures.

The political and social context of community-based spaces informs their construction, philosophies, and practices. As Educational Excellence struggled to maintain its identity as an asset-based academic and youth development program, the organization was met with both external and internal pressures to concentrate on a growth model that did more harm than good. Coupled with a mismatch of values and ideologies about youth participants, staff at EE found themselves caught in a very tenuous situation. The internal conflict emerging within the organization presented challenges for EE, including the imposition of deficit narratives and struggles to maintain self-determination while meeting the demands of outside funders and its biggest benefactor, the founder, Richard Dunn. As shown in Chapter 3, the proliferation of charter school networks under neoliberal reforms increased competition for funding. The Board of Directors and Gina may not have understood how their decisions regarding the program were linked to broader political realities surrounding education and neoliberalism. Yet their choices regarding expansion, growth, and scaling up were directly influenced by and connected to the broader neoliberal shifts within public education. These external political pressures created a very real weight for youth workers.

With external political factors influencing the decisions and day-to-day practices at Educational Excellence, internal turmoil was inevitable. Distrust among staff (and between staff and program leadership), mismatched expectations, and a lack of understanding of education and youth development all contributed to the breakdown of the organization as it was formally known. Rapid turnover among youth workers, distrust of leadership, and a breakdown in relationships and camaraderie also contributed to these changes. Considering both external politics and internal conflict, youth workers at EE knew that leaving the organization meant that a radical restructuring of the program would occur, which would erase what EE had previously stood for. Youth workers sensed that with their leaving, there would be no way that the essence of EE would remain. As culture bearers and committed educators, youth workers understood that EE's transformation would be aligned with privatized notions of education whereby community-based spaces for youth are reduced to spaces either of academic achievement (neglecting social, cultural, and political needs) or of containment and control.[3] As youth workers struggled to resist the deficit and paternalistic framing of youth participants, they also understood that leadership embraced these frames and failed to understand their negative implications for EE's pedagogical and organizational practices. Without the support of leadership, youth workers had no chance of continuing an organization that affirmed academic and racial/ethnic identities of Black youth. Put another way, the imagining and framing of Black youth matters to how they are engaged— community-based leaders who understand this know that the imagining of youth informs their treatment, and thus shapes the organization's community of practice. Leaders of community-based youth programs must be attentive to an organization's culture of practice in order to sustain and nurture it.[4]

Although some youth workers departed for other professional opportunities or personal reasons, many cited EE's leadership and the new direction of the organization as their cause for leaving. An overwhelming number of changes occurred in personnel, direction, and scope of Educational Excellence, and a wealth of emotions consumed those who worked there. I wanted to understand the processes youth workers underwent in making the decision to leave the program, and I wanted to explore the external and internal conditions that influenced their decisions to leave.

In the sections that follow, through the narratives of youth workers at EE, I discuss the tensions and conflicts they experienced as their place in the organization shifted. Many staff members noted that their decision to leave was a direct result of the change in values and priorities of the organization under new leadership. Despite the frustration and tension youth workers shared with me, they also discussed their professional and personal growth, deep connection with youth and families from EE, and the rare community EE was able to create for over a decade.

Narratives of Leaving

As a community-based youth worker, I have worked with a number of organizations across the country. My engagement with youth organizations typically began every time I moved to a new city. But leaving my colleagues and students was always hard, and the decision to leave is never an easy one. Within a short year-and-a-half period, many youth workers moved on from EE. The decision to leave was quite difficult for many of them; this decision was especially hard for those that worked directly with youth.

The changes within Educational Excellence rest on three important factors: the application of market-based and corporate-style approaches in education to youth work under a neoliberal paradigm; the persistent neglect of a critical understanding of the ways in which race functioned in the lives of EE youth under new leadership; and a breakdown in trusting relationships between youth workers as a result of dramatic shifts and turnover within the program. The radical shift in EE's approach to education and youth work and the lack of intentionality (and understanding) about the persistence of race and its intersections with neoliberalism undermined the long-standing work of EE. Under Leah Davis's leadership, EE had established a space that acknowledged structural inequality and its role in the educational experiences and outcomes of Black youth, affirmed and celebrated racial and ethnic identity, and created rich pedagogical practices that disrupted anti-Black ideology and deficit-based thinking and practices. The predominantly Black staff at EE can also not be understated or ignored during its "Golden Era." In reflecting on the importance of students in the program seeing staff and teachers of color, Monica shared a memory of an exchange she had with the director of the middle school program, a white woman, prior to Walidah's arrival:

> We had a middle school director and the question I asked was, "Do you think it's important that young people see themselves reflected in the individuals that are in their classrooms?" She said, "No, I don't think that's important because anybody and everybody here can teach whatever." What I would have preferred her to say was, "I do think it's important. I don't think that it's always essential in every situation but that, if young people knew that you cared about them, that you believed in them, that you respected who they are and where they come from, that it becomes less essential. But representation also is important, because young people do need models that look like them as well." That would

have been my preference. And as it turned out, she had a preference for Latino kids and sort of couldn't deal with Black kids at all, really.

Having educators of color does not automatically presume a certain type of racial consciousness (awareness of how racism informs social progress and social life), but in the case of EE, it did. There is also evidence to suggest that Black teachers have more positive perceptions of Black students than white teachers do.[5] The transition from Leah to Gina signaled a very different understanding of race, inequality, and education and that was reflected in the framing of EE's work with young people post the "Golden Era."

Problem of Leadership

The problem of leadership as a reflection of the shift occurring with public and community-based education was a challenge for many youth workers who ultimately decided to leave the organization. Walidah, a longtime community-based educator (a former middle school teacher and teacher-coach), had a clear understanding that the radical shift to Educational Excellence had a lot to do with changes in leadership. Although she did not place the blame for the organization's demise squarely on Gina, the difference between having an all-Black leadership with a very particular imagining of Black youth and Gina's leadership, which ignored race and allowed Richard's paternalistic and anti-Black practices to filter through the organization, was palpable. Even more, under Gina's leadership, it was clear that the desire to compete and take up the language and practices of the market was connected to the broader shifts and changes in the landscape of public education and the implications for all educational spaces youth occupy. In discussing EE's evolution, Walidah pointed directly to the persistent rise of public education as a business enterprise and the push for youth organizations to mirror the tactics used to privatize public education. Below, Walidah reflects on her work with EE and shares her thoughts on the need for community-based program leaders to be clear about the approach and intention of their work. In particular, for spaces that purport to support and educate Black youth, the intentionality of the work is critical. Walidah explained:

> While politics exist in any field, I think there's a degree of courage that is required for you to stand against some of the pressures that are given to you, whether it be by funders or by your board. I think you have to be someone who is embedded in the work to some degree. Like I said, I don't believe just because

you're a businessperson you should think you know all there is to know about creating a successful youth program. If you believe that this is the calling you have, go find some people who are gonna help you make it really great and value their experience and what they have to offer in that regard. You can provide that vision but get some input on how that vision works with the real lived experiences of the young people you're trying to serve, and then let that information drive what you do for the kids. You have to be brave enough to stand by that and I think that's the piece because, just like anybody else, I think executive directors can get lost in trying to keep their own skin tight that they forget about what the focus of the work should be. You have to always keep that at the forefront of everything you do.

Walidah's focus on executive leadership is important to the story of Educational Excellence. Leaders set the tone and vision for an organization. As reflected in the work of Educational Excellence, Leah's vision for Black youth and educational opportunity was at the forefront of her vision for the program and the strategies and decisions she engaged, supported, or even resisted. According to participants, success in the minds of Richard, Gina, and the Board of Directors meant that EE would "expand its footprint" and "serve more students." Under new leadership, the "success" of EE was separate from the well-being of youth in the program. This approach signaled a major detachment on the part of new leadership to connect the work of EE, its programming, and culture to the socioemotional, political, cultural, and academic identities of youth. The hyperfocus on expansion and neoliberal notions of success neglected the structural factors that contribute to the subjugation of Black youth in schools and in larger society. Their lived realities are misunderstood, ignored, or rationalized as pathological and not as a result of structural harms.

Race and Distrust

Many participants shared that race was no longer a part of the conversation youth workers had even among themselves. Although social identity courses were still in place under Gina's tenure, staff members could no longer process the meaning of race and other social identities in the lives of youth participants and in their own lives during staff meetings and retreats or during the lunch hour as previously done. There was once an explicit and open dialogue about race in the program. New leadership, however, did not articulate an understanding of how race, class, and systemic oppression informed the need for Educational Excellence. Daniel, one of EE's lead grant writers, worked to understand the implications of race in the organization's attempt to obtain funding and paid attention to the dynamics of race and class in the organization's search for donors. Through his time in the program, Daniel became quite reflective about issues of race and open to learning from staff members at EE. He argued that Gina had an ingrained fear of Black people and of the Dunbar neighborhood evidenced by their walk through Dunbar, when Gina told him that "Dunbar is not safe for whites." The centrality of race during Leah's tenure was apparent and forced all staff members to confront various manifestations of racism as a part of their work with youth. Daniel believed that Gina's agreeable nature and affirmation of everyone's ideas helped to perpetuate the "board's mentality" regarding race, class, and Black youth.

This "mentality" was one of racialized and classed, deficit-oriented discourse about youth of color and the families from which they come. As discussed in casual conversations over lunch with staff members as well as in professional development meetings, it was often communicated that the board understood the role of Educational Excellence as needing to "fix" youth in Dunbar instead of recognizing the need for the program because of structural inequality. As Leah often shared, this orientation is a long-standing one by Richard and not new to the board that he crafted. Leah, however, was able to prevent this kind of thinking from being represented in the organizational culture and curricula at EE. Given Leah's contentious relationship with Richard, many staff members suspected that he sought more influence over the programming of EE after Leah's departure.

The changes in leadership and circumstances surrounding Gina's hire (where department directors felt their input was ignored during the hiring process) created a deep sense of distrust. As a steady stream of staff members left, new ones came and quickly left. Cynthia Gladys, who was in charge of the organization's finances, and Monica Matthews joined Leah at her new organization approximately six months after Leah left. Within the first few months of Gina's hire, Ms. Allan, a longtime staff member in charge of admissions decisions, resigned under contentious circumstances that continue to haunt the organization and former staff members. Longtime staff Terry and Walidah remained with EE under significant stressors and during organizational changes that created deep fears for the future of youth in the program, the organization itself, and for their own professional lives. Terry was promoted after Leah's departure and felt isolated in his new role. He recognized that long-standing relationships suffered as a result of his tenuous position following through on demands from Gina and the board while overseeing programming and the department directors. Echoing Daniel's thoughts, Terry expressed that Gina often said "yes" to every idea the board had, even if it was outside of the organization's mission and had racist undertones. Terry later reflected on feeling "stuck" in an organization in which he was no longer working toward a mission but working for Gina and for the board. Tension surfaced between Terry and the department directors as they were unclear where he stood on the orders coming from the board. Conflict surfaced between Terry and Faith after Terry told Gina that Faith was leaving EE to work with Leah, Monica, and Cynthia Gladys:

> TERRY: I do feel a little bit like I'm selling my soul to the devil. But the reality is there are no positions out there for me to go apply to. I need a job.
>
> INTERVIEWER: Why do you feel like that?
>
> TERRY: Because there aren't. I don't have the educational qualifications.
>
> INTERVIEWER: No, why do you feel like you are selling your soul?
>
> TERRY: Because, you know, and this may be off topic, so tell me if it is. The reason that Faith's response is pissing me off is because I'm like you're free. You're free. Everyone that worked at EE was led by their commitment to the mission, their call to the mission. You are free to continue your call somewhere else. And I'm stuck under this new leadership . . . I'm still locked up. And I told her you're mad because I'm not emotional, but I'm on a sinking ship. I don't have time to wave goodbye. I gotta keep bailing the water. That's what I go to do. So, like I said, that's probably off topic but . . . I feel like I sold my soul to the devil 'cause this is not [pause] I'm not working for the kids. I'm working for them, for [Gina]. And I have to make the transition and in the process of working for her I'm still working for the kids.

The friction between Terry and Faith stems from Faith asking that Terry not reveal that she was leaving to work with Leah right away. Terry was unable to do that, and Faith's departure was announced by Gina in front of the staff. This fueled the belief, started by Richard, that Leah was "taking" core staff members away from EE. During my interviews with other youth workers, there was a deep sense of mistrust of all leadership, including Terry. The nature of Terry's role put him in an awkward position of having previously been an ally to the rest of the department directors while trying to embrace a new role of leadership in which he felt constrained by the board's demands and Gina's leadership style. Terry's comment about being on a "sinking ship" was disconcerting to hear, but it was a feeling also shared by Walidah. Even in Terry's frustration and pain, he had a clear understanding that the new direction of EE under Gina's and the board's leadership was incongruent with the mission of the organization and not aligned with the values and norms previously established. Further, the uncritical adoption of market-based logics under new leadership led to the organization's expansion into new neighborhoods, a quest to serve more students at any cost, and a more corporate-like environment with little joy.

As youth workers, both old and new, began to depart Educational Excellence, Walidah's fear that people without an understanding of the lived realities of EE youth would lead the organization ultimately came to fruition. During follow-up conversations with youth workers, fear and uncertainty was often expressed about EE's direction. Long-term youth workers were concerned with the direction of Educational Excellence under Gina's leadership and greater influence from Richard and the board. As the culture of the organization began to shift in ways that were incompatible with the professional and personal values of many staff members, they began to consider opportunities outside of the organization. For many community-based youth workers and other individuals deeply connected to youth and families through community and neighborhood organizations, leaving to work elsewhere is a difficult decision to make. For any educator working in school or in out-of-school spaces, the connections made with students and families are precious and meaningful. The transformation of Educational Excellence occurred right before the eyes of youth workers who felt like they had little control. Once it became an organization that did not align with their ideology about youth and education, youth workers began to rethink their job opportunities and left EE.

Even for staff members who did not directly engage with young people, the decision to leave EE was also difficult. Daniel, a member of the Development team as a lead grant writer, chose to leave because he refused to work with Gina any longer. Although his new job was closer to his own personal interests in environmental justice, Daniel was candid that he was unwilling to take any further direction from Gina:

DANIEL: I think it's just been one extreme to another. It was too intense intellectually now it's too—there's no . . . I can't put my finger on it, Bianca, I don't know what it is. Maybe it's the knowledge I have that things are the way they are and there's not much hope of it getting better for the foreseeable future anyway. I'm leaving.

INTERVIEWER: Have you processed that at all? I'm always curious about these stories of leaving and when people transition and move on. How are you in the process? What's going through your head?

DANIEL: I did think of it as a big deal before, and now I'm certainly struck by the realization that I'm here, today, right now and that literally tomorrow I'm going to be somewhere else. I think that's why people take breaks before starting. But, it'll be interesting. I've never not transitioned somewhere. That's what I'm thinking about now.

Daniel discussed his excitement about his new position because it was closely aligned to the work he wanted to do in the long term:

I'm very excited about that. That's the pull factor. The push factor would be unquestionably Gina, as much as I hate to say it because I do think she's a nice person and means well, she was a terrible fit for that position. I fear it's going to be more . . . she doesn't really care much for me. She was reticent to my being promoted in the summer. I think I'm just very assertive with her and I think that rubs her the wrong way. I make faces when she says things and I can't help it. I think she knows that I don't respect her intellectually, and that there's nothing I can do about it. If I don't respect my [executive director] intellectually, how is that sustainable? So I'm going to miss the place and I hope that everything I've set up, in transition, will be continuing, but I don't have a high degree of confidence that it will.

Daniel's candidness about Gina's leadership and the direction of the organization was shared by many staff members who felt that what once made EE strong was its leadership and the culture fostered by both staff and students who understood and believed in the mission of the organization and the humanity of Black youth. Similarly, Patrick, the head of Development and Daniel's immediate supervisor, explained his thoughts on how massive turnover in the organization shaped the organization and staff members' faith in the programming:

And everybody's been very clear, "If you leave, I'm gone." So, I can see a whole new staff. Or at least a 90 percent. You know, when we did the staff meeting yesterday, more than 50 percent of the staff has been here less than a year. So, it's already a very new place and will just continue moving in that direction. I think we'll be closer to 100 percent in under two years. That's just my take, just looking around. I don't have any data, I just look at people and they don't look happy.

People look miserable. What's worse is I get the sense, and I'm including myself in this, that there's nowhere to go with it. I'm really frustrated because I don't understand where the program's going, who it's going to serve, how is recruitment going to change. How do you ever resolve it? Or if you do resolve, how do you talk to a white person like, "You don't really understand Black people's issues." How do you broach that conversation? We have to talk differently to them than we did with Leah. We can't shorthand. We can't use the references we did.

Patrick's comments capture how long-term staff turnover prompted younger staff members to leave. For younger youth workers like Dana and Frank, working with Faith and Terry was important for them because they were once students in the organization and looked up to these staff members. Patrick also highlights how the organization has shifted racially, pointing out how staff members no longer have space to discuss race in ways they had before. Patrick's references to talking "differently" to the board under Leah's direction captures the kind of conversations the leadership would have had in the past among themselves about how to manage Richard and the board. Further, Patrick's comments speak to how Leah, as a director, was well versed in the ways in which structural inequality shaped the lives of Black youth. She recognized the importance of understanding the lived realities of youth and the structural resources needed to make them not only academically successful but socially and politically aware and active. More concretely, Richard often relied on cultural and individual explanations for the outcomes of Black and Latinx youth; in contrast, Leah countered with larger questions about political constraints, historical context, and social realities affected by institutional racism and capitalism. The absence of this more sociologically informed thinking allowed Richard's anti-Blackness to surface in tangible ways and resulted in anger and deep unhappiness in the organization and among staff. Unhappiness, as Patrick addresses, seemed to be the prevailing feeling among youth workers at EE during my final visit. The emotions youth workers shared were difficult to witness as I observed and heard their unhappiness during my interviews. It was difficult not to notice how unhappy people were and how desperate they were to find other places to work while feeling guilty about leaving students to whom they had grown close.

Camille originally began working for EE as counseling coordinator. She supervised master's students at a nearby counseling psychology program who served as EE students' counselors. Camille, a doctoral student, remained at EE until she left to pursue an internship as a condition of her doctoral program.

Her departure occurred in the same year as those of Faith Davenport, Benjamin Tucker, and Daniel Morris but at the end of the school year. As Camille reflected on her process of leaving the organization, she described the Youth Lead office being totally vacant. She was disappointed by her departure experience. "I felt like the 'goodbye' was very anticlimactic. I felt like I had worked there for almost five years and it was kind of like, 'Alright good luck!' [laughter] . . . It didn't matter that I was leaving. I left the same week as three other people." After reflecting on her last day in the program, Camille shared that although she enjoyed working with youth, she no longer wanted to be a part of the program. "I don't really want to be in this environment. I'm gonna miss the kids and really that's it. That's really the only thing I miss about the work now is the kids, because it's not like what I first experienced when I developed my love for the organization."

Camille's analysis of her departure from EE speaks volumes to the detached relationships that now characterized the organization. Being physically present but psychologically absent captures the way many other staff members began to function in the organization. Her emphasis on being present for students and enjoying engaging with them seemed to be the primary reason why many youth workers remained at EE for as long as they did. To learn that the "love for the organization" was no longer present was disheartening, but it was the reality for other youth workers as well, including Walidah, who remained at EE longer than most after the transition.

Walidah joined EE as the director of High Achievers in 2007, and after receiving her doctorate in education in 2013, she was promoted to the director of High Achievers and Expansion. As the only remaining original staff member under the new transition in 2015, Walidah was concerned about the direction of the organization, the responsibility that fell on her lap as a result, and the stark differences in program culture. Walidah also witnessed everyone else depart EE and move into different positions within education or nonprofit community-based youth work. Walidah remained committed to her work with young people despite her unhappiness. "I haven't been happy about it. I've been trying to weather the storm and I think what has kind of kept me from going off the deep end, I think, [I have] just been trying to remind myself that I'm doing the work for the kids. The kids are who we're supposed to be working for, and I'm always trying to do the best that I can for them," explained Walidah.

In a few cases, staff members left EE without lining up another job. Many people were desperate to leave EE but felt conflicted about leaving students behind. For example, Faith recalled some of the conversations she held with high school and college students who were saddened by her decision to leave:

> Initially they were very tearful. One guy accused me . . . no, he said, "Why would I do this to them? Things are changing." And, one other student, in a one-on-one conversation was like, "with all the staff leaving things are going to change. They're not gonna be the same. I'm not gonna want to come here." . . . And we tried to encourage them that you're still going to be an alum, you still have to give back, it's very important to give back. But [long pause] it's just been difficult because, they see you as a parent figure, you know? Or someone who has supported them throughout, and I think by the end of the day, because I talked to them at the beginning of the day, by the end of the day some of them came to me and said, "I'm really happy for you," and what I said to them is that I'm not leaving you, I'm leaving EE. To help them understand that I will be in touch like I mentor you now from afar 'cause you're in college. Same thing applies, it just means you are not gonna come here on this floor. You know? But they connect the people with the organization, and it's like if you are then out of the organization, it's sort of like you don't exist anymore. And I'm trying to help them to hold on to that relationship. That's the psychologist in me.

In my follow-up surveys of youth alumni, several former participants talked about feeling "obligated" to return to the organization to visit. Most return during the winter for alumni gatherings or to volunteer for career events. As one person wrote, "I try to visit EE as often as I can." Relationships established between adult and youth participants in community-based organizations can be meaningful and critical to building meaningful social networks, as many scholars contend.[6] The connections established between youth workers and students go far beyond role model or mentor. At EE, youth workers engaged with students during formative years of their lives and were connected to their families as well. Some youth participants had siblings who were alumni of the program, so EE held relationships with entire families for several years. Youth workers therefore had a difficult time deciding to leave the organization despite the professional and personal growth now lacking in the program. For instance, Solomon shared that he was considering leaving EE prior to Leah's departure. In addition to his family transitioning out of the city, Solomon wanted to "spread his wings" because he had been working for EE for seven years. As he reflected on leaving the organization, he shared how he might miss out on upcoming cohorts of students that he had connections with and was reminded of advice Faith had given him:

And then I started thinking about the new freshman class. The eighth graders who are gonna become freshman. I'm not gonna be there. And I was like, man, these guys, they got flavor. They got character that I would have loved to be a part of that energy . . . And then I was, like, trying to draw off of vicariously some of other people's process, particularly Faith, who [said] you can't think about the past work that you've done, which has been momentous, versus what you are not gonna be able to do this year, next year, or moving forward. Right? There's so many seeds and so many lives that you already have helped shape that you can't let that idea that you won't still be there undermine that. You have to honor that work. You have to honor yourself and be like, yo, I did that.

Solomon and I shared a laugh as he expressed his excitement for the incoming class of ninth graders. He had worked with them as sixth, seventh and eighth graders. I also had worked with them as sixth and seventh graders and was able to empathize with Solomon's enthusiasm for working with students and the regret he felt that he would no longer be around to see future cohorts move through the program. As participants reflected back on their experiences as staff members and the students they have supported during their tenure in the organization, there was a sense of accomplishment and disappointment that the work could no longer continue. Solomon, a husband and father of two, had widespread interests in youth development specifically for Black boys and wanted to grow professionally. Solomon had been instrumental in the lives of boys at EE, and his departure was tough as he and other youth workers wanted to see students move through the continuum. However, leaving EE under its new leadership and goals of expansion felt like youth workers were leaving an entirely different organization than the one they had initially joined.

As EE became "a revolving door of youth workers," long-term staff members began to see the impact departures had on students. Students would come to programming after school expecting to hear an announcement that someone else was leaving. Alums of the program who are now in college and or have progressed in their careers shared how staff turnover also affected them. When asked if they had returned to the program, one respondent wrote,

> I did go and I was very disappointed. I reached out this summer in hopes to connect with an old faculty member. However, I was met with great deceit. I found out that none of the old staff worked there any longer. I was met with new faces who were also planning to leave EE. They told me about the high

turnover rates and the lack of love in [the] environment. I too could feel that sense of emptiness when I walked into that building.

Many of the alumni who completed the questionnaire explained that lack of time or living out of state prevented them from visiting. Some did mention that they were "afraid that the atmosphere won't be the same." Some alumni planned to return but were skeptical about what they would experience because of what their peers told them about the current state of the program. "I will visit soon to meet the new staff members running the program. Have not visited because I hear it is unfamiliar and unrecognizable. Many of my old peers had strange experiences visiting," wrote another alum.

Cultivating meaningful relationships with students in the program was critical to the success of the program. For youth workers who remained long after Leah's departure, leaving the students proved to be a challenging decision for them as they were torn between disappointing students and feeling that they were dying professionally. Being able to let go and celebrate the work that has been done with youth is sometimes difficult. Some youth workers recognized that although EE had changed, the work that had been done with youth proved to be meaningful and important to their lives. For that reason, staff members like Faith and Monica frame EE as existing beyond the physical space. Monica, for example, suggests that EE is "located in young people who have moved through the continuum" and who are reflections of the mission of the organization.

As I spoke with youth workers about their understanding of the organization's transformation and their feelings about leaving or staying in the program, it was apparent that their decision to leave was never because of issues they were having with the students. On the contrary, many staff members stayed longer than they wanted to because of the relationships they held with students. Camille reflected: "it just got crazy how many people were leaving and realizing that they'd rather do other things really. I mean, I don't think it was about the kids. I mean everybody loves working with the kids, but at the end . . . that wasn't the type of work environment they wanted to be in."

Under (Internal) Pressure

During the period of transition between 2012 and 2015, the breakdown in professional and personal relationships proved to be one of the most challenging and unexpected consequences of the shift in leadership. During my follow-up research, the distrust of the board and Gina was apparent. There was a heightened fear that all that had been established in ten years under Leah's tenure would be washed away—from the subtle ways youth workers spoke to youth, uplifting them and each other during their darkest days, to the explicit ways leadership and youth workers spoke about racism and structural inequality and raised the critical consciousness of both youth and youth workers. Coming back to EE after two years, I expected to hear more stories of resistance and refusal against the anti-Black and deficit ideology of Richard and the board members aligned with his thinking. I expected that youth workers who had known each other for several years would become even closer personally as they collectively resisted the neoliberal push to make EE into something drastically different than what they fought so hard to build. Instead, I found a staff that was disjointed and experiencing very different emotions under the new direction of the program. While some spoke of their utter disappointment at the gross levels of anti-Blackness, neoliberal paternalism, and outright incompetence and lack of understanding of education, others felt betrayed, while some described feelings of "emptiness" and being "stuck." Many staff members wanted to resist and push back against Richard, Gina, and the board's demands. Although some did so in subtle ways, there was the reality that pushing back against institutional power might jeopardize their livelihood.

At the same time, youth workers had trouble walking away abruptly, because of the relationships they had built with youth and families over the years. For some, the fear of losing their job was very real. Additionally, although there are hundreds of nonprofit community-based youth organizations in the city, the professional networks encompassing those organizations is small, and the prospect of leaving under questionable circumstances scared many youth workers. While some left once they secured other employment, others made the decision to leave without securing another job. For them, the culture of EE had shifted so much that they refused to stay any longer regardless of their next or future positions. The direction of leadership reflected neoliberal strategies for success that increased racial and class-based tensions that made the majority staff of color uneasy. Terry and Walidah, who had been employed in professional positions for decades, both left EE without securing other jobs. To them, being unemployed with no job prospects in sight was far better than being a part of an organization they no longer believed in.

During my conversations with former EE youth workers, they often reflected on their personal and professional growth and their deep engagement with youth over many years. Each of them pointed to their growth and development as professionals and educators during their time with EE. Youth workers were able to capture what made EE special in comparison to other community-based youth spaces. Though their experiences came with some frustration as with any job, they were overjoyed with their accomplishments as a program and were extremely proud of the young people who came through the organization. Camille expressed gratitude for the time she spent getting to know youth in the program. She reflected on the relationships she was able to cultivate with other staff members, youth, and her professional and personal growth:

> I learned a lot about myself. I mean clinically, the type of work I like to do. I think something that always stood out to me even despite the change is just how close the staff was. Even though it didn't hold to the end, I think that was something unique about EE that I hadn't experienced in other organizations. How that cohesion and really feeling like everyone is about the same purpose. And I hadn't experienced that in the same way prior. So that was something that I loved and would hope to find in another organization. But I think when everyone was on it and connected and had the same purpose, like I think you know we did a lot. We got a lot done. We were really successful, and I think at the end of the day it really is about the kids. Despite the change, I still think there's that—the people that are working there—some of them [slight laugh], it's still what motivates them. Even in chaos, it should really be about the kids. Despite the craziness, I think that's something that I held onto and a lot of the staff held onto for as long as they could. You know, for some, it just couldn't be about the kids, it really had to be about their well-being, but I mean I think for me, I learned that staff cohesion is important.

The focus on youth or "just the kids," as Camille stated, kept youth workers engaged for as long as it did despite the drastic organizational shifts. Camille is pointing out a very valid and real concern that many educators are faced with, whether they are in schools or working in community-based programs. Prioritizing personal well-being or that of a student is an extremely difficult decision to make. And, to stress again, EE youth workers had known many young people from the ages of eleven to eighteen. Even more, former youth participants like Frank, Samira, and Dana who served as program coordinators for Youth Lead, Step 2 College, and High Achievers, respectively, returned for employment and volunteer opportunities during and after college. Entire families came through the program, which made it extremely difficult for staff to walk away.

Camille worked with students at EE for five years. For her, there was no question that the young people at EE sustained her during the most difficult moments of the transition. "Just the kids," she said. "That's literally the only thing—like at the end of the day, regardless of how stressed or overwhelmed I was feeling, I still loved meeting with the kids. You know, going into the classroom when they needed me, I still enjoyed. But, that was really it."

The changes to EE's culture and climate as an organization felt extreme to longtime youth workers. The constant changes in staff also proved to be challenging for participants. Prior to all of these changes, youth workers like Camille found joy and hope in what the organization was able to do with young people, as well as the relationships she established with her colleagues. Although most were saddened by the changes occurring, they were always grateful for the relationships they established with youth. These relationships established between youth workers, between youth workers and students, and between the young people proved to be the thing that participants reflected on warmly with fondness and a sense of accomplishment.

Beyond the Brick and Mortar

The full essence of Educational Excellence in its Golden Era is best captured by what was instilled in young people and what they carry with them through college and their careers. Longtime youth workers at EE who had been with the organization for four years or more had deep connections with young people. Many saw youth mature and matriculate from middle to high school to college. Former youth participants, like Frank, Samira, and Dana, often returned to work for EE as counselors for summer programs and to work as part-time or full-time staff members if positions were available. During an interview once Monica was well settled into her new role, she shared that she would hear from former staff members about their frustration with the changes being made to EE. Although Monica appeared sympathetic to their concerns, she articulated a broader conception of what the organization stood for:

> You know, I try to get the people that I've seen that come and are worried in that way to think more broadly about what it is, what EE is . . . What it is so powerful and so expansive is that it can't be contained by the confines of structure and titles. You know, we did programs and we did activities, but what we did was love, we did truth, we did knowledge, we did belief, we did faith. Those were

the things that were enacted in those methodologies. Youth development is just an approach. It's a tool. I've always said that all of the things that we've ever done, every approach and methodology that we've done is just an approach . . . I think that it's when we recognize that EE exists beyond the confines of brick and mortar and curriculum and data. It is experiences. It is its truth. It joins the ether and ethos of experience. It's not bound by that. People don't really understand that. It's a hokey kind of thing and people are really concrete and so on and so forth, but it's a truth. You know that when you have relationships with people. You know that when there are people you can pick up the phone and talk to. So it's hard to see the physical EE or the way in which you imagine or believe or understand EE to have been changed, but you can't deny all of what came before it. So we have to be willing and open to looking at it differently. It also means we have to be willing and open to walking away from and letting go of attachment a lot of times driven by our own sense of importance. "I was there, I did this thing. It was amazing. I'm fucking amazing!" . . . Letting that go, knowing that EE moves and travels in the Maishas, and the Nasirs, and the Jamals [student participants enrolled in college at the time of study]. You know, a little bit of EE goes everywhere you go.

Monica's comments are powerful in that they capture the consistency of change. Even more, her reflections capture the constant change that occurs within organizations and institutions as the actors within them grow, change, or disengage. It would be far too simplistic to speak of organizational change as "good" or "bad"—that dichotomy isn't sufficient and social organizations are complex.[7] Monica's understanding of EE occurring outside of the physical space is important as it speaks to the significance of the work of staff members and community building to create opportunities and experiences for young people. Below, she refers to EE as a "collection of experiences" that were meaningful, life changing, and life affirming for many who came through the doors of EE:

It only reinforced what I know to be true. The experiences that people have and the opportunity that people have to learn, and grow, and engage, and analyze, and sit with, and meld, and ruminate, and you know mesh with creates who we are. I mean we're just a collection of experiences, you know . . . I tell my staff all the time, you can never un-ring a bell. You cannot go back and recapture that sound. It's out in the universe. It's done. Victory's already been claimed. There are hundreds of kids that are moving through the world in a way that might not have been possible had not Leah been there, or me. But me, Leah, Terry, you, Walidah . . . all of that came together in a very unique and special way. You can't undo that. You cannot undo that. And the experiences of the kids coming together themselves are even beyond the importance of the brick, the mortar.

EE exists beyond the brick and mortar of its physical space. As Monica passionately articulated, the organization exists within the collective experiences shared by students and staff. These collective experiences between youth and staff members reflect the deep relationships created in a space that deliberately fostered these relationships. This space was intentional and led to staff and youth showing up in tangible ways for youth and families—whether to console students or staff during family loss, support the family of a former youth participant who took her life, or raise funds for a former staff member who lost their belongings in a fire.

The collapse of EE's Golden Era might have been inevitable, but there are many lessons to learn from the story of Educational Excellence and of the experiences of youth workers. Educators situated within community-based youth spaces are not immune to the political realities that shape public education. As the persistent privatization efforts of public education continue, community-based after-school programs will continue to be vulnerable in similar ways as schools. As this book reveals, these macro-level political realities are deep and penetrating as they inform the day-to-day processes within community organizations. EE was shaped by broader political changes to treat education as a business under a neoliberal framework, which reifies and reflects racialized deficit discourses of individualism and pathological explanations for the experiences of minoritized youth in urban settings.

Neoliberal Paternalism and the Persistence of Race

So, when Leah said that she was gonna leave, I really thought about economics. I was like, damn. It's economics. It's all economics. Right? . . . Because if we were running this shit, Leah wouldn't be leaving. We would have none of this beef with this dude. And we were doing crazy stuff, right? So I kind of started feeling like, should I focus solely on building economics? Like really going full force with my entrepreneurial pursuits and transforming that into a lifestyle of philanthropy, however small, and slowly build that up. And so that was part of my process. Like, okay, I need to really just leave and just be entrepreneurial 100 percent. And because of my experience with social justice and now with education, just kind of have a

social justice consciousness while being an entrepreneur . . . But at the end of the day, hopefully that's not too much of a trite thing to say, is we need to build our own institutions. And we need to run our own institutions. And we need to fund them as heavily and as aggressively as a place like EE is funded because [Richard Dunn] has the damn money.
    —*Solomon Youth Lead Coordinator/Instructor, 2005–2013*

During EE's Golden Era, race proved to be a central organizing factor in the program. Under the direction of Leah, and with the support of Monica, Terry, Walidah, and Faith, dialogues about how race shaped the educational experiences and opportunities for youth in the program were paramount. EE not only established and held high expectation for achievement among youth participants, but it also stressed that youth be knowledgeable about the world around them. Through after-school courses and throughout engagement between staff and students, critical conversations about racism, and racial and other social identities, were a significant element of the EE experience. As part of the continuum model, a deep understanding of race was key for both academic achievement and healthy social identities. Youth workers shared important insights about educational policy and its influence on community-based youth work. Race continued to be an important factor at the forefront of youth workers' minds as they reflected on their past work with youth at EE.

Despite EE's deep focus and intentionality around racial consciousness among staff and youth participants, contradictions did emerge. The weight of white supremacy shapes and reshapes how racialized groups understand, interpret, and make sense of the world.[8] The performative aspects of the program related to student culture, expression, and language were often determined through a number of things like age, class status, and the gaze of whiteness. Youth workers like Walidah and Solomon sometimes used the word "conservative" to describe some practices in the organization. These practices have to be understood from two specific frameworks. First, how youth workers engage students, construct pedagogy, and instill cultural practices in the organization is filtered through their own understanding of their social worlds, not only through their racial lens, but also class, gender, age, and education levels, among other things. Even more, operating within a system of white supremacy often means that contradictions emerge in the ideology and practices of those who operate from an affirming, anti-racist, and social justice framework. Second, the power and control of Educational Excellence was never in the hands of its leader or executive director. The organization belongs to Richard Dunn. He held the financial power and wielded that power whenever he could. As Walidah shared, repeating the advice of Felicia, who served as the interim executive director prior to Gina's hire, "the sooner we understand that this organization belongs to Richard Dunn, the better off we all will be."

Richard used his wealth as a tool of control and power over Leah and the organization. According to the directors, the persistent use of race (as a form of cultural superiority) and class (as a tool of control by Richard) was how Richard hired Gina against the wishes of staff members and to justify his interference in programming. As a white male philanthropist, Richard's history of racist deficit comments about Black communities were reflected in his speeches, essays, and interaction with staff members during board meetings. They also appeared during his visits to the program and were manifested in the imposition of cultural hegemonic and racialized practices on the program. The story of EE helps us understand the nature of race and how it functions within the neoliberal educational policy context. Within an organizational context, race permeates organizational culture and practices as the actors carry racial meaning with them in their social interactions.[9] Under Leah's direction, learning about and understanding how racism and capitalism play a critical role in determining youths' educational opportunities were core aspects of the professional and personal development training for staff members. And, as explored in previous chapters, youth participants were engaged in conversations about how racial identity and structural oppression shaped their experiences as youth of color.

The absence of discourse around race does not mean that racism is not present.[10] Although race was no longer discussed at EE in tangible ways, race still proved to be a factor in the experiences of youth workers at EE. The relationship Richard held with EE following Leah's departure resulted in his ideas about Black communities surfacing in the culture of the program in ways that were problematic and that elevated white middle-class values and cultural norms. According to youth workers, Gina did not talk about how race, and its intersections with social class, had an impact on the lives of youth participants. This seeming discomfort in discussing race eroded a fundamental practice of the program—placing race at the table to be deconstructed, analyzed, and understood. Instead, she advocated color-blind approaches in which silence about race allows white supremacy to continue unchallenged.

In contrast to Gina's silence about race, Richard's attitudes toward Black communities resulted in him making decisions for the program that aligned with the types of cultural values he felt youth at EE needed to hone—middle-class white values and norms of speaking and existing in the world. Even more, Richard's control and power over EE as its founder and primary funder are reflected in a troubling relationship between white neoliberal paternalism, benevolence, and capitalism.[11] The relationship dynamics between Richard and Leah included racism, paternalism, and patriarchy functioning in toxic ways that ultimately played a role in Leah's resignation. Solomon put it best when he said, "Leah definitely gave up something to ride until she couldn't give that anymore. And it was the race thing. It was the racist relationship" with Richard. Solomon went on to explain that once Leah exited the relationship with Richard and EE, the extent of Richard's attitude toward Black people became abundantly clear: "So, I guess once that severance happened, then we really got to see what he thought of us. What he thought of the children. What he thought of how we should be doing things as Black people who aren't on the same level as white people."

Richard's anti-Black rhetoric was once hearsay, passed down to directors Terry, Monica, and Walidah by Leah and other colleagues who attended monthly board meetings with Richard. Leah was able to serve as an important buffer between Richard and the rest of the staff and young people. Once she left, Richard's attitudes became more visible in the program. For instance, he pressed Gina to engage EE participants in cultural experiences rooted in "cultural" programming that ignored racial and cultural dynamics (the kinds of programming that Leah often resisted). According to Walidah, who began attending board meetings once she was promoted, Richard often chided students in the program for their speaking patterns.

The story of EE and its ties to Richard Dunn, its founder, is complex but not uncommon given the nature of philanthropists' and foundations' relationship with communities of color. Philanthropic organizations that engage poor communities of color often locate the power to create social change within the foundations themselves rather than in grassroots community organizing and social movements.[12] Rooted in false generosity,[13] racist paternalistic ideologies, and practices that seek to discipline and control poor people of color through neoliberal governmentality,[14] nonprofit community-based organizations must not forget that donors often seek private gain rather than social change for the greater good.[15]

In the organizations that I have been fortunate enough to engage with as a participant, staff member, or researcher, youths and adults alike feel a sense of ownership and responsibility for the program. That feeling is in part tied to the deep cultural practices cultivated in those organizations over time. Young people and youth workers often play a significant role in creating cultural practices that are sustained over the years. Although this feature of an organization can be palpable, the financial ownership does not lie with youth participants and youth workers. In many cases, community-based organizations are tethered to their funders—whether that is a foundation or influential individual donors. Although the depth of control may vary from program to program, money often denotes ownership. And yet it is also true that youth and youth workers owned EE via the cultural practices they were able to cultivate, the power of relationships, and the concerted effort to meet the academic, political, and cultural needs of young people. That sense of ownership among EE staff also encouraged an impression of having a broader, material form of ownership as well. However, that ownership was illusory, according to Solomon:

> We ruled EE. We ruled that thing, but it was never ours . . . It was never Dunbar's. It was never the children's. What was ours were our relationships and our love for our people. And while that love was informed by various levels of probably problematic politics, I definitely didn't have as much as a legitimate consciousness as I like to believe I have now.

"We ruled EE . . . but it was never ours." Indeed, Solomon's statement reflects so much truth about the nature of community-based organizations that rely on financial support from outside of the community they serve to remain afloat.

• • •

Leaders and youth workers at EE were once cognizant of the political landscape of education marked by privatization, an influx of charter management organizations, and market-based approaches to public education. The onslaught of neoliberal ideology and reform efforts also reify racism and individual explanations for failure while touting equal opportunity for all. These external political pressures proved to be a challenge for Educational Excellence, one that was compounded by the transition of leadership and the subsequent turnover among the staff. Ultimately, there were a variety of push and pull factors contributing to participants' decisions to leave the organization. These factors include the macro-level neoliberal political shifts informing public education and their impact on the micro-level practices among youth workers. Other factors included the growing corporate-style culture of the organization, which prevented youth workers from communicating from a place of joy with each other by not being allowed to laugh; a hyperfocus on expansion and serving more students at any cost; and the subtle shift of the language of the program to reflect racialized deficit narratives instead of affirming and humanizing language to define the young people in the program.

The landscape of community-based youth work is not immune from the political shifts and reforms occurring within public education. The privatization and marketization of education has led to a fundamental shift in how young people are engaged within schools. However, community-based after-school spaces are also shaped by the political context and political economy of public education. Funding patterns and philanthropy within education is and has always been informed by the current politics of education. Thus, community-based spaces are often forced to follow trends in the education world that can reinforce neoliberal logics of practice and racist deficit and damage-centered models of engagement. Community-based after-school programs have been liberatory spaces for Black youth; however, in the current era of education reform, the flexibility of these spaces is being threatened as they are forced to consider more "efficient" models of engagement and expansion instead of the comprehensive approach that sets them apart from schools.

Conclusion

*Reclaiming Community-Based Youth Work
in the Neoliberal Era*

THE STORY OF EDUCATIONAL EXCELLENCE is a powerful example of how larger political structures and educational policy constrain and inform the day-to-day practices of community-based youth workers within youth organizations. In many ways, the story of EE is about the ways that community organizations fight for the right to self-determination, setting the organization's direction while negotiating, disrupting, and sometimes adapting to the demands of the state and the donors that financially support them. More broadly, this story shows how these larger political structures shape Black self-determination over the community's educational spaces.

In its "Golden Era," Educational Excellence was shaped by a set of community-based leaders, directors, and youth workers fueled by the mission to get youth in Dunbar to and through college, using a youth-centered and identity-affirming approach. They recognized that setting high expectations for academic success through culturally relevant and sustaining practices and pedagogies,[1] coupled with opportunities for sociopolitical and cultural development and emotional support, was vital to the success of the program. During the staff-proclaimed "Golden Era," 100 percent of students in the program graduated from high school and 95 percent of students completed college within six years. Educational Excellence celebrated success that was measurable and quantifiable to appease donors and its Board of Directors. In addition to helping youth achieve academic success, EE supported after-school courses taught by the Youth Lead department that fostered racial and political consciousness and helped students deconstruct systemic inequality in social institutions, including schools and the criminal justice system. Educational Excellence offered these opportunities because of the orientation of the leadership and staff—who themselves were educators of color with strong racial awareness and a specific humanizing approach in working with minoritized youth. Under the leadership of Leah Davis, EE strived to protect the framing and imagining of racialized youth and avoided deficit and damage-centered[2] portrayals of these youth in its presentation of their work with students to families, media outlets, and potential donors. EE did not view Black youth as "at risk" or "broken" or as needing to be "fixed" by the organization. Rather, staff understood that because education is administered in the context of white supremacy, additional support, tools, and strategies are needed to combat the structural harm Black youth experience in schools and in larger society.[3] As the data from this research reveal, the community of practice established at EE, which included an imagining of youth of color as whole and complete beings; cultural and pedagogical practices rooted in identity affirmation; high expectations; and authentic relationships of radical care between staff and students anchored the program in ways that were meaningful for both youth participants and staff members.

Despite these triumphs, internal challenges and problematic politics emerged in ways that were sometimes difficult to grasp for youth workers. Contradictions in racial framing connected to various forms of youth expressions were reflected through class and generational differences, while other internal conflicts proved to be directives passed down from the organization's founder through the Board of Directors. Challenges also emerged when program leaders, grant writers, and department directors sought funding in ways that may have contradicted their stance on a comprehensive approach where academics were weighted as equally as youth development in the program. This sometimes resulted in an overreliance on their academic college preparation work to funders because policy trends and broader educational discourses relied on measurable results and "numbers" with youth rather than their more critical youth development work. Changes to the program after the departure of Leah Davis radically shifted the culture of the program as more interference from the founder and Board of Directors began to influence program offerings.

On the surface, the transformation of Educational Excellence may appear to be the result of natural shifts and changes that all organizations are susceptible to, especially in light of leadership and member turnover. Although some aspects of typical changes in organizations is part of the Educational Excellence story, there are a specific set of external pressures that contributed to the changes within the organization—many of which mirror the current changes in public education. Under new leadership, language aligned with the markets flourished, and Educational Excellence began to focus on expansion, growth, and increasing its numbers. These decisions resulted in EE expanding into new neighborhoods without much thought and moving toward a drop-in model that jeopardized the organization's comprehensive approach and intimate relationship building between staff and students. The organization shifted to be more "business-like" and "corporate-like," according to long-term youth workers as well as youth participant alumni of the program. The trend toward privatization, which treats schools like for-profit enterprises focused on measurable outcomes based on success in the form of test scores and other measures of accountability, is mirrored in community-based youth work where programs are incentivized to focus on increasing numbers for funding or narrowing the academic "achievement gap" while diminishing other components that make these programs distinct from schools. These external pressures coupled with the internal politics within Educational Excellence contributed to its transformation. These internal conflicts rested on shifts in racial consciousness, power and control over money and ownership of the organization, and competing understandings of youth work engaging minoritized youth. The story of Educational Excellence shows more broadly the potential authoritative influence of macro-level politics in education, including privatization discourses shaped by neoliberal logics about how to best educate students and the permanence and persistence of racism through those discourses, and the micro-level organizational impacts on community-based educational spaces.

Research on youth experiences in community-based programs is critically important and helps keep them supported politically and funded. This book, however, seeks to draw closer attention to the community-based educators and youth workers who engage youth in community spaces. A more robust investigation into their pedagogies, philosophies, and understanding of education and youth development are essential to community-based education and school-based, classroom teacher–led education.[4]

Future Directions for Research and Practice

Given the experiences of educators at Educational Excellence and the current context of education rooted in market-based neoliberal approaches to reform that rely on racialized deficit framing of minoritized poor youth, it is imperative for practitioners, policy makers, and educational leaders to consider the critical relationship between framing, pedagogy, and funding practices. Specifically, the problematic narratives about Black youth shape how they are framed in discourse in after-school and community-based organizations. For instance, former U.S. secretary of education Arne Duncan, has written about his experiences working with young people in community-based after-school programs in Chicago. While speaking about the important role these spaces play in the lives of youth living in low-income environments, he suggests that the most important "problem for low-income urban youth is that they can't imagine a world they can't see." These, and other remarks he made, epitomize the paternalistic deficit narrative plaguing education policy and community-based youth work. He writes:

> The only life they see is the one in front of them—single-parent families, drug dealing, street gangs, a few if any men going to work each morning and coming home each night, police patrols, and violence. Asking them what they want to do with their lives and how they might fit in the larger world is like asking a fish to imagine what it's like to fly. If you've never worked in an office building and don't know anyone who does, you can't imagine doing it yourself. Programs like CYCLE (Community Youth Creative Learning Experience) understand that poverty is not the defining obstacle to success. The real barrier is the lack of opportunity to see and experience the larger world.[5]

He then continues by discussing the ways that children from more affluent families are engaged in a wide range of extracurricular and after-school activities and that out-of-school activities need to be made available for "low-income children." He concludes this statement by saying, "They need mentors, relationships, internships, work, and play opportunities, and sometimes just friends from outside their immediate environment."

Indeed, it is true that children from affluent families have the resources to participate in a wide range of activities during nonschool hours that lead to greater access to social mobility.[6] It is also true that all young people need a wide range of supports as they navigate schools, families, and larger society. However, what is sorely missing from Duncan's comments is an analysis of deep structural inequality that constrains and limits opportunities for young people of color and youth residing in low-income contexts. The framing of his analysis is also not uncommon throughout broader discourses about community-based spaces at the policy, philanthropic, educational, and organizational level. Black youth are discussed from a position of "lack," which dismisses their agency, assets, and what they bring to their schools, neighborhoods, and the after-school community-based spaces they participate in. Unpacking why affluent families have greater resources through a lens of capitalism, opportunity, and resource hoarding (particularly among white families),[7] and legacies of racial discrimination through housing, education, and employment that has left Black poor neighborhoods disproportionately dispossessed, disenfranchised, and rendered disposable is rarely interrogated. Whether intended or not, these comments by Duncan are pervasive and reify pathological discourses about communities of color even as CYCLE's mission sought to move away from pathological discourses of "fixing" youth.

The refusal to identify, disrupt, and eradicate the structural conditions that shape the lives of Black youth is dangerous as it places their lack of access to "opportunity" squarely on them and their families. It shifts the responsibility not only to youth and families but also to community-based organizations to "fix" youth rather than investing in dismantling white supremacy. I believe in the power of community-based educational spaces for racialized youth, in particular as a form of survivance[8] in an inherently racist and deeply capitalist society. As a former youth worker, I understand the value of these spaces and support the contributions they make to the educational and developmental experiences of youth. Yet the trends in research and the public discourse that follows treats them as sites where Black youth go to be "saved"—they are discussed from a position of "lack," and these spaces ultimately become racialized as a resource needed by these groups because of something they inherently lack and not as a response to systemic oppression.

Deficit-oriented rhetoric ascribed to Black and other minoritized youth shapes not only how they are framed and imagined but also the ways in which they are engaged in a variety of educational contexts. The problematic narratives about Black youth within diverse educational contexts powerfully shape educational policy, youth work, and the public's imagination of Black youth.[9] Disrupting and refusing such narratives is imperative. Changing these narratives is imperative in the current moment as neoliberal logic makes it easy to position community-based after-school programs as sites of control and governmentality over youth of color.

Community-based youth work as a field—as an approach to youth development, as a way of "seeing" youth—needs protection now more than ever. Greater attention and acknowledgment of those who work in these spaces are crucial to a full understanding of the multiple contexts and spheres of influence in the lives of young people. The heterogeneity and flexibility of these spaces have always supplemented what schools may be lacking and have also been sites of repair for the violence Black and other minoritized youth experience in schools. Furthermore, what community-based youth workers are able to do in after-school spaces can augment and support classroom-based education.[10] Sociologists, community-based leaders, and teachers committed to education must begin to theorize youth workers as pedagogues and cultural workers who operate from a particular kind of praxis that is significant to the academic, social, and political identities of young people. Acknowledging and engaging them in broader discourse is essential as they are also stakeholders and education providers who hold a critical position in students' lives.[11] This will require an ideological shift from viewing classroom teachers as the only bearers of knowledge. It also requires a reimagining of youth workers as pedagogues and of community-based educational spaces as legitimate places of academic, cultural, and political support for minoritized youth. In many ways, society's belief in the myth of meritocracy and education as the "great equalizer" limits learning to inside of schools. Although this is patently untrue, more research should document the pedagogical practices youth workers employ for educating youth beyond academic development, to include cultural, political, and social development. More work is needed to capture the depth of youth workers' praxis. Youth workers exist in a complex and intimate space in the lives of youth as cultural workers guiding them through myriad circumstances in multiple stages in their lives.[12] Youth workers must contend with and negotiate through and alongside family structures, neighborhood and community issues, and schools. In this position, youth workers become catalysts for learning, increased social consciousness, and activism, and they also serve as institutional agents and advocates on behalf of youth.[13]

An Uncertain Future?

Community-based spaces of learning have long existed within communities of color that have experienced structural violence and exclusion. These spaces have offered respite, opportunities to develop deep connections between youth and their peers and caring adults, and opportunities to develop transferable skills useful for higher education, future employment, and personal growth.[14] As the assault on public education and urban communities prevails under neoliberal restructuring of communities, community-based after-school spaces are implicated in these changes. Bearing the brunt of these shifts are the lives of the most vulnerable—youth of color in poor settings. As a racialized class-based project, neoliberalism "shapes and reshapes racial subjects," and in this way, neoliberalism is a process of racial formation and racism.[15] There-fore, rhetoric espousing meritocracy and notions of individualism under neo-liberal logics ignore structural inequality and open the door for rhetoric that positions marginalized communities of color as problems to be fixed and as threats to be destroyed. Community-based youth spaces have long provided a buffer against hostile school and arduous neighborhood circumstances. Yet, as social organizations, in the same way as schools, they are privy to forms of stratification and can reproduce inequality and harm. In some cases, they are beholden to the State or donors who have a very specific imagining and under-standing of social problems and of communities of color. Although many community-based leaders and youth workers fight like hell for self-determination over the direction of their programs, the landscape of public education and nonprofit philanthropy threatens this desire. Even still, they are important to the landscape of education and the political development of youth.

Under the Trump administration, threatened budget cuts and reductions in federal funds to after-school programs will eliminate opportunities to sup-port youth and families who rely on these spaces.[16] Community-based or school-based after-school programs provide support to parents who work mul-tiple jobs and long hours who need after-school care for their children.[17] The threat to eliminate federally supported after-school programs and the contin-ued privatization of public education pose immense threat to young people. The proposed federal cuts to after-school programming demonstrates the need for additional research and public discourse so that the public and policy makers understand the significance of these spaces. Although they are not perfect and vary across region and site, they are essential fixtures in commu-nities and neighborhoods across the country. As many schools prove to be major sites of suffering for Black youth,[18] it is imperative not only that community-based programs exist but that they are structured in ways that do not reproduce harm and exacerbate inequality.

In addition to the proposed federal cuts to after-school programming, the privatization of public education under the Trump administration could fundamentally shift what these spaces can do on behalf of young people and communities. As time and money is spent weakening public schools and in-creasing "choice" through charter management organizations and voucher programs, the "public" in public schools will no longer have any meaning. As this book reveals, the privatization of public education can have devastating consequences on the academic and social progress of Black children. The clos-ing of Black schools has destabilized the cities of Philadelphia, Chicago, and

New Orleans, something that will ultimately inflict more physical and psychic violence upon Black and other minoritized youth.[19]

The third sector or third space that community-based nonprofits exist within will be constrained not just by the lack of funding (as it shifts to charter schools or is cut by the current administration) but by the logics of neoliberalism that rely on technical skills, efficiency models, accountability determined by audit culture, and high-stakes testing as a function of these paradigms.[20] Increasing attention to solely improving test scores or basing success on the number of students who enter community-based after-school programs only reifies and mirrors the ways youth of color are engaged within schools.[21] It causes young people to become objects whose abilities and values can only be measured quantitatively, misappropriated, or dismissed, instead of encouraging young people to pursue their growth through an exploration of intersecting racial, ethnic, gender, social class, and sexual identities. Relegating youth to simply objects and reducing youth workers to actors within organizations who check off a list as students just "drop in" creates community-based programs that are detached from the lived realities of youth.

This same dynamic occurs within community-based after-school spaces as seen in the case of Educational Excellence. These organizations can be filled at the leadership level and at the level of direct engagement with people who lack educational backgrounds, who carry anti-Black logics and discourses, and who fail to understand the structural constraints that inform their lived realities. As more and more white leaders with progressive "good intentions" lead these programs embedded within Black communities, they will be positioned and promoted in ways that make them "saviors" to Black youth. Therefore, the culture established within these spaces will be developed on ideas about Black inferiority and Black suffering. In this way, Black youth will have little to no educative spaces where their identities, intellect, and creativity are nurtured and affirmed. Community-based leaders and youth workers of all racial backgrounds must resist and refuse this position as it reifies the notion that Black youth must be saved and fixed within the context of community-based youth work.

Reclaiming Community: The Promise of Community-Based Education

Although previous scholarship captures the significance of community-based youth workers in the lives of marginalized youth, their voices and experiences are absent from broader educational discourse. Subsequently, community-based youth workers' relationships with schools, families, engagement with youth, and their pedagogical practices remain underutilized and undervalued. Some community-based educational spaces have been instrumental in shifting the discourse by challenging dominant deficit narratives stemming from schools about minoritized youth because of their flexibility and fewer political constraints that traditional schools and classroom teachers experience. Yet youth work within community-based after-school programs is particularly vulnerable in the current political educational context in a way that poses major threats to their flexibility and capacity to employ broad pedagogical approaches that humanize youth by engaging their full lives. Community-based programs should be supported in ways that allow them to meet the demands of their contexts. For sociologists of education who challenge the impact of neoliberal education restructuring on schools and cities, community-based youth organizations must be included.

Although federal funding is significant for specific kinds of after-school programs, many community-based nonprofit programs engaging youth rely on foundations and donors for support. As seen through the findings from my research, economic control over an organization often determines its leadership, structure, and cultural dynamics. Solomon's words stay etched in my mind: "It was never ours." The economic control Richard Dunn possessed loomed over Educational Excellence. Although the organization was able to establish a vibrant culture in which youth participants and youth workers developed meaningful relationships and learned useful skills critical to their development, it was short-lived. For youth workers, being able to create and sustain an organization for a community with their own vision is imperative. In circumstances where economic control is not in their hands, how can youth workers or organizational leadership respond to and resist actions that are antithetical to the organization they seek to create? What options exist for Black communities that have little economic power who seek to establish and define community-based programs for young people in the ways they desire and are not invested in neoliberal logics?

The importance of youth work should not rest on Black and other minoritized youth needing these programs because something is inherently wrong with them. All too often, these programs are propped up as spaces of refuge that end up reifying pathological discourses about minoritized youth or their families. They are often discussed as places of containment and operated as a form of surveillance and governmentality to contain Black youth. I am a supporter of diverse learning spaces for young people that are humanizing and dignifying. Yet the policies and discourses driving schooling and education reform are terrifying and can dictate how community-based youth work is constructed and sustained. Community-based program leaders should be deliberate and intentional about how they approach youth work; understand its ties to the politics of education and the politics of race, capitalism, and philanthropy; and recognize the ways in which their work will be informed by macro-level educational policies, social contexts, and political conflict. As participants in this study shared, resistance and pushing back on racist and cultural pathological explanations for failure is critical in neoliberal times. The triumphs, contradictions, and resistance of educators in this study are significant and parallel to those of teachers in traditional school contexts. Youth workers are educators working in an inherently racist society exacerbated by neoliberalism.

There has been a long tradition of Black communities creating alternative spaces of dignity, learning, and respite for Black children amid racially and culturally hostile educational experiences. At various stages of history, resistance movements within Black communities (for example, Civil Rights, Black Power, and Black Arts movements) have fostered spaces to nurture and provide Black youth with an understanding of who they are and who they are perceived to be in a country where racism is a permanent fixture,[22] while also adapting to new circumstances.[23] As the system of oppression shifts and racism becomes altered, resistance can also take on new forms. Resistance within organizations can be difficult depending on a member's locus of power, but subtle and more forceful push-backs to education privatization and its impact on community-based youth work are vital. As part of this resistance, there must be intentionality in identifying and naming how the dynamics of race and paternalism flourish through philanthropy and nonprofit community-based youth work. The long history of organizing and resistance among minoritized communities for educational freedom and dignity has resulted in a number of spaces created and sustained within and by communities.[24] If history is a guide, resistance and refusal against the rise of market-driven education reform and the corporatization of after-school community-based educational spaces will continue to take on new forms.

Policy changes that have informed Black life in productive ways were often generated by acts of refusal and resistance from community-based efforts. Given this, changes in policies, a re-imagining of Black youth, and the positioning of community-based after-school programs will be seen only if there is greater theorization in scholarship, a meaningful inclusion of youth workers' experiences and pedagogies, and continued resistance and acts of refusal within communities that seek to engage Black youth on their own terms.

Appendix

Methodological Reflections, Considerations, and Accountability

QUALITATIVE RESEARCH HAS BEEN DEFINED as a systematic and planned empirical inquiry into meaning, an orientation grounded in the world of experience that seeks to understand how others make sense of their experiences, and a perspective that involves both an interpretive and naturalistic approach.[1] In short, qualitative researchers "study" individuals, communities, and phenomena in their own "natural settings, attempting to make sense of, or to interpret, phenomena in terms of the meanings people bring to them."[2] I chose a qualitative approach with ethnographic methods in order to learn and, in my case, relearn the cultural practices of staff members at Educational Excellence, and also to capture—while being immersed in the organization—the rich meaning making taking place there.

A critical approach to this study was paramount to understand how individuals construct meaning from their experiences by examining the social and political context in which participants operate.[3] I was able to pay attention to the dialectical relationship between the structural conditions and constraints that inform the lives of educators and communities, forms of agency they possess and enact, and the interlocking systems of dispossession that inform the lives of people and communities.[4] My intention to uncover, name, and problematize the structures that exist and inform Educational Excellence's transformation (for example, neoliberalism, privatization of public education, and racism) and the experiences, perspectives, and lives of participants was an important theoretical task for this research.[5] Rather than reify pathological discourses about minoritized communities, a critical lens allowed me to situate the lives of participants in a historical, social, and political context, which is necessary for removing deficits from individuals and communities and indicting systemic oppression and "interlocking circuits of dispossession and privilege."[6]

I recognize that the term "critical" is used often without a clear definition. I use it as a way to examine and analyze the structural conditions that shape the lives of my participants, while also being committed to naming these oppressions and thinking through ways to eradicate them.[7] This critical lens binds together the youth workers in my study with the structures and histories that inform their lived realities and approach to their work with youth. Studying youth workers at Educational Excellence could not be disentangled from the structural conditions and political problems that shaped Dunbar, the framing of race and Black youth, educational experiences of youth participants in the program, broader economic and education reforms, and the sense making of youth workers connected to their own understanding of race, class, and educational change. Because I was an insider at Educational Excellence and youth worker-researcher, a critical approach to ethnographic research provides a way to uncover, name, and problematize political and social problems, while charting pathways for humanization and liberation.[8]

Access to Community

I began part-time work with Educational Excellence in 2009. As a youth development instructor, I worked with girls in the eighth through twelfth grades. I made a conscious decision to conduct research at Educational Excellence for a few important reasons: (1) The asset-based, identity-affirming, and youth-centered program operated (at the organizational level) almost entirely by Black staff members and that deserved attention. Far too often, damage-centered research on minoritized communities is lauded while ignoring strengths, joy, and history within communities. (2) My rapport with staff and students offered a level of access to the program that I would not have otherwise held had I not been involved with the program. (3) Staff members at Educational Excellence generously allowed me access to spaces outside of the scope of my regular workday, and this access gave me the opportunity to employ ethnographic methods in spaces that I would not have had access to had I not cultivated a strong relationship with the program.

Community-based organizations serving minoritized youth frequently receive requests from researchers. Many organizations I have been connected with have very strict policies about outside researchers—as they should. There is a long history of scholars researching "on" vulnerable communities to extract information.[9] Many community-based groups serving marginalized groups have concerns about researchers entering their sites and exiting without commitment or awareness of the impact their presence has on individuals or the community as a whole.[10] The colonizing research methods most students are trained to use rarely center people or communities in humanizing and caring ways.[11] This issue was deeply important to me as a researcher and as a community-based youth worker and stayed present in my thoughts throughout my research. Given these issues, I tried my best to engage in the process of reciprocity with Educational Excellence. Reciprocity, or the responsibility to not only study and disclose educational and social problems but to assist in eradicating them—through building knowledge that can inform practice or by being of service in other ways to the people and institutions we research—is an important critical lens at the crux of this research.[12] Reciprocity as an exchange with or deep commitment to the study's participants is critical in community-based settings, especially where young people or other vulnerable groups are present.

As a youth worker at EE, I continued to teach youth development courses after school to middle and high school students during the week and on Saturdays throughout the data collection period. I also participated in a few tasks I would not have normally been assigned, such as writing course outlines for EE's summer program and leading professional development workshops for fellow youth workers. My contribution, in the spirit of reciprocity, was to create opportunities for research and evaluation for the Youth Lead division. I co-developed a proposal to have high school students serve as "research fellows" to develop a youth participatory action research project for the organization.

Youth Worker-Researcher: Joys and Tensions

In my role as a youth worker part-time, I spent approximately four to five hours each day working with students. As a part-time staff member, I also participated in yearly staff retreats and student retreats that were led by the Youth Lead and Step 2 College departments. As part of the staff, I participated in celebratory events for students and families, such as holiday parties and graduation ceremonies. In my thirteen months as a researcher, I conducted interviews outside of my work schedule with staff members, came in during my time off to attend and observe professional development trainings (meetings I never attended as a part-time youth worker), observed parent orientation meetings, and came in early to sit in with staff members as they ate lunch together.

"Are you Bianca or the researcher?" or "Are *you* here?" These kinds of questions were asked during professional development sessions and curriculum planning meetings I joined as an observer. These types of questions always sparked laughter from everyone, but they also brought up interesting questions and tensions to work through. During a professional development session with staff members, everyone was asked to brainstorm themes for the six-week summer program for middle school students. Everyone always respected when I wanted to stay silent, but I often struggled when, where, or how to enter. This tension of when and where to jump into and out of the researcher role can be tricky.[13] Staff members viewed me as a valuable member of the team and I felt like a valued member of the team. My identities, my history with the people that made up the organization, and my knowledge as a youth worker meant that I was part of the community. Straddling these multiple roles was sometimes complex but important for data collection and analysis. I carefully noted these moments in my field notes, separating my observations from the thoughts and feelings I held in order to ensure I captured what was discussed accurately.

Some suggest these dual roles are incompatible and position the employee and study participants in a difficult situation. Other scholars have presented counterarguments against this perspective and make the claim for "insider" research or "self-ethnography" in which an individual has "natural access" to a community or organization.[14] "Insider" research should be more formal, structured, and well thought out; a reflexive awareness is a critical element to conducting research as an insider. Although complete "objectivity" is considered to be ideal and what makes research the most valid, I, alongside many others, argue that objectivity is a fallacy—all researchers hold a number of subjectivities that they bring with them to their research.[15] I remained cognizant of the biases and preconceived notions I held and could potentially bring to this study. In order to ensure that my role as an insider did not jeopardize the research process and results, I employed validity checks, by having a group of colleagues from different fields read my formal interview protocol guides to ensure that questions were not leading.[16] I also used member-checking strategies and gave youth workers the opportunity to review their interview transcripts and discussed findings and insights with them regularly. My knowledge of and comfort with the organization situated me as the researcher in a reflexive position knowledge of the site and access assisted me with gaining the trust of my participants.[17]

Phase 1: 2011–2012

For almost two decades, I have worked with young people in community programs, and I recognize the dearth of academic scholarship on the youth workers who carry out this valuable work. The first phase of this study examined how a predominantly Black-led organization understood how social and political problems informed the educational experiences of Black youth. Additionally, I examined how youth workers' sense making of the racialized framing of Black youth in the context of community-based organizations and how that framing and imagining informed their engagement and pedagogical practices. My focus on the framing of Black youth in this study was not meant to render Latinx students who didn't identify, or were not read racially as Black, invisible. My investigation and analysis was informed by the constructs of Blackness as a problem as EE served majority Black youth and was perceived as a Black organization. This phase of data collection included participant observations, individual interviews, focus groups, and document analysis.

Participant Observations and Field Notes   Approximately two hundred hours of participant observations occurred at large-scale program events for youth and their families, including middle and high school retreats, staff retreats, parent orientation meetings, and Programs staff's curriculum and planning meetings. I was given permission to attend one board meeting toward the end of my data collection period but was unable attend. I took descriptive and reflective field notes after each workday, including of conversations with fellow staff members that related to the study's guiding questions.[18] Participant observations were essential to answering my research questions for a few reasons. First, as this study explored how youth workers frame and imagine young people, observing how Black youth are discussed in spaces where they are not present (that is, curriculum planning meetings, professional development meetings, parent orientations, and so forth) was critical to understand how they are discussed with curriculum planning and pedagogy in mind. Second, it was also important to observe large-scale events where youth are present. Understanding youth workers' pedagogical practices and engagement with youth, and students' reaction to these practices, was important.

Interviews   Individual interviews were held with all twenty ($N = 20$) youth workers and staff. Individual interviews with participants were critical for the purpose of the study and research questions. I wanted to understand how youth workers frame and imagine the Black students they work with. My aim was to seek an understanding of how they make sense of the structural constraints

TABLE 1. Phase 1 Participant Table, Educational Excellence Staff, 2011–2012

Participant	Age Range	Race/Ethnicity	Educational Background	Time Employed (Years)	Title	Position Description
Leah Davis	40–50	Black	BA, EdM, EdD	10	Executive director	Serves on Board of Directors, raises funds, makes media appearances
Monica Matthews	40–50	Black	BA, MFA	10	Director of Programs	Supervises department directors; oversees all youth programming—academic, elective, and youth development
Walidah Thomas	30–40	Black	BA, EdM	4	Director of middle school programming	Curriculum developer, hires instructors, oversees Saturday and Summer programs
Terry Niles	30–40	Black	BA, JD	9	Director of high school and alumni programming	Curriculum developer, hires instructors, prepares students for college
Faith Davenport	40–50	Black	BA, MA, PhD	9	Director of youth leadership and counseling	Curriculum developer, student therapist, coordinates student retreats and parent conferences
Solomon Modupe	30–40	Black	Some college	6	Youth development instructor	Youth development instructor for male students
Camille Kent	20–30	Black	BA, MA	1	Associate director of counseling	Supervises counseling interns, student therapist, assists with youth development instruction
Alexandria Jimenez	20–30	Afro-Latina (biracial)	BA, MS	5	Associate director of high school and alumni programs	Coordinates college program, guides senior students, mentors college students
Benjamin Tucker	20–30	White	BA	1.5	Volunteer coordinator	Recruits volunteers, provides logistical support to S2C, manages database for high school students, oversees student leadership group

Name	Age	Race	Education	Tenure	Title	Duties
Omari Anderson	20–30	Black	BA	<1 year[a]	High school coordinator	Provides logistical support to S2C, manages database for high school students, oversees student leadership group
Michaela Delgado	20–30	Dominican/Puerto Rican	BA	7	Associate director of middle school programming	Curriculum developer, conducts teacher development, provides logistical support to HA
Patrick Denny	30–40	Black	BA	<1 year	Director of development	Sits on Board of Directors, seeks funds, writes grants
Patricia Douglas	20–30	Black	BA, MA	<1 year[a]	Development assistant	Supports the director of development, writes grants, creates organization newsletter
Bernice Allan	Over 60	Black	BA, MS	5	Director of admissions	Recruits students, interviews and orients new students and parents
Cynthia Gladys	40–50	Black	BA	4	Director of finance	Finance executive, advises Board of Directors, manages organization budget
Simone Classon	20–30	Black	BA	3	Assistant to the director of finance	Assists financial director, assists with audits/budgets, human resources
Janelle Campbell	20–30	Black	BA	2	Assistant to the executive director	Administrative liaison between all departments, manages organization's database
Ayoka Taiwo	20–30	Black	BA	1[b]	Volunteer fellow	Recruits and hires volunteers
Rachel Atkinson	20–30	White	BA	1[b]	Volunteer fellow	Recruits and hires volunteers
Belinda Arrington	20–30	Black	BA, MA	<1 year[a]	Associate director of high school programming	Coordinates college program, guides senior students, and mentors colleges students

NOTE: BA = bachelor of arts; EdM = master of education; EdD = doctorate of education; MFA = master of fine arts; JD = juris doctorate; MA = master of arts; PhD = doctorate of philosophy; MS = master of science.

[a] Terminated

[b] Temporary positions

their program exists within and how they might shape either their pedagogical practice, treatment of youth, or feelings about their work. I sought an indepth exploration of how and why youth workers came to this particular field of work and the site of study. Questions centered on participants' social identities, including but not limited to their understanding of race, ethnicity, and social class, as well as the meaning they make from these understandings. It was important to understand how they "see" inequality and how they understand and imagine Black youth. Using individual interviews allowed participants to reflect deeply on their experiences as current educators within a community-based space. All individual interviews were semi-structured, indepth, open-ended interviews that lasted between sixty and 150 minutes and were audio-recorded. These open-ended, semi-structured interviews were important in eliciting deeper and reflective responses from participants.[19] Interviews were conducted in participants' offices, in empty classrooms, and, in one instance, in a public library. The organization and participants are referred to throughout the book by a pseudonym to protect their identities.

Focus Groups   Focus group conversations gave participants an opportunity to discuss their curricula—how the curriculum currently operates and how they wished it could be. The absence of supervisors and supervisees allowed conversation to flow more candidly. A total of three focus groups, lasting between one hour and an hour and a half, were held with participants. Groups were formed based on job responsibilities and the power dynamics between positions. For example, all participants who were the heads of their departments were participants in the same focus group. They all report to the same person and are responsible for supervising a small group of staff members. The first focus group, held in April of 2011, was conducted with assistant directors and program coordinators; each of these participants are directly supervised by a director. The second focus group, held in June of 2011, included three temporary employees who were hired to assist the organization in hiring and organizing short-term and long-term volunteers. The final focus group, conducted in July 2011, gathered the directors from High Achievers, Step 2 College, and Youth Lead. Participants were grouped in this way for a few reasons. First, most staff members have worked together for many years and have amazing rapport with one another. While observing staff meetings during the collection period, I noticed that not only do staff members solicit ideas and feedback from each other about their work; they actually enjoyed being with each other. Although this was not true for all participants, I knew that holding focus groups would generate much debate and conversation about important issues that affect their jobs and relationship with students. Second, in order to understand how staff frame and imagine Black youth in the program, it was important for them to engage in dialogue about the political, social, and educational issues that affect Black youth. Utilizing focus groups allowed greater understanding of the similarities and differences in thought and practice of youth workers.

Document Analysis   I gathered organizational literature including brochures; parent newsletters (via e-mail or hard copies); annual reports from 2006 to 2012; literature posted around the public space (posters and flyers in bathrooms and elsewhere); admissions literature; instructors' class reports, which assess student behavior; and course curricula descriptions. I chose all of these documents because I wanted to understand how the imagining of students was reflected in the framing of youth within organizational literature. I gathered a wide range of documents from the organization—those that are disseminated to potential funders, youth participants, and their families, as well as those presented to student members. Collecting organizational literature helped me assess how the program frames youth throughout literature distributed to not only its youth participants but also to parents and potential funders. Using this method was important because it helped to elicit data that may not come up in the other methods incorporated in this study. EE youth participants are often framed in program literature as a selling point to donors and in advertisements to schools, parents, and potential youth participants. This is important to note as the way youth are framed in program literature can reflect the ways that youth workers imagine the young people they serve. Whereas individual interviews and focus groups can provide critical data that show how youth workers make sense of their experiences in their role and how they frame and imagine the Black students they serve, organizational literature captured how this framing and imagining is distributed, which also shapes additional narratives about Black youth in the program.

Exclusions   I would have liked to include youth as participants during this phase of study. However, I recognized that there was a dearth of research on youth workers, their reasons for choosing their professions, their imagining and framing of youth, and how they approach youth work. I also did not conduct interviews with the founder, Richard Dunn, or members of the Board of

Directors. Although I would have liked to include youth and board members to compare how framing of youth affects their role, the focus on youth workers contributes to a lack of scholarship about them.

Phase 2: 2013–2015, 2017

My approach to follow-up data collection between 2013 and 2015 was to contact youth workers who were previously in my study and employed at Educational Excellence during the time of transition in leadership and staff turnover.

Follow-up Interviews, New Interviews, and Site Visits   Between 2013 and 2015, I conducted fourteen interviews with staff members—some of whom were currently employed at Educational Excellence at the time of my follow-up visits or who had already left the organization but were present during the leadership transition and major staff turnover. I had previously interviewed ten of these participants during the first phase of study. Four new participants were added to the study. The first was Daniel Morris, whose role as temporary, part-time grant writer had changed to a full-time lead grant writer. He was also present for the transition. Second, Sara Montes, Dana Baldon, and Frank Robertson began working during the transition, and they all had the unique experience of being former youth participants in the program. The majority of the interviews were held in person near or around Dunbar, while others were held via phone. One staff member during the first phase of study, Cynthia Gladys, was unable to participate in a follow-up interview because of scheduling conflicts. I made three visits to Dunbar and Educational Excellence during the follow-up data collection period to examine how the neighborhood and organization had changed.

Questionnaire with Former Youth Participants   In 2017, I developed and administered a questionnaire to former Educational Excellence youth participants. I remain in contact with many former students, as many seek me out to discuss decision making around pursuing advanced degrees or transferring colleges or just for personal updates every now and then. The majority of contact I have with former students is through social media, where I receive regular updates about their college, work, and family lives. Approximately seventy-five former students had access to the questionnaire, and thirty responded. The questionnaire asked participants about the length of time they spent in the organization, their relationship with staff members and other students, the culture of the program—its benefits and challenges—and their thoughts about the staff turnover and transitions in the program in the preceding several years. It should be noted that alumni involvement in the program is important. College students and graduates are expected and encouraged to maintain contact with the program. About half of the respondents had visited the program recently while others were out of state for school or were reluctant to visit because of the ongoing changes.

Analysis

After obtaining all data, using critical discourse analysis,[20] I read and reread interview transcripts, observational notes, field notes, and data retrieved from organizational literature. I used discourse analysis to review after-school instructor and staff training handbooks, promotional literature, and annual reports and observed engagement between students and staff. Qualitative studies often produce a tremendous amount of data, and careful selection of which data to use is an important part of the analytical process. After obtaining all data, I read and reread through interview transcripts, observational notes, field notes, and data retrieved from organizational literature. Descriptive and reflexive note taking occurred after each data collection method.[21] Central to my analysis was an ongoing transcribing and coding process throughout the study. First, I applied a descriptive coding process, in which I summarized attributes of a particular case with an easily identifiable label. Second, I used "topic coding" to label text as categories, followed by an analytical coding process in which I created new categories based on the concepts and ideas that emerged as I reflected on the data collected.[22]

In analyzing interviews, I took each transcript (individual and group interviews) to review statements that adequately described participants' experience; recorded relevant statements and eliminated repetitive ones; organized the meaning of these experiences into relevant themes; and used these themes to generate concepts in order to describe the experiences of participants. This process resulted in twelve codes that described the cases and experiences of participants. Using a constant comparative method, the coding process required constant revision and modification until all categories were formed.[23] Through an inductive process, open coding involves reviewing all text for descriptive categories and developing and refining each category until no new information yields any additional meaning. Following the systematic coding process, I developed major themes and subthemes in which the initial twelve themes were collapsed and modified down to seven core themes and codes.

TABLE 2. Phase 2 Participant Table, Educational Excellence Staff, Follow-up Interviews, 2013–2015

Participant	Age Range	Race/ Ethnicity	Educational Background	Departure	Current/Former Title(s)	Position Description
Walidah Thomas	30–40	Black	BA, EdM	Left in 2015[a]	Director of HA and expansion to Bayside	Curriculum developer, hires instructors, oversees Saturday and Summer programs
Terry Niles	40–50	Black	BA, JD	Left in 2014[a]	Director of programs	Supervises department directors; oversees all youth programming—academic, elective, and youth development
Solomon Modupe	30–40	Black	Some college	Left in 2013[a]	Former Youth Lead coordinator/instructor	Youth development instructor for male students
Faith Davenport	40–50	Black	BA, MA, PhD	Left in 2014[b]	Former director of Youth Lead and counseling	Curriculum developer, student therapist, coordinates student retreats and parent conference
Frank Robertson	30–40	Black	Some college	Left in 2015[b]	Youth development coordinator/instructor	Youth development instructor for male students
Camille Kent	20–30	Black	BA, MA	Left in 2014[b]	Counseling coordinator	Supervises counseling interns, student therapist, assists with youth development instruction
Samira Montes	20–30	Dominican	BA, MS	Left in 2015[a]	Director of S2C alumni programming	Coordinates college program, guides senior students, mentors college students
Benjamin Tucker	20–30	White	BA	Left in 2014[b]	Program coordinator, S2C	Provides logistical support to S2C, manages database for high school students, oversees student leadership group

Daniel Morris	30–40	White	BA	Left in 2014[b]	Lead grant writer	Writes grants, maintains relationships with donors
Dana Baldon	20–30	Black	BA	Left in 2014[a]	Assistant director of HA	Curriculum developer, teacher development, logistical support to HA
Patrick Denny	40–50	Black	BA	Left in 2015[b]	Director of development	Sits on Board of Directors, seeks funds, oversees all donors
Monica Matthews	40–50	Black	BA	Left in 2012[b]	Director of programs	Supervises department directors; oversees all youth programming—academic, elective, and youth development
Bernice Allan	60–70	Black	BA, MS	Left in 2013[a]	Director of admissions	Recruits students, interviews and orients new students and parents
Leah Davis	40–50	Black	BA, EdD	Left in 2012[b]	Executive director	Serves on Board of Directors, raises funds, makes media appearances

NOTE: BA = bachelor of arts; EdM = master of education; EdD = doctorate of education; MFA = master of fine arts; JD = juris doctorate; MA = master of arts; PhD = doctorate of philosophy; MS = master of science.

[a] Resigned
[b] New job opportunity

These themes were then refined and considered for theoretical implications. After completing the coding process by hand, I uploaded all data into Dedoose, a qualitative and mixed methods online software program. This was incredibly helpful for organizing interview transcripts, field notes, organizational literature, and media images.

Accountability

After the first year of study, I shared findings with participants in a meeting specifically designed for me to share my research. While it was not easy to share what I observed as contradictions in how youth were framed in the program, participants were open to listening even if they disagreed. This presentation also generated new information as I learned that some contradictions existed because of tension between the founder/Board of Directors and the desires of leadership and staff. Since that time, I continue to share my research with former participants. As a form of accountability, I share everything I publish with a note of gratitude to participants, and sometimes seek public forums to share my work to make it more accessible to communities that are shut out of academic spaces. It matters to me that participants in all of my research have access to what I write; their insights, experiences, triumphs, vulnerabilities, and challenges have direct implications for their current engagement with youth, their future work in other spaces, and can validate the experiences of other youth workers in similar contexts. Researchers often publish for the academy with no way for participants to access the writing. Sharing my research findings as a form of accountability is imperative because the knowledge I have gained is a direct result of the dedication and sacrifices youth workers in this study have made, and continue to make through their engagement with youth.

Notes

Chapter 1: Community-Based Youth Work in Uncertain Times

1. The neighborhood of Dunbar, Educational Excellence, and all participant names are pseudonyms.

2. Ginwright and James, "From Assets to Agents of Change," 27; Ginwright and Cammarota, "New Terrain in Youth Development," 82.

3. Patel, "Pedagogies of Resistance and Survivance"

4. Dumas, "Losing an Arm," 11; Ladson-Billings, "From the Achievement Gap to the Education Debt," 465; Tuck, "Suspending Damage."

5. Patel, "Pedagogies of Resistance and Survivance."

6. Baldridge, "Relocating the Deficit"; McKenzie, "Reconsidering the Effects."

7. Apple, *Educating the "Right" Way*; Au, "Meritocracy 2.0"; Bartlett, Frederick, Gulbrandsen, and Murillo, "The Marketization of Education"; Buras, "Race, Charter Schools, and Conscious Capitalism"; Ewing, *Ghosts in the Schoolyard*; Lipman, *The New Political Economy of Urban Education*; White, "Teach for America's Paradoxical Diversity Initiative"; Stovall, *Born Out of Struggle*.

8. There is considerable debate about the field of youth work as practice and also a discipline. As Dana Fusco notes in her chapter, "On Becoming an Academic Profession," in *Advancing Youth Work: Current Trends, Critical Questions* (New York: Routledge, 2012), "Is this discipline called youth work, youth development, social education, after-school education, out-of-school time, informal education, youth studies, nonformal learning, community education, community development, or something else?," 113.

9. Fusco, "On Becoming an Academic Profession."

10. Halpern, "A Different Kind of Child Development Institution."

11. Ibid.

12. See Carnegie Council on Adolescent Development, *Task Force on Youth Development and Community Programs, Carnegie Council on Adolescent Development. A Matter of Time: Risk and Opportunity in the Nonschool Hours* (New York: Carnegie Corporation of New York, 1992).

13. Halpern, "A Different Kind of Child Development Institution."

14. Ibid.

15. Ginwright and James, "From Assets to Agents of Change."

16. Ginwright, *Black Youth Rising.*

17. Kwon, *Uncivil Youth,* 9.

18. Carnegie Council on Adolescent Development, *Task Force on Youth Development.*

19. Fashola, *Building Effective Afterschool Programs,* 3–6; U.S Department of Education, *National Study of Before- and After-School Programs.*

20. Ibid.; Halpern, "A Different Kind of Child Development Institution."

21. Halpern, "A Different Kind of Child Development Institution"; Vasudevan, "The Occupational Culture."

22. Yohalem and Pittman, *Putting Youth Work on the Map.*

23. See: Carnegie Council on Adolescent Development, *Task Force on Youth Development.*

24. Baldridge, Beck, Medina, and Reeves, "Toward a New Understanding of Community-Based Education"; Ginwright, *Black Youth Rising;* Watson, *Learning to Liberate.*

25. Baldridge, Beck, Medina, and Reeves, "Toward a New Understanding of Community-Based Education," 381–402; Ginwright, *Black Youth Rising;* Watson, *Learning to Liberate.*

26. Ginwright, *Black Youth Rising;* Baldridge, Beck, Medina, and Reeves, "Toward a New Understanding of Community-Based Education."

27. Baldridge, Hill, and Davis, "New Possibilities," 124.

28. Hirsch, Deutsch, and DuBois, *After-School Centers and Youth Development.*

29. In some spaces youth workers may be referred to as program directors, youth specialists, or community-based educators. See Yohalem and Pittman, "Putting Youth Work on the Map."

30. Fusco, "On Becoming an Academic Profession."

31. Baldridge, "'It's Like This Myth of the Supernegro,'" 781–795.

32. Halpern, "A Different Kind of Child Development Institution"; Hirsch, "Learning and Development in After-School Programs."

33. Baldridge, "Relocating the Deficit," 440–472.

34. Kwon, *Uncivil Youth.*

35. Ibid.; Ray, *The Making of a Teenage Service Class.*

36. Heath and McLaughlin, "The Best of Both Worlds."

37. Baldridge, "On Educational Advocacy and Cultural Work"; Watson, *Learning to Liberate.*

38. McLaughlin, *Community Counts,* 34–35.

39. Watson, *Learning to Liberate,* 8.

40. Zeldin, "Foreword," *Advancing Youth Work.*

41. Halpern, "A Different Kind of Child Development Institution."

42. Metcalf, "Neoliberalism: The Idea That Swallowed the World," *Guardian*, August 18, 2017.

43. Harvey, *A Brief History of Neoliberalism*; Spence, "The Neoliberal Turn in Black Politics," 139.

44. Metcalf, "Neoliberalism."

45. Apple, *Educating the "Right" Way*.

46. Brown, *A Good Investment*; Henry and Dixson, "'Locking the Door Before We Got the Keys,'" 218; Buras, "Race, Charter Schools, and Conscious Capitalism."

47. Lipman, *The New Political Economy of Urban Education*.

48. Goffman, *Frame Analysis*.

49. Young, "New Life for an Old Concept,"55.

50. Cohen, *Democracy Remixed*; Collins, *Another Kind of Public Education*.

51. Soung, "Social and Biological Constructions of Youth," 428–429.

52. Nunn, "Race, Crime and the Pool of Surplus Criminality," 381; Lesko, "Denaturalizing Adolescence"; "Social and Biological Constructions of Youth."

53. Greene, "Imagining Futures: The Public School and Possibilities," *Curriculum Studies* 32, no. 2 (2000): 267–280.

54. Ibid.; Dimitriadis and Weis, "Imagining Possibilities."

55. Kwon, *Uncivil Youth*.

56. Lipman, "Neoliberal Education Restructuring," 117–118.

57. Rhee, "The Neoliberal Racial Project," 561.

58. Sanders, Stovall, and White, *Twenty-First-Century Jim Crow Schools*.

59. Henry and Dixson, "'Locking the Door Before We Got the Keys'"; Lipman, "Neoliberal Education Restructuring," 118.

60. Tuck, "Suspending Damage."

61. Beatty, "Rethinking Compensatory Education."

62. Martinez and Rury, "From 'Culturally Deprived' to 'At Risk.'"

63. Ibid.; Valencia, *Dismantling Contemporary Deficit Thinking*.

64. Martinez and Rury, "From 'Culturally Deprived' to 'At Risk.'"

65. See United States, National Commission on Excellence in Education, *A Nation at Risk: The Imperative for Educational Reform*.

66. Kwon, *Uncivil Youth*, 8.

67. Dumas, "My Brother"; Rhee, "The Neoliberal Racial Project"; Melamed, "Racial Capitalism,"

68. Dumas, "My Brother"; Baldridge, "'It's Like This Myth of the Supernegro'"; Dawson, "Hidden in Plain Sight."

69. Dumas, "My Brother"; Rhee, "The Neoliberal Racial Project."

70. Allen, *Black Awakening*; Kwon, *Uncivil Youth*; Rhee, "The Neoliberal Racial Project;" Soss, Fording, and Schram, *Disciplining the Poor*.

71. Henry and Dixson, "'Locking the Door Before We Got the Keys'"; Sanders, Stovall, and White, *Twenty-First-Century Jim Crow Schools*.

72. Giroux, "Spectacles of Race and Pedagogies of Denial;" Rhee, "The Neoliberal Racial Project," 3.

73. Toward the end of the first data collection period, Omari Anderson was terminated. His position was filled by Benjamin Tucker, who was a temporary volunteer coordinator during the first data collection period.

74. See Cammarota and Fine, "Youth Participatory Action Research: A Pedagogy for Transformational Resistance," 1–12; Morrell, "Six Summers of YPAR."

75. Denzin and Lincoln, *Strategies of Qualitative Inquiry*.

76. Dimitriadis, "'In the Clique.'"

77. Kincheloe and McLaren, "Rethinking Critical Theory and Qualitative Research," 87–138; Madison, *Critical Ethnography: Method, Ethics, and Performance*.

78. Bhachattarya, "Consenting to the Consent Form"; Paris and Winn, *Humanizing Research*; Patel, *Decolonizing Educational Research*.

79. Guba, "Criteria for Assessing the Trustworthiness."

80. Geertz, *The Interpretation of Cultures* (New York: Basic Books, 1973).

81. Baldridge, "Relocating the Deficit."

Chapter 2: "The EE Family"

1. Baldridge, "It's Like This Myth of the Supernegro"; Lee, *Unraveling the Model Minority Stereotype*.

2. Du Bois, *Darkwater*.

3. Dumas, "Against the Dark"; Dumas and ross, "Be Real Black for Me"; Sharpe, *In the Wake*.

4. Hill, *Nobody*.

5. Baldridge, "'It's Like This Myth of the Supernegro.'"

6. Omi and Winant, *Racial Formation in the United States*; Ladson-Billings and Tate, "Toward a Critical Race Theory of Education," 47.

7. Bonilla-Silva, *Racism Without Racists*.

8. Baldridge, "It's Like This Myth of the Supernegro"; Rhee, "The Neoliberal Racial Project," 561.

9. Giroux, "Spectacles of Race and Pedagogies of Denial," 198.

10. Hill, *Nobody*; Teasley and Ikard, "Barack Obama and the Politics of Race," 411.

11. Schlichtman, Patch, and Hill, *Gentrifier*.

12. Ibid.

13. Freeman, *There Goes the Hood*.

14. Schlictman, Patch, and Hill, *Gentrifier, 13*.

15. Pattillo, *Black on the Block*.

16. Freeman and Cai, "White Entry into Black Neighborhoods."

17. Wilson, *The Truly Disadvantaged*.

18. Baltodano, "The Pursuit of Social Justice"; Buras, "Race, Charter Schools, and Conscious Capitalism"; Ewing, *Ghosts in the Schoolyard*.

19. Lipman, *The New Political Economy of Urban Education*; Schlictman, Patch, and Hill, *Gentrifier*.

20. Spence, *Knocking the Hustle.*

21. The Dunbar neighborhood is heavily policed and located in a large urban city where "stop and frisk" policies were widespread and disproportionately targeted Black and Latinx young men. See Victor Rios's *Punished: Policing the Lives of Black and Latino Boys* (New York: New York University Press, 2011) for an important analysis of the "youth control complex" and how Black and Latino boys are hyper-surveilled.

22. Baldridge, "On Educational Advocacy and Cultural Work."

23. Baldridge, Beck, Medina, and Reeves, "Toward a New Understanding of Community-Based Education."

24. Gilmore, "In the Shadow of the Shadow State."

25. Alexander, *The New Jim Crow.*

26. Ginwright, *Black Youth Rising;* Halpern, *Thought and Knowledge;* Kwon, *Uncivil Youth.*

27. Baldridge, "'It's Like This Myth of the Supernegro,'" 781.

28. Baldridge, "Relocating the Deficit"; Gorski, *Unlearning Deficit Ideology and the Scornful Gaze;* Kwon, *Uncivil Youth;* Dumas, "Against the Dark."

29. Wilson, "Toward a Framework for Understanding Forces."

30. Evelyn Brooks Higginbotham, "African American Women's History and the Metalanguage of Race," *Signs* 17, no. 2 (1992): 251–271.

31. Valencia, *Dismantling Contemporary Deficit Thinking.*

32. Beatty, "Rethinking Compensatory Education."

33. Martinez and Rury, "From 'Culturally Deprived' to 'At Risk.'"

34. Jackman, *The Velvet Glove.*

35. Allen, *Black Awakening;* Incite! Women of Color Against Violence, *The Revolution Will Not Be Funded: Beyond the Non-Profit Industrial Complex* (Boston: South End Press, 2007).

36. Brown, *A Good Investment?;* Moeller, *The Gender Effect.*

37. Anderson, *The Education of Blacks in the South.*

38. Anderson and Larson, "'Sinking, like Quicksand,'" 71; Baldridge, "Relocating the Deficit," 440; Baldridge, Hill, and Davis, "New Possibilities"; Ginwright, Cammarota, and Noguera, *Beyond Resistance!;* Ginwright, *Black Youth Rising;* Woodland, Martin, Hill, and Worrell, "The Most Blessed Room in the City," 233.

39. Ginwright and James, "From Assets to Agents of Change," 27.

40. Ginwright and Cammarota, "New Terrain in Youth Development," 82.

41. Ibid.; Ginwright, *Black Youth Rising.*

42. Pittman and Fleming, "A New Vision."

43. Ginwright and Cammarota, "New Terrain in Youth Development," 86.

44. Freire, *Pedagogy of the Oppressed.*

45. Ginwright and Cammarota, "Youth Activism in the Urban Community"; Dimitriadis, "Coming Clean at the Hyphen," 578–597; Ginwright, *Black Youth Rising;* Kwon, *Uncivil Youth;* Watson, *Learning to Liberate.*

46. Baldridge, Beck, Medina, and Reeves, "Toward a New Understanding of Community-Based Education."

47. Rhodes, "The Critical Ingredient," 145.

48. Hirsch, Deutsch, and DuBois, *After-School Centers and Youth Development*.

49. Dumas, "Against the Dark."

50. Students at Educational Excellence who required additional mental health support would be referred to other professionals and, in some cases, other organizations that were better resourced to support particular emotional or cognitive challenges.

51. Fusco, *Advancing Youth Work*.

52. Fusco, "On Becoming an Academic Profession."

53. Heathfield, "A Chicago Story."

54. Baldridge, "On Educational Advocacy and Cultural Work."

55. Nicole Yohalem and Alicia Wilson-Ahlstrom, "Inside the Black Box: Assessing and Improving Quality in Youth Programs," *American Journal of Community Psychology* 45, 350.

56. Freire, *Cultural Action for Freedom*.

57. Baldridge, "On Educational Advocacy and Cultural Work"; Ginwright, "Black Youth Activism," 403.

58. Ibid.; Ginwright and Cammarota, "New Terrain in Youth Development."

59. Ginwright and James, "From Assets to Agents of Change"; McKenzie, "Reconsidering the Effects of Bonding Social Capital"; Sullivan, "Hip-Hop Nation," 235.

60. Baldridge, "Relocating the Deficit."

61. Stanton-Salazar, "A Social Capital Framework," 1066.

62. DuBois and Silverthorn, "Natural Mentoring Relationships and Adolescent Health," 518; Hirsch, Deutsch, and DuBois, *After-School Centers and Youth Development*.

63. Bourdieu, "The Forms of Capital"; Carter, *Keepin' It Real*.

64. Hosang, "Beyond Policy."

65. Du Bois, *The Souls of Black Folk*.

66. Carter, "Straddling Boundaries"; Emdin, *For White Folks Who Teach in the Hood*; O'Connor, "Dispositions Toward (Collective) Struggle and Educational Resilience," 593.

67. Hill, *Nobody*.

68. Saidiya Haartman, *Lose Your Mother: A Journey Along the Atlantic Slave Route* (New York: Macmillan, 2008).

69. Higginbotham, "'The Metalanguage of Race,'" 628; Dumas, "Against the Dark."

70. Du Bois, *The Souls of Black Folk*.

71. Ibid.

72. Dumas, "My Brother as Problem"; Goldberg, *The Threat of Race;* Melamed, "Racial Capitalism."

73. Emirbayer and Johnson, "Bourdieu and Organizational Analysis."

Chapter 3: "We're Not Saving Anybody"

1. Jennings, "School Choice or Schools' Choice?," 227.

2. Sanders, Stovall, White, and Pedroni, *Twenty-First Century Jim Crow Schools*.

3. Picower, "The Unexamined Whiteness of Teaching," 197; Ladson-Billings, "Toward a Theory of Culturally Relevant Pedagogy," 465; White, "Teach for America's Paradoxical Diversity Initiative."

4. Apple, *Educating the "Right" Way*; Baltodano, "The Power Brokers of Neoliberalism," 141; Harvey, *A Brief History of Neoliberalism*; Lipman, *The New Political Economy of Urban Education*; Saltman, *The Gift of Education*; Spence, "The Neoliberal Turn in Black Politics," 139.

5. Harvey, *A Brief History of Neoliberalism*, 3.

6. Rich, "Neoliberalism and Black Education," 26.

7. Michael Apple, *Ideology and Curriculum* (New York: Routledge, 2004); Apple, *Educating the "Right" Way*; Baltodano, "The Power Brokers of Neoliberalism," 141; Lipman, *The New Political Economy of Urban Education*.

8. Apple, *Educating the "Right" Way*.

9. Apple, *Ideology and Curriculum*; Baltodano, "The Power Brokers of Neoliberalism," 141; Giroux, *On Critical Pedagogy*; Lipman, *The New Political Economy of Urban Education*; Wells, Slayton, and Scott, "Defining Democracy in the Neoliberal Age," 337.

10. Ewing, *Ghosts in the Schoolyard*.

11. Salazar Perez and Cannella, "Disaster Capitalism as Neoliberal Instrument," 47; Spence, "The Neoliberal Turn in Black Politics"; Buras, "Race, Charter Schools, and Conscious Capitalism"; Stovall, "Born Out of Struggle."

12. Henry and Dixson, "'Locking the Door Before We Got the Keys,'" 218.

13. Lipman, *The New Political Economy of Urban Education*.

14. Theodore, Peck, and Brenner, "Neoliberal Urbanism."

15. Apple, "Understanding and Interrupting Neoliberalism."

16. Wells, Slayton, and Scott, "Defining Democracy in the Neoliberal Age," 337.

17. Lipman, *The New Political Economy of Urban Education*; Miron, Urschel, Mathis, and Tornquist, "Schools Without Diversity."

18. Baldridge, "Relocating the Deficit"; Marwell, "Privatizing the Welfare State," 265; Saltman, *The Gift of Education*.

19. Lipman, *The New Political Economy of Urban Education*.

20. Leah and other staff members at EE used the term "forgotten middle" to describe a population of students who are not the highest performing but are not the lowest performing either. On a few occasions, I heard Leah and some directors state that the landscape of youth programming was dominated by programs that participated in a "creaming process" (taking the cream of the crop or the best of the best) by engaging high-performing students or students who were struggling, but there were rarely services that engaged students who were not in any of those groups or in the middle.

21. Nygreen, "Negotiating Tensions," 42.

22. Larson and Gootman, "Features of Positive Developmental Settings," 8; Fashola, "Developing the Talents of African American Male Students," 398; Ginwright, "Black Youth Activism"; Ginwright, *Toward a Politics of Relevance*; Hirsch, Deutsch, and DuBois, *After-School Centers and Youth Development*; McLaughlin and Irby, "Urban Sanctuaries," 300; Woodland, "'Whatcha Doin' After School?,'" 537.

23. Noguera and Cannella, "Youth Agency, Resistance, and Civic Activism"; Ginwright, "Black Youth Activism"; Kwon, *Uncivil Youth*.

24. Students were separated by gender in "girls" and "boys" groups. Responding to a questionnaire of youth alumni, one student who transitioned while in college shared that gender-based programming "seemed to be heteronormative and I wonder how they would have handled someone who was gender non-conforming or questioning their gender at the time." This is certainly an important point that I have thought about during my time working and researching the program. To my knowledge, three students have transitioned since being in the program, and they have maintained contact with EE staff members and are fully supported.

25. Freire, *Pedagogy of the Oppressed*.

26. Anderson and Larson, "'Sinking, like Quicksand,'" 71.

27. Ibid.; Nicholson, Collins, and Holmer, "Youth as People," 55.

28. Ginwright and Cammarota, "Youth Activism in the Urban Community."

29. Baldridge, "Relocating the Deficit"; Marwell, "Privatizing the Welfare State"; Nygreen, "Negotiating Tensions."

30. Lopez, Wells, and Holme, "Creating Charter School Communities"; Sanders, Stovall, White, and Pedrino, *Twenty-First Century Jim Crow Schools*.

31. KIPP is a network of 224 nonprofit college preparatory public charter schools.

32. U.S. Department of Education, "Race to the Top Fund," last modified June 2016, https://www2.ed.gov/programs/racetothetop/index.html.

33. Small, Pope, and Norton, "An Age Penalty in Racial Preferences," 730.

34. Small, Pope, and Norton, "An Age Penalty in Racial Preferences."

35. Ferguson, *Bad Boys*.

36. Brown, *A Good Investment*.

37. Martinez and Rury, "From 'Culturally Deprived' to 'At Risk.'"

38. de St. Croix, "Youth Work, Performativity and the New Youth Impact Agenda."

39. Baldridge, Beck, Medina, and Reeves, "Toward a New Understanding of Community-Based Education."

40. Heath and McLaughlin, "The Best of Both Worlds," 278; Noguera and Cannella, "Youth Agency, Resistance, and Civic Activism"; Ginwright, "Black Youth Activism"; Ginwright, "Toward a Politics of Relevance"; McLaughlin and Irby, "Urban Sanctuaries"; Woodland, "'Whatcha Doin' After School?'"

41. Martinez and Rury, "From 'Culturally Deprived' to 'At-Risk.'"

42. Paris and Winn, *Humanizing Research*; Tuck, "Suspending Damage."

Chapter 4: "Expanding EE's Footprint"

1. Feldman and Pentland, "Reconceptualizing Organizational Routines."

2. Gersick and Hackman, "Habitual Routines in Task-Performing Groups."

3. Buras, "Race, Charter Schools, and Conscious Capitalism"; Trujillo and Scott, "Superheroes and Transformers"; White, "Teach for America's Paradoxical Diversity Initiative."

4. Brown, *A Good Investment*; Lipman, *A New Political Economy of Urban Education*; Sanders, Stovall, White, and Pedroni, *Twenty-First Century Jim Crow Schools*.

5. Clarke and Newman, *The Managerial State*; Spence, *Knocking the Hustle*.

6. Ginwright and Cammarota, "New Terrain in Youth Development."

7. Eccles and Gootman, *Community Programs to Promote Youth Development*; Ginwright, *Black Youth Rising*; Hirsch, Deutsch, and DuBois, *After-School Centers and Youth Development*; Nicholson, Collins, and Holmer, "Youth as People."

8. Baldridge, Beck, Medina, and Reeves, "Toward a New Understanding of Community-Based Education."

9. Rios, *Punished*.

10. Ladson-Billings and Tate, "Toward a Critical Race Theory of Education"; Leonardo, *Race Frameworks*.

11. King and Osayande, "The Filth on Philanthropy."

12. Jackman, *The Velvet Glove*.

13. Gilmore, "In the Shadow of the Shadow State."

14. Brown, *A Good Investment*.

15. Moeller, *The Gender Effect*; Brown, *A Good Investment*.

16. Golden-Biddle and Rao, "Breaches in the Boardroom."

17. Baldridge, *Relocating the Deficit*; Beatty, *Rethinking Compensatory Education*; Valencia, *Dismantling Contemporary Deficit Thinking*.

18. Baldridge, "'It's Like This Myth of the Supernegro.'"

Chapter 5: "The Family Is Dead"

1. Wenger, McDermott, and Snyder, *Cultivating Communities of Practice*.

2. Baldridge, Hill, and Davis, "New Possibilities"; Heath and McLaughlin, "The Best of Both Worlds"; Ginwright, *Black Youth Rising*; Ginwright, "Black Youth Activism"; Watson, *Learning to Liberate*.

3. Emirbayer and Johnson, "Bourdieu and Organizational Analysis."

4. Baldridge, "On Educational Advocacy and Cultural Work"; Ginwright, *Black Youth Rising*.

5. Drame and Irby, *Black Participatory Research*.

6. Carter, "'Black' Cultural Capital."

Chapter 6: "It Was Never Ours"

1. Apple, *Educating the "Right" Way*; Lipman, *The New Political Economy of Urban Education*.

2. Baldridge, "Relocating the Deficit"; Baldridge, "'It's Like This Myth of the Supernegro'"; Halpern, "A Different Kind of Child Development Institution"; Kwon, *Uncivil Youth*.

3. Baldridge, "Relocating the Deficit."

4. McLaughlin, *You Can't Be What You Can't See*.

5. Downey and Pribesh, "When Race Matters."

6. Ginwright, "Black Youth Activism"; Hirsch, Deutsch, and DuBois, "After-School Centers and Youth Development."

7. Emirbayer and Johnson, "Bourdieu and Organizational Analysis."

8. Du Bois, *The Souls of Black Folk*.

9. Lewis and Diamond, *Despite the Best Intentions*.

10. Bonilla-Silva, *Racism Without Racists*.

11. Soss, Fording, and Schram, *Disciplining the Poor*; King and Osayande, "The Filth of Philanthropy."

12. Ahn, "Democratizing American Philanthropy."

13. Freire, *Pedagogy of the Oppressed*.

14. Dumas, "My Brother as 'Problem'"; Soss, Fording, and Schram, *Disciplining the Poor*; Rhee, "The Neoliberal Racial Project."

15. Ahn, "Democratizing American Philanthropy."

Conclusion

1. Paris, "Culturally Sustaining Pedagoy," 93–97; Ladson-Billings, "Toward a Theory of Culturally Relevant Pedagogy."

2. Tuck, "Suspending Damage."

3. Ladson-Billings, "Toward a Theory of Culturally Relevant Pedagogy."

4. Watson, *Learning to Liberate*.

5. McLaughlin, *You Can't Be What You Can't See*.

6. Nelson, *Why Afterschool Matters*.

7. Lewis and Diamond, *Despite the Best Intentions*; Lewis-McCoy, *Inequality in the Promised Land*.

8. Patel, "Pedagogies of Resistance and Survivance: Learning as Marronage," 397–401.

9. Cohen, *Democracy Remixed*.

10. Watson, *Learning to Liberate*.

11. Baldridge, "On Educational Advocacy and Cultural Work."

12. Ibid.

13. Stanton-Salazar, "A Social Capital Framework."

14. Baldridge, Beck, Medina, and Reeves, "Toward a New Understanding of Community-Based Education."

15. Rhee, "The Neoliberal Racial Project."

16. Emma Brown, "Trump Budget Casualty: Afterschool Programs for 1.6 Million Kids. Most Are Poor," *Washington Post*, March 16, 2017, https://www.washingtonpost.com/local/education/trump-budget-casualty-afterschool-programs-for-16-million-kids-most-are-poor/2017/03/16/78802430-0a6f-11e7-b77c-0047d15a24e0_story.html?utm_term=.eea69ab54d9f.

17. After School Alliance, *America After 3 p.m.*; McLaughlin, *You Can't Be What You Can't See*.

18. Dumas, "Against the Dark."
19. Sanders, Stovall, White, and Pedroni, *Twenty-First-Century Jim Crow Schools.*
20. Nygreen, "Negotiating Tensions"; de St. Croix, "Youth Work."
21. Baldridge, "Relocating the Deficit"; de St. Croix, "Youth Work."
22. Bell, "Racial Realism," 363–379.
23. Gillborn, "Heads I Win, Tails You Lose," 1–12.
24. Warren, *Lift Us Up.*

Appendix

1. Denzin and Lincoln, *Strategies of Qualitative Inquiry.*
2. Ibid.
3. Dimitriadis, "Coming Clean at the Hyphen"; Kincheloe and McLaren, "Rethinking Critical Theory and Qualitative Research."
4. Anderson, "Critical Ethnography in Education"; Weis and Fine, "Critical Bifocality and Circuits of Privilege."
5. Weis and Fine, "Critical Bifocality and Circuits of Privilege," 196.
6. Ibid.
7. Leonardo, *Race Frameworks.*
8. Madison, *Critical Ethnography.*
9. Bhachattarya, "Consenting to the Consent Form"; Patel, *Decolonizing Educational Research.*
10. Marwell, "Privatizing the Welfare State"; Siddle-Walker, "Culture and Commitment."
11. Patel, *Decolonizing Educational Research.*
12. Marwell, "Privatizing the Welfare State"; Siddle-Walker, "Culture and Commitment"; Winn, "A-Words."
13. Bhachattarya, "Consenting to the Consent Form."
14. Brannick and Coghlan, "In Defense of Being 'Native.'"
15. Bhachattarya, "Consenting to the Consent Form"; Peshkin, "The Nature of Interpretation in Qualitative Research."
16. Denzin and Lincoln, *Strategies of Qualitative Inquiry.*
17. Lincoln and Guba, "Establishing Trustworthiness," 331.
18. Dewalt and Dewalt, *Participant Observation.*
19. Bogdan and Biklen, *Qualitative Research for Education.*
20. Fairclough, *Critical Discourse Analysis.*
21. Bogdan and Biklen, *Qualitative Research for Education.*
22. Lyn Richards, *Handling Qualitative Data: A Practical Guide* (Thousand Oaks, CA: Sage, 2005).
23. Barney Glaser and Anselm L. Strauss, *The Discovery of Grounded Theory: Strategies for Qualitative Research* (Chicago: Aldire, 1967).

Bibliography

Afterschool Alliance. *America After 3 p.m.: Afterschool Programs in Demand.* Washington, DC: Afterschool Alliance, 2014.

Ahn, Christine E. "Democratizing American Philanthropy." In *The Revolution Will Not Be Funded: Beyond the Non-Profit Industrial Complex*, edited by INCITE! Women of Color Against Violence, 63–79. Boston: South End Press, 2007.

Alexander, Michelle. *The New Jim Crow: Mass Incarceration in the Age of Colorblindness.* New York: New Press, 2012.

Anderson, Gary. "Critical Ethnography in Education: Origins, Current Status, and New Directions." *Review of Educational Research* 59, no. 3 (1989): 249–270

Anderson, James D. *The Education of Blacks in the South, 1860–1935.* Chapel Hill: University of North Carolina Press, 1998.

Anderson, Noel S., and Colleen L. Larson. "'Sinking, like Quicksand': Expanding Educational Opportunity for Young Men of Color." *Education Administration Quarterly* 45, no. 1 (2009): 71–114.

Apple, Michael W. *Educating the "Right" Way: Markets, Standards, God and Inequality.* New York: Routledge, 2006.

———. "Understanding and Interrupting Neoliberalism and Neoconservatism in Education." *Pedagogies: An International Journal* 1, no. 1 (2006): 21–26.

Au, Wayne. "Meritocracy 2.0: High-Stakes, Standardized Testing as a Racial Project of Neoliberal Multiculturalism." *Educational Policy* 30, no. 1 (2016): 39–62.

Baldridge, Bianca J. "'It's Like This Myth of the Supernegro': Resisting Narratives of Damage and Struggle in the Neoliberal Educational Policy Context." *Race Ethnicity and Education* 20, no. 6 (2017): 781–795.

———. "On Educational Advocacy and Cultural Work: Situating Community-Based Youth Work[ers] in Broader Educational Discourse." *Teachers College Record* 1, no. 20 (2018): 1–28.

———. "Relocating the Deficit: Reimagining Black Youth in Neoliberal Times." *American Educational Research Journal* 51, no. 3 (2014): 440–472.

Baldridge, Bianca J., Nathan Beck, Juan Medina, and Marlo Reeves. "Toward a New Understanding of Community-Based Education: The Role of Community-Based Educational Spaces in Disrupting Inequality for Minoritized Youth." *Review of Research in Education* 41, no. 1 (2017): 381–402.

Baldridge, Bianca J., Marc Lamont Hill, and James Earl Davis. "New Possibilities: (Re) Engaging Black Male Youth within Community-Based Educational Spaces." *Race Ethnicity and Education* 14, no. 1 (2011): 121–136.

Baltodano, Marta P. "The Power Brokers of Neoliberalism: Philanthrocapitalists and Public Education." *Policy Futures in Education* 15, no. 2 (2016): 141–156.

Bartlett, Lesley, Marla Frederick, Thaddeus Gulbrandsen, and Enrique Murillo. "The Marketization of Education: Public Schools for Private Ends." *Anthropology & Education Quarterly* 33, no. 1 (2002): 5–29.

Beatty, Barbara. *Rethinking Compensatory Education: Historical Perspectives on Race, Class, Culture, Language, and the Discourse of the "Disadvantaged Child."* New York: Teachers College Press, 2012.

Bell, Derrick. "Racial Realism." *Connecticut Law Review* 24 (1991): 363–379.

Bhachattarya, Kakali. "Consenting to the Consent Form: What Are the Fixed and Fluid Understandings between the Researcher and the Researched?" *Qualitative Inquiry* 13, no. 8 (2007): 1095–1115.

Bogdan, Robert, and Sari Knopp Biklen. *Qualitative Research for Education: An Introduction to Theories and Methods.* Upper Saddle River, NJ: Pearson Education, 2006.

Bonila-Silva, Eduardo. *Racism Without Racists: Color-Blind Racism and the Persistence of Racial Inequality in the United States.* Lanham, MD: Rowman & Littlefield, 2006.

Bourdieu, Pierre. "The Forms of Capital." In *Handbook of Theory and Research for the Sociology of Education*, edited by J. Richardson, 241–258. New York: Greenwood Press, 1986.

Brannick, Teresa, and David Coghlan. "In Defense of Being 'Native': The Case for Insider Academic Research." *Organizational Research Methods* 10, no. 1 (2007): 59–74.

Brown, Amy. *A Good Investment: Philanthropy and the Marketing of Race in an Urban Public School.* Minneapolis: University of Minnesota Press, 2015.

Buras, Kristen L. "Race, Charter Schools, and Conscious Capitalism: On the Spatial Politics of Whiteness as Property (and the Unconscionable Assault on Black New Orleans)." *Harvard Educational Review* 81, no. 3 (2011): 296–330.

Cammarota, Julio, and Michelle Fine. "Youth Participatory Action Research: A Pedagogy for Transformational Resistance." In *Revolutionizing Education: Youth Participatory Action Research in Motion*, edited by Julio Cammarota and Michelle Fine, 1–12. New York: Routledge, 2008.

Carter, Prudence L. "'Black' Cultural Capital, Status Positioning, and Schooling Conflicts for Low-Income African American Youth." *Social Problems* 50, no. 1 (2003): 136–155.

———. *Keepin' It Real: School Success Beyond Black and White.* New York: Oxford University Press, 2005.

———. "Straddling Boundaries: Identity, Culture, and School." *Sociology of Education* 79, no. 3 (2006): 304–328.

Clarke, John, and Janet Newman. *The Managerial State: Power, Politics and Ideology in the Remaking of Social Welfare*. Thousand Oaks, CA: Sage, 1997.

Cohen, Cathy J. *Democracy Remixed: Black Youth and the Future of American Politics*. New York: Oxford University Press, 2010.

Collins, Patricia Hill. *Another Kind of Public Education: Race, Schools, the Media, and Democratic Possibilities*. Boston: Beacon Press, 2009.

Dawson, Michael C. "Hidden in Plain Sight: A Note on Legitimation Crises and the Racial Order." *Critical Historical Studies* 3, no. 1 (2016): 143–161.

De St. Croix, Tania. "Youth Work, Performativity and the New Youth Impact Agenda: Getting Paid for Numbers?" *Journal of Education Policy* 33, no. 3 (2018): 414–438.

Denzin, Norman, and Yvonna Lincoln. *Strategies of Qualitative Inquiry*, vol. 2. Thousand Oaks, CA: Sage, 2008.

Dewalt, Kathleen Musante, and Billie R. Dewalt. *Participant Observation: A Guide for Fieldworkers*. New York: Alta Mira, 2002.

Dimitriadis, Greg. "Coming Clean at the Hyphen: Ethics and Dialogue at a Local Community Center." *Qualitative Inquiry* 7, no. 5 (2001): 578–597.

———. "'In the Clique': Popular Culture, Constructions of Place, and the Everyday Lives of Urban Youth." *Anthropology & Education Quarterly* 32, no. 1 (2001): 29–51.

Dimitriadis, Greg, and Lois Weis. "Imagining Possibilities with and for Contemporary Youth: (Re)writing and (Re)visioning Education Today." *Qualitative Research* 1, no. 2 (2001): 223–240.

Downey, Douglas B., and Shana Pribesh. "When Race Matters: Teachers' Evaluations of Students' Classroom Behavior." *Sociology of Education* 77, no. 4 (2004): 267–282.

Drame, Elizabeth, and Decoutea Irby. *Black Participatory Research: Power, Identity, and the Struggle for Justice in Education*. New York: Palgrave Macmillan, 2016.

DuBois, David L., and Naida Silverthorn. "Natural Mentoring Relationships and Adolescent Health: Evidence from a National Study." *American Journal of Public Health* 95, no. 3 (2005): 518–524.

Du Bois, W. E. B. *Darkwater: Voices from Within the Veil*. New York: Harcourt, Brace and Howe, 1920.

———. *Souls of Black Folk*. New York: Routledge, 2015.

Dumas, Michael J. "Against the Dark: Antiblackness in Education Policy and Discourse." *Theory into Practice* 55, no. 1 (2016): 11–19.

Dumas, Michael J., and kihana miraya ross. ""Be Real Black for Me": Imagining BlackCrit in Education." *Urban Education* 51, no. 4 (2016): 415–442.

———. "My Brother as 'Problem': Neoliberal Governmentality and Interventions for Black Young Men and Boys." *Educational Policy* 30, no. 1 (2016): 94–113.

———. "'Losing an Arm': Schooling as a Site of Black Suffering." *Race Ethnicity and Education* 17, no. 1 (2014): 1–29.

Eccles, Jacquelynne, and Jennifer Appleton Gootman. *Community Programs to Promote Youth Development*. Washington, DC: National Academy Press, 2002.

Emirbayer, Mustafa, and Victoria Johnson. "Bourdieu and Organizational Analysis." *Theory and Society* 37, no. 1 (2008): 1–44.

Espinoza, Manuel L., and Shirin Vossoughi. "Perceiving Learning Anew: Social Interaction, Dignity, and Educational Rights." *Harvard Educational Review* 84, no. 3 (2014): 285–313.

Ewing, Eve L. *Ghosts in the Schoolyard: Race, History and Discourse amid Chicago's School Closures*. Chicago: University of Chicago Press, 2018.

Fairclough, Norman. *Critical Discourse Analysis: The Critical Study of Language*. New York: Routledge, 2013.

Fashola, Olatokunbo S. "Developing the Talents of African American Male Students during the Nonschool Hours." *Urban Education* 38, no. 4 (July 2003): 398–430.

———. *Building Effective Afterschool Programs*. California: Corwin Press, 2002.

Feldman, Martha S., and Brian T. Pentland. "Reconceptualizing Organizational Routines as a Source of Flexibility and Change." *Administrative Science Quarterly* 48, no. 1 (2003): 94–118.

Ferguson, Ann Arnett. *Bad Boys: Public Schools in the Making of Black Masculinity*. Ann Arbor: University of Michigan Press, 2000.

Freeman, Lance. *There Goes the Hood: Voices of Gentrification from the Ground Up*. Philadelphia: Temple University Press, 2006.

Freeman, Lance, and Tiancheng Cai. "White Entry into Black Neighborhoods: Advent of a New Era?" *Annals of the American Academy of Political and Social Science* 660, no. 1 (2015): 302–318.

Freire, Paulo. *Cultural Action for Freedom*. Cambridge, MA: Harvard Educational Review, 1970.

———. *Pedagogy of the Oppressed*. New York: Continuum, 2007.

Friedman, Sam. "Habitus Clivé and the Emotional Imprint of Social Mobility." *Sociological Review* 64, no. 1 (2016): 129–147.

Fusco, Dana. "On Becoming an Academic Profession." In *Advancing Youth Work: Current Trends, Critical Questions*, 111–126, New York: Routledge, 2011.

Gersick, Connie J. G., and J. Richard Hackman. "Habitual Routines in Task-Performing Groups." *Organizational Behavior and Human Decision Processes* 47, no. 1 (1990): 65–97.

Gillborn, David. "Heads I Win, Tails You Lose: Anti-Black Racism as Fluid, Relentless, Individual and Systemic." *Peabody Journal of Education* (2018): 1–12.

Gilmore, Ruth Wilson. "In the Shadow of the Shadow State." In *The Revolution Will Not Be Funded: Beyond the Non-Profit Industrial Complex*, 41–51, edited by Incite! Women of Color Against Violence. Boston: South End Press, 2007.

Ginwright, Shawn. "Black Youth Activism and the Role of Critical Social Capital in Black Community Organizations." *American Behavioral Scientist* 51, no. 3 (2007): 403–418.

———. *Toward a Politics of Relevance: Race, Resistance and African American Youth Activism*. Last modified in 2006. http://ya.ssrc.org/african/Ginwright/.

———. *Black Youth Rising: Activism and Radical Healing in Urban America*. New York: Teachers College Press, 2009.

Ginwright, Shawn, and Julio Cammarota. "New Terrain in Youth Development: The Promise of a Social Justice Approach." *Social Justice* 29, no. 4 (2002): 82–95.

———. "Youth Activism in the Urban Community: Learning Critical Civic Praxis within Community Organizations." *International Journal of Qualitative Studies in Education* 20, no. 6 (2007): 693–710.

Ginwright, Shawn, Julio Cammarota, and Pedro Noguera. *Beyond Resistance! Youth Activism and Community Change: New Democratic Possibilities for Practice and Policy for America's Youth.* New York: Routledge, 2006.

Ginwright, Shawn, and Taj James. "From Assets to Agents of Change: Social Justice, Organizing, and Youth Development." *New Directions for Student Leadership* 2002, no. 96 (2002): 27–46.

Giroux, Henry. *On Critical Pedagogy.* New York: Bloomsbury Academic Press, 2012.

———. "Spectacles of Race and Pedagogies of Denial: Anti-Black Racist Pedagogy Under the Reign of Neoliberalism." *Communication Education* 52, no. 3–4 (2003): 191–211.

Glaser, Barney, and Anselm L. Strauss. *The Discovery of Grounded Theory: Strategies for Qualitative Research.* Chicago: Aldire, 1967.

Goffman, Erving. *Frame Analysis: An Essay on the Organization of Experience.* Cambridge, MA: Harvard University Press, 1974.

Golden-Biddle, Karen, and Hayagreeva Rao. "Breaches in the Boardroom: Organizational Identity and Conflicts of Commitment in a Nonprofit Organization." *Organization Science* 8, no. 6 (1997): 593–611.

Gorski, Paul C. "Unlearning Deficit Ideology and the Scornful Gaze: Thoughts on Authenticating the Class Discourse in Education." *Counterpoints* 402 (2011): 152–173. http://www.jstor.org/stable/42981081.

Greene, M. *Releasing the Imagination: Essays in Education, the Arts, and Social Change.* San Francisco: Jossey Bass, 2011, 61–70.

Guba, Egon G. "Criteria for Assessing the Trustworthiness of Naturalistic Inquiries." *Educational Communication and Technology Journal* 29, no. 2 (1981): 75–91.

Halpern, Diane. *Thought and Knowledge: An Introduction into Critical Thinking.* New York: Psychology Press, 2002.

Halpern, Robert. "A Different Kind of Child Development Institution: The History of After-School Programs for Low-Income Children." *Teachers College Record* 104, no. 2 (2002): 178–211.

Harvey, David A. *Brief History of Neoliberalism.* Oxford: Oxford University Press, 2007.

Heath, Shirley Brice, and Milbrey W. McLaughlin. "The Best of Both Worlds: Connecting Schools and Community Youth Organizations for All-Day, All-Year Learning." *Educational Administration Quarterly* 30, no. 3 (1994): 278–300.

Heathfield, M. "A Chicago Story: Challenge and Change." In *Advancing Youth Work: Current Trends, Critical Questions,* edited by Dana Fusco, 85–99. New York: Routledge, 2011.

Henry, Kevin Lawrence, Jr., and Adrienne D. Dixson. "'Locking the Door Before We Got the Keys': Racial Realities of the Charter School Authorization Process in Post-Katrina New Orleans." *Educational Policy* 30, no. 1 (2016): 218–240.

Higginbotham, Evelyn Brooks. "'The Metalanguage of Race,' Then and Now." *Journal of Women in Culture and Society* 42, no. 3 (2017): 628–642.

Hill, Marc Lamont. *Nobody.* New York: Atria Books, 2016.

Hirsch, Barton. "Learning and Development in After-School Programs." *Phi Delta Kappan* 92, no. 5 (2011): 66–69.

Hirsch, Barton J., Nancy L. Deutsch, and David L. DuBois. *After-School Centers and Youth Development: Case Studies of Success and Failure.* New York: Cambridge University Press, 2011.

Hosang, Daniel. "Beyond Policy: Ideology, Race and the Reimagining of Youth." In *Beyond Resistance! Youth Activism and Community Change: New Democratic Possibilities for Practice and Policy for America's Youth,* edited by Shawn Ginwright, Pedro Noguera, and Julio Cammarota, 3–20. New York: Routledge, 2006.

Jackman, Mary. *The Velvet Glove: Paternalism and Conflict in Gender, Class, and Race Relations.* Berkeley: University of California Press, 1994.

Jennings, Jennifer L. "School Choice or Schools' Choice?" *Sociology of Education* 83, no. 3 (July 2010): 227–247.

Kincheloe, Joe L., and Peter McLaren. "Rethinking Critical Theory and Qualitative Research." In *Ethnography and Schools: Qualitative Approaches to the Study of Education,* edited by Yali Zhou and Enrique T. Trueba, 87–138. Lanham, MD: Rowman & Littlefield, 2002.

Kincheloe, Joe L., Peter McLaren, and Shirley R. Steinberg. "Critical Pedagogy and Qualitative Research: Moving to the Bricolage." In *The SAGE Handbook of Qualitative Research,* edited by Norman K. Denzin and Yvonna S. Lincoln, 163–177. Thousand Oaks, CA: Sage, 2011.

King, Tiffany Lethabo, and Ewuare Osayande. "The Filth on Philanthropy: Progressive Philanthropy's Agenda to Misdirect Social Justice Movements." In *The Revolution Will Not Be Funded: Beyond the Non-Profit Industrial Complex,* edited by Incite! Women of Color Against Violence, 79–90. Boston: South End Press, 2009.

Kirshner, Ben, and Shawn Ginwright. "Youth Organizing as a Developmental Context for African American and Latino Adolescents." *Child Development Perspectives* 6, no. 3 (2012): 288–294.

Kwon, Soo Ah. *Uncivil Youth: Race, Activism, and Affirmative Governmentality.* Durham, NC: Duke University Press, 2013.

Ladson-Billings, Gloria. "From the Achievement Gap to the Education Debt: Understanding Achievement in U.S. Schools. *Educational Researcher* 35, no. 7 (2006): 3–12.

———. "Toward a Theory of Culturally Relevant Pedagogy." *American Educational Research Journal* 32, no. 3 (September 1995): 465–491.

Ladson-Billings, Gloria, and William F. Tate IV. "Toward a Critical Race Theory of Education." *Teachers College Record* 97, no. 1 (1995): 47–68.

Larson, Reed, Jacquelynne Eccles, and Jennifer Appleton Gootman. "Features of Positive Developmental Settings." *Prevention Researcher* 11, no. 2 (2004): 8–13.

Lee, Stacey J. *Unraveling the Model Minority Stereotype: Listening to Asian American Youth.* New York: Teachers College Press, 2009.

Leonardo, Zeus. *Race Frameworks: A Multidimensional Theory of Racism and Education*. New York: Routledge, 2013.

Lewis, Amanda E., and John B. Diamond. *Despite the Best Intentions: How Racial Inequality Thrives in Good Schools*. Oxford: Oxford University Press, 2015.

Lewis-McCoy, R. L'Heureux. *Inequality in the Promised Land: Race, Resources, and Suburban Schooling*. Stanford, CA: Stanford University Press, 2014.

Lincoln, Yvonna S., and Egon G. Guba. "Establishing Trustworthiness," *Naturalistic Inquiry* (1985): 289–331.

Lipman, Pauline. *The New Political Economy of Urban Education: Neoliberalism, Race, and the Right to the City*. New York: Routledge, 2011.

———. "Neoliberal Education Restructuring: Dangers and Opportunities of the Present Crisis," *Monthly Review* 63 no. 3 (2011).

Lopez, Alejandra, Amy Stuart Wells, and Jennifer Jellison Holme. "Creating Charter School Communities: Identity Building, Diversity and Selectivity." In *Where Charter School Policy Fails*, edited by Amy Stuart Wells, 129–158. New York: Teachers College Press, 2000.

Madison, Soyini D. *Critical Ethnography: Method, Ethics, and Performance*. Thousand Oaks, CA: Sage, 2011.

Martinez, Sylvia, and John Rury. "From 'Culturally Deprived' to 'At Risk': The Politics of Popular Expression and Educational Inequality in the United States, 1960–1985." *Teachers College Record* 114, no. 6 (2012): 1–31.

Marwell, Nicole. "Privatizing the Welfare State: Nonprofit Community-Based Organizations as Political Actors." *American Sociological Review* 69, no. 2 (2004): 265–291.

Maxwell, Joseph. *Qualitative Research Design: An Interactive Approach*, vol. 41. Thousand Oaks, CA: Sage, 2012.

McKenzie, Brian D. "Reconsidering the Effects of Bonding Social Capital: A Closer Look at Black Civil Society Institutions in America." *Political Behavior* 30 (2007): 25–30.

McLaughlin, Milbrey. *Community Counts: How Youth Organizations Matter for Youth Development*. Washington, DC: Public Education Network, 2000.

———. *You Can't Be What You Can't See: The Power of Opportunity to Change Young Lives*. Cambridge, MA: Harvard Education Press, 2018.

McLaughlin, Milbrey, and Merita Irby. "Urban Sanctuaries: Neighborhood Organizations That Keep Hope Alive." *Phi Delta Kappan* 76, no. 4 (1994): 300–306.

Melamed, Jodi. "Racial Capitalism," *Critical Ethnic Studies* 1, no. 1 (2015): 76–85.

Miron, Gary, Jessica L. Urschel, William J. Mathis, and Elana Tornquist. *Schools Without Diversity: Education Management Organizations, Charter Schools, and the Demographic Stratification of the American School System*. Boulder, CO: Education and the Public Interest Center, 2010.

Moeller, Kathryn. *The Gender Effect: Capitalism, Feminism, and the Corporate Politics of Development*. Oakland: University of California Press, 2018.

Morrell, E. "Six Summers of YPAR." In *Revolutionizing Education: Youth Participatory Action Research in Motion*, edited by Julio Cammarota and Michelle Fine, 155–184. New York: Routledge, 2008.

Nelson, Ingrid A. *Why Afterschool Matters*. New Brunswick, NJ: Rutgers University Press, 2017.

Nicholson, Heather Johnston, Christopher Collins, and Heidi Holmer. "Youth as People: The Protective Aspects of Youth Development in After-School Settings." *Annals of the American Academy of Political and Social Science* 591, no. 1 (2004): 55–71.

Noguera, Pedro, and Chiara Cannella. "Youth Agency, Resistance, and Civic Activism: The Public Commitment to Social Justice." In *Beyond Resistance! Youth Activism and Community Change: New Democratic Possibilities for Practice and Policy for America's Youth*, edited by Shawn Ginwright, Pedro Noguera, and Julio Cammarota, 333–348. New York: Routledge, 2006.

Nunn, Kenneth B. "Race, Crime and the Pool of Surplus Criminality: Or Why the War on Drugs Was a War on Blacks." *Journal on Gender Race & Justice* 6 (2002): 381–445.

Nygreen, Kysa. "Negotiating Tensions: Grassroots Organizing, School Reform, and the Paradox of Neoliberal Democracy." *Anthropology and Education Quarterly* 48, no. 1 (2017): 42–60.

Nygreen, Kysa, Soo Ah Kwon, and Patricia Sanchez. "Urban Youth Building Community: Social Change and Participatory Research in Schools, Homes, and Community-Based Organizations." *Journal of Community Practice* 14, no. 1 (2006): 107–123.

O'Connor, Carla. "Dispositions Toward (Collective) Struggle and Educational Resilience in the Inner City: A Case Analysis of Six African-American High School Students." *American Educational Research Journal* 34, no. 4 (1997): 593–629.

Omi, Michael, and Howard Winant. *Racial Formation in the United States: From the 1960s to the 1990s*. New York: Routledge, 1994.

Paris, Django. "Culturally Sustaining Pedagogy: A Needed Change in Stance, Terminology, and Practice." *Educational Researcher* 41, no. 3 (2012): 93–97.

Paris, Django, and Maisha Winn. *Humanizing Research: Decolonizing Qualitative Inquiry with Youth and Communities*. Thousand Oaks, CA: Sage, 2013.

Patel, Leigh. *Decolonizing Educational Research: From Ownership to Answerability*. New York: Routledge, 2015.

———. "Pedagogies of Resistance and Survivance: Learning as Marronage." *Equity and Excellence in Education* 49, no. 4 (2016): 397–401.

Pattillo, Mary. "Black on the Block." In *Racial Structure and Radical Politics in the African Diaspora*, edited by James L. Conyers Jr., 13–44. New York: Routledge, 2017.

Peshkin, Alan. "The Nature of Interpretation in Qualitative Research." *Educational Researcher* 29, no. 9 (2000): 5–9.

Picower, Bree. "The Unexamined Whiteness of Teaching: How White Teachers Maintain and Enact Dominant Racial Ideologies." *Race Ethnicity and Education* 12, no. 2 (June 2009): 197–215.

Pittman, K., and W. Fleming. "A New Vision: Promoting Youth Development." *Academy for Education Development*, 1991.

Ray, Ranita. *The Making of a Teenage Service Class: Poverty and Mobility in an American City*. Oakland: University of California Press, 2017.

Rhee, Jeong-Un. "The Neoliberal Racial Project, Governmentality, and the Tiger Mother." *Educational Theory* 63, no. 6 (2013): 561–580.

Rhodes, Jean. "The Critical Ingredient: Caring Youth–Staff Relationships in After-School Settings." *New Directions for Student Leadership* 2004, no. 101 (2004): 145–161.

Rich, John Martin. "Neoliberalism and Black Education." *Journal of Negro Education* 55, no. 1 (Winter 1986): 21–28.

Richards, Lyn. *Handling Qualitative Data: A Practical Guide.* Thousand Oaks, CA: Sage, 2005.

Rios, Victor M. *Punished: Policing the Lives of Black and Latino Boys.* New York: New York University Press, 2011.

Salazar Perez, Michelle, and Gaile Cannella. "Disaster Capitalism as Neoliberal Instrument for the Construction of Early Childhood Education/Care Policy: Charter Schools in Post-Katrina New Orleans." *International Critical Childhood Policy Studies Journal* 6, no. 1 (2011): 47–68.

Saltman, K. *The Gift of Education.* New York: Palgrave Macmillan, 2010.

Sanders, Raynard, David Stovall, Terrenda White, and Thomas Pedroni. *Twenty-First Century Jim Crow Schools: The Impact of Charters on Public Education.* Boston: Beacon Press, 2018.

Schlichtman, John, Jason Patch, and Marc Lamont Hill. *Gentrifier.* Toronto: University of Toronto Press, 2017.

Sharpe, Christina. *In the Wake: On Blackness and Being.* Durham, NC: Duke University Press: 2016.

Siddle-Walker, Vanessa. "Culture and Commitment: Challenges for the Future Training of Education Researchers." In *Issues in Education Research: Problems and Possibilities*, edited by E. C. Lagemann and L. S. Shulman, 224–244. San Francisco: Jossey-Bass, 1999.

Small, Deborah A., Devin G. Pope, and Michael I. Norton. "An Age Penalty in Racial Preferences." *Social Psychological and Personality Science* 3, no. 6 (2012): 730–737.

Soss, Joe, Richard C. Fording, and Sanford Schram. *Disciplining the Poor: Neoliberal Paternalism and the Persistent Power of Race.* Chicago: University of Chicago Press, 2011.

Soung, Patricia. "Social and Biological Constructions of Youth: Implications for Juvenile Justice and Racial Equity." *Northwestern Journal of Law and Social Policy* 6 (2011): 428–444.

Spence, Lester K. *Knocking the Hustle: Against the Neoliberal Turn in Black Politics.* New York: Punctum Books, 2015.

———. "The Neoliberal Turn in Black Politics." *Souls* 14, no. 3–4 (2013): 139–159.

Stanton-Salazar, Ricardo D. "A Social Capital Framework for the Study of Institutional Agents and Their Role in the Empowerment of Low-Status Students and Youth." *Youth and Society* 43, no. 3 (2011): 1066–1109.

Stovall, David. *Born Out of Struggle: Critical Race Theory, School Creation, and the Politics of Interruption.* New York: State University of New York Press, 2016.

Sullivan, Lisa Y. "Hip-Hop Nation: The Undeveloped Social Capital of Black Urban America." *National Civic Reviewer* 86, no. 3 (1997): 235–243.

Teasley, Martell, and David Ikard. "Barack Obama and the Politics of Race: The Myth of Postracism in America." *Journal of Black Studies* 40, no. 3 (2010): 411–425.

Theodore, Nik, Jamie Peck, and Neil Brenner. "Neoliberal Urbanism: Cities and the Rule of Markets." In *The New Blackwell Companion to the City*, edited by Gary Bridge and Sophie Watson, 15–25. Malden, MA: Blackwell Publishing, 2011.

Trujillo, Tina, and Janelle Scott. "Superheroes and Transformers: Rethinking Teach for America's Leadership Models." *Phi Delta Kappan* 95, no. 8 (2014): 57–61.

Tuck, Eve. "Suspending Damage: A Letter to Communities." *Harvard Educational Review* 79, no. 3 (2009): 409–428.

United States. *National Commission on Excellence in Education. A Nation at Risk: The Imperative for Educational Reform: A Report to the Nation and the Secretary of Education, United States Department of Education.* Washington, DC: The Commission: [Supt. of Docs., U.S. G.P.O. distributor], 1983.

U.S. Department of Education. "National Study of Before and After-School Programs." Washington, DC: Office of Policy and Planning, 1993.

Valencia, Richard R. *Dismantling Contemporary Deficit Thinking: Educational Thought and Practice.* New York: Routledge, 2010.

Vasudevan, Deepa. "The Occupational Culture and Identity of Youth Workers: A Review of the Literature." http://nrs.harvard.edu/urn-3:HUL.InstRepos:33797252, (2017): 1–62.

Warren, Mark R., and David Goodman. *Lift Us Up Don't Push Us Out! Voices from the Front Lines of the Educational Justice Movement.* Boston: Beacon Press, 2018.

Watson, Vajra. *Learning to Liberate: Community-Based Solutions to the Crisis in Urban Education.* New York: Routledge, 2011.

Weis, Lois, and Michelle Fine. "Critical Bifocality and Circuits of Privilege: Expanding Critical Ethnographic Theory and Design." *Harvard Educational Review* 82, no. 2 (2012): 173–201.

Wells, Amy Stuart, Julie Slayton, and Janelle Scott. "Defining Democracy in the Neoliberal Age: Charter School Reform and Educational Consumption." *American Education Research Journal* 39, no. 2 (2002): 337–361.

Wenger, Etienne, Richard Arnold McDermott, and William Snyder. *Cultivating Communities of Practice: A Guide to Managing Knowledge.* Boston: Harvard Business Press, 2002.

White, Terrenda C. "Teach for America's Paradoxical Diversity Initiative: Race, Policy, and Black Teacher Displacement in Urban Public Schools." *Education Policy Analysis Archives* 24, no. 16 (2016): 1–42.

Wilson, William Julius. "Toward a Framework for Understanding Forces That Contribute to or Reinforce Racial Inequality." *Race and Social Problems* 1, no. 1 (2009): 3–11.

———. *The Truly Disadvantaged: The Inner City, the Underclass, and Public Policy.* Chicago: University of Chicago Press, 2012.

Winn, Maisha. "A-Words: Action, Activism and Activating Research Agendas." In *Humanizing Research: Decolonizing Qualitative Inquiry with Youth and Communities*, edited by Django Paris and Maisha Winn, 59–62. Thousand Oaks, CA: Sage.

Woodland, Malcolm. "After-School Programs: A Resource for Young Black Males and Other Urban Youth." *Urban Education* 51, no. 7 (2016): 770–796.

———. "'Whatcha Doin' After School?' A Review of the Literature on the Influence of After-School Programs on Young Black Males." *Urban Education* 43, no. 5 (2008): 537–560.

Woodland, Malcolm, Justin F. Martin, R. LeRoi Hill, and Frank Worrell. "The Most Blessed Room in the City: The Influence of a Youth Development Program on Three Young Black Males." *Journal of Negro Education* 78, no. 3 (2009): 233–245.

Yohalem, Nicole, and Karen Pittman. "Putting Youth Work on the Map." Washington, DC: *Forum on Youth Investment* (2006): 1–10.

Yohalem, Nicole, and Alicia Wilson-Ahlstrom. "Inside the Black Box: Assessing and Improving Quality in Youth Programs." *American Journal of Community Psychology* 45, no. 3–4 (2010): 350–357.

Young, Alford A. "New Life for an Old Concept: Frame Analysis and the Reinvigoration of Studies in Culture and Poverty." *Annals of the American Academy of Political and Social Science* 629, no. 1 (2010): 53–74.

Zeldin, Shepherd. "Foreword." In *Advancing Youth Work: Critical Questions, Current Trends*, edited by Dana Fuscso, xi–xiv. New York: Routledge, 2012.

Index

Italicized page numbers refer to material in figures and tables.

academic achievement: and after-school programs, 10, 11; EE's focus on, 36; and structural racism, 17; versus whole child development, 67

accountability: and competition for funding, 99–100; and EE, 95; and market-based approaches, 7; and neoliberal reforms, 80; and objectification of youth, 208

achievement gaps, 10, 84–85, 88, 93, 122, 203

adolescent psychology, 48, 63

affirming language, 43, 66, 144, 153, 171

after-school programs: and 21CCLC, 10; as community-based educational spaces, 35–36; and competition for funding, 94; as containment spaces, 18; emergence of, 8–9; and market-based approaches, 13; and neoliberalism, 92; and youth-centered classes, 57

agency: and Blackness, 29; of Black youth, 149, 204–205, 210; and

community-based educational spaces, 36; and EE culture, 177; and framing, 100; and white rescue trope, 47, 145, 146

Anderson, James, 47

anti-blackness, 5, 16, 26, 28–29, 71, 74, 104, 186, 191

asset-based ideology: Board of Directors' lack of, 143; and deficit framing, 68–69; and EE Golden Era, 149; and funding, 75; and high expectations, 57; and leadership changes, 117; versus neoliberal ideology, 100–102, 177; and study methodology, 212; of youth workers, 50, 96–99, 149. See also framing

Baldwin, James, 28–29

Bayside (pseudonym), 127, 129–135

Beatty, Barbara, 41

Benjamin (S2C coordinator; pseudonym): on cultural shift, 158; departure from EE, 113, 186; described, 216, 222; on education

Benjamin (*continued*)
policy, 91; and EE structure, 55; on expansion, 125–126, 130; hiring of, 228n73

Bernice (EE admissions; pseudonym), 19, 22, 50–51, 55, 84, 182, *217, 223*

Black churches, 6, 9, 45

Black communities: activism within, 26; and agency, 47; and civil society organizations, 63; and deficit framing, 16, 29; Richard Dunn's ideas about, 197–198; and economic control, 209; and neoliberal reforms, 33–34; resistance within, 210; and respectability politics, 41; and white rescue trope, 208; and white supremacy, 74; and youth work, 5–6, 9

Black English, 128–129

Black Freedom Struggle, 6, 35

Black Lives Matter, 71

Black Panther Party, 6

Black youth: and adolescent development research, 48–49; agency of, 149; and Board of Directors, 182; and charter schools, 18, 78, 92; and community-based educational spaces, 6, 36, 63, 69, 210; and competitive high school admission, 76–77; criminalization of, 70–71; and deficit framing, 13, 15–17, 29–30, 39; Richard Dunn's ideas about, 45, 47, 128–129, 134–135, 172, 180; and education policies, 83, 204–205; and EE philosophy, 4–5, 50, 59; and EE staff, 74–75, 158, 218–219; and ethnographic research, 212, 215; and faith-based organizations, 9; framing of, 24–25, 67–68, 96, 98–100, 101–103, 141–147, 168–169, 178; and Leah, 37–38, 139, 181, 202; and neoliberal reforms, 26–27, 80–82; pathologization of, 40–42, 43; and

schools, 58, 207; and social justice youth development, 90–91; and stereotypes, 95; and structural racism, 12; and white rescue trope, 28, 97

Board of Directors: and day-to-day control, 117; and deficit framing, 41, 43, 98, 153; and EE power dynamics, 171; and EE staff, 67, 86, 144, 150, *216–217, 223*; and EE structure, 55, 102; and emphasis on fundraising, 123–124; and Gina, 121–122; and leadership changes, 165, 202; and Leah, 38, 52, 93, 107, 177; and neoliberalism, 103, 157; and pro-abstinence curriculum, 44; push for expansion by, 176, 181; racial attitudes of, 191; and racial framing, 143, 146; and Richard, 37, 113; and search for Leah Davis's replacement, 111, 118–119; and statistics, 95–96, 201

bootstraps rhetoric, 39, 115

Boys and Girls Club, 37

Boy's Clubs, 9

Brown, Amy, 141

Bush administration, 81

Butler, Octavia, 35

Camille (EE counseling coordinator; pseudonym): on cultural shift, 111; departure from EE, 186–187; and EE structure, 55; on leadership changes, 120, 137, 140–141, 171; on pro-abstinence curriculum, 44; on relationships, 150–151, 152, 153–154, 192–193; on removing pregnant students, 73; and respectability politics, 70; on Richard's racism, 128–129; and students, 59; on Terry's isolation, 166; workshops by, 21

Cammarota, Julio, 48

Canada, Geoffrey, 29–30

capitalism: and achievement gap, 122; and Black youth, 186, 197; and Harlem Children's Zone, 30; and neoliberalism, 14, 17, 80; and race, 198, 204–205; and youth work, 11; and youth workers, 68, 74

charter schools: appeal to parents of, 77; and competition for funding, 92–95, 208; and gentrification, 31–32; and neoliberal reforms, 16, 25, 78–79, 80–82, 176; and public education, 7, 232n31

Chicago: and community-based educational spaces, 12–13, 204; and gentrification, 32; and Hull House, 8; and neoliberal reforms, 18, 33, 78, 81, 121, 207

Children's Aid Society, 37

civil society, 6, 63

class, 146; and privilege, 170; as tool of control, 197

Clinton administration, 9–10

college students, 4, 19, 57, 66, 221

color blindness, 7, 18, 115

community-based educators. *See* youth workers

community-based organizations: and 21CCLC, 9–10; and after-school programs, 37; appreciation for, 11; and charter schools, 82; defined, 26; diversity of, 157; and market-based approaches, 7; and neoliberal reforms, 25; and philanthropy, 46, 198–199; and Race to the Top, 95; and racial disparities, 8; versus school-based organizations, 132; and schools, 12–13; and social justice youth development, 48–49; and youth work, 6, 63, 204–205

competition: and charter schools, 77–78; at EE, 6, 13; and EE expansion, 157; for funding, 10, 92–95, 177; and neoliberalism, 14; and public

education, 80–81; and standardized testing, 7

conscientização, 48

counseling: and EE culture, 54, 60; and EE programs, 19, 21, 56, 59–61; and EE promotional video, 90; and EE structure, 55; and personal success, 64–65; and Youth Lead, 20, 44

critical media literacy, 21, 35, 56

Cynthia (EE finance director; pseudonym): on Board of Directors, 143–144; departure from EE, 109, 110, 117, 122, 159, 182–183; described, *217*; and EE culture, 155; and EE structure, 20, 55

Dana (HA coordinator; pseudonym), 123–124, 186

Daniel (EE grant writer; pseudonym): on deficit framing, 144–145; departure from EE, 112, 184–185, 186; and EE structure, 55; and Gina's leadership, 143; on Gina's leadership, 155–156; on leadership changes, 124–125; on racial power dynamics, 182

deficit discourses, 7, 36, 195. *See also* deficit framing

deficit framing: and after-school programs, 9, 12; versus asset-based ideologies, 50; and Black youth, 15–17; Leah Davis's campaign against, 38–42; and education policies, 204; and funding, 96–97; and informal cultural practices, 69; and leadership changes, 140–142; need to challenge, 101–102. *See also* deficit discourses; low expectations

demographics, 6, 19, 37, 119

Detroit education privatization, 82

DeVos, Betsy, 82

double-consciousness, 74

dress codes, 69–70. *See also* respectability politics

Du Bois, W. E. B., 74
Dunbar (pseudonym): and after-school programs, 37; versus Bayside EE site, 133; and charter schools, 77–79; and EE, 3, 19, 36, 201; and EE expansion, 131, 165, 169–170; and EE students, 61; and ethnographic research, 212, 220; and ethnoracial tensions, 52–53; gentrification of, 30–34, 82, 111–112; Gina Roy's attitude toward, 146, 182
Dunbar, Paul Laurence, 53
Duncan, Arne, 204–205

educational discourse: and accountability, 202; and community-based educational spaces, 100–101; and structural racism, 16–17; and youth workers, 62, 208–209
educational policy: and after-school programs, 27; and deficit framing, 205; and neoliberalism, 16, 81, 94–95, 197; and racism, 14–15, 17–18; and youth work, 196, 201
education management organizations (EMOs), 79
education reform: and accountability, 99; and Black youth, 26, 75; and charter schools, 92–94; and community-based educational spaces, 100–101, 200, 209–210; and competition for funding, 24; and ethnographic research, 212; and neoliberalism, 79–80; and privatization, 121; versus Youth Lead philosophy, 88; and youth workers, 27, 86
EE (Educational Excellence; pseudonym): admission requirements, 19, 84–85, 99–100; Career Day at, 3–4; conflict within, 177–178; culture of, 59–62, 155–168, 169–173; and deficit framing, 17; described, 19–22, 34–35; and dress codes, 69–70; and Dunbar, 30; educational hierarchy of, 55;

ethnographic research in, 22–26; existence beyond physical space, 190–195; Golden Era of, 52, 148–149, 179, 201–202; and individualized intervention, 63–66; and leadership changes, 110–111; leadership of, 6; and Leah, 38–42; and neoliberalism, 103–104; and neoliberal reforms, 203; and outreach, 50–51; and politics of respectability, 71; and privatization of public education, 82; promotional video for, 89–90; relationships within, 150–154; and social justice youth development, 49; structure and pedagogy of, 56–62; structure of, 55; and student fears of rejection, 72–73; tensions within, 67, 113–117, 122; and whole child development, 47–48; and youth-centered classes, 57–58
ethnographic research, 22–24, 211–215, 216–217, 218–221, 222–223, 224

Faith (YL and Counseling director; pseudonym): on academics versus youth development, 90–91; and asset-based ideologies, 50; background of, 54, 83; on Board of Directors, 128; departure from EE, 112, 183, 186, 187–188; and EE culture, 60, 164; on EE culture, 159–160, 161; and EE structure, 21, 55; on gentrification, 31; hiring of, 53; and individualized intervention, 64–65; and leadership changes, 111; and pro-abstinence curriculum, 44; and search for Davis's replacement, 108, 109, 118; on social development, 86–87; and social identity curriculum, 88; and Youth Lead, 56
faith-based organizations, 9, 10
Felicia (EE board member; pseudonym), 107–109, 113, 143, 197

framing: of Black youth, 24–25; and competition for funding, 97–99; defined, 15; and EE culture, 202; and leadership changes, 139, 140–144; and youth work, 67–68. *See also* asset-based ideology

Frank (YL coordinator; pseudonym), 123–124, 135–136, 186

Freedom Schools, 6

Freire, Paulo, 48, 62–63

funding: for academics versus youth development, 90–91; and after-school programs, 11, 36; and community-based educational spaces, 207–208; competition for, 92–95; Richard Dunn's withholding of, 131; and education policies, 91; and EE admissions, 85; and framing, 145–146; and Gina's leadership, 155–156; versus programs, 123–124; tenuousness of, 12; and Youth Lead, 56, 87

Gates, Bill, 92–93

gender: and privilege, 170; and Youth Lead, 88

gender bias, 73

gentrification, 31–32

Gilmore, Ruth, 45

Gina (new EE CEO; pseudonym): background of, 156–157; and Board of Directors, 122, 136–137, 183; and EE culture, 139–140, 163; and expansion, 124–125, 126, 129–135, 158; and framing, 169; hiring of, 113, 119–120, 142, 166; and neoliberal reforms, 157; racial attitudes of, 143, 146, 168, 180; and Richard, 128–129; and staff relationships, 152; and turnover, 121, 182–183, 184–185

Ginwright, Shawn, 48

Giroux, Henry, 30

Great Migration, 9

HA (High Achievers), 20, 56, 160

Harlem Children's Zone (HCZ), 29, 95

Hartman, Saidiya, 29

Harvey, David, 80

health care, 29, 33

healthy choices, 21

Higginbotham, Evelyn Brooks, 41

high schools: and charter schools, 78; and community-based educational spaces, 50–51; and competitive admissions, 56, 76–77, 83–84, 130; and transition to college, 21

Hull House, 8, 9

individualism, 13, 18, 205–206

inequality: and critical consciousness, 196, 201–202; and framing, 36, 40, 102; and funding trends, 95; and neoliberalism, 30, 176; reproduction of, 8, 26; and school choice, 14; study of, 51–52; understanding of, 104; youth workers on, 218. *See also* structural inequality; structural racism

institutional agents, 61, 63, 206

intentionality, 137–138, 167

internalized racism, 74

intersectionality, 170–171

Jackman, Mary, 135

Janelle (pseudonym), 55, 85

Jimenez, Alexandria, 20, 113

Johnson, Felicia, 107–109

Knowledge Is Power Program (KIPP), 94

Latinx youth: and adolescent development research, 48–49; and charter schools, 78; and deficit framing, 39; pathologization of, 41–42

Leah (EE CEO; pseudonym), 20; approach to education of, 37–42; and asset-based ideologies, 50; on asset-rich perspective, 97–98; as buffer, 137–138, 177, 186, 198; on charter schools, 93; and EE culture, 6, 7, 60, 148–149, 155; and EE Golden Era, 202; and EE mission, 19; and EE staff hired away, 183; and EE structure, 55; and framing, 139–140; on funding trends, 95; holistic perspective of, 146–147; impact on EE of, 25; and individualized intervention, 63–65; and minoritized youth, 52; on pregnant students, 73; resignation from EE by, 107–109; and Richard, 43–44, 45, 47, 113–117, 131, 134; and structural inequality, 179; on students served by EE, 83–84; and Youth Lead, 56, 87

Lipman, Pauline, 16, 81, 82

The Lottery, 93

low expectations, 39–42, 69. *See also* deficit framing

mass incarceration, 9, 29

McLaughlin, Milbrey, 12–13

media literacy, 21

mental health, 21, 60, 61, 230n50

meritocracy, 18, 30, 205–207

Metcalf, Stephen, 14

Mexican American communities, 16

Michaela (HA coordinator; pseudonym): on charter schools, 93; on competitive high school admission, 77; departure from EE, 111; and EE structure, 55; on gentrification, 32, 61; and High Achievers, 20; on standardized testing, 84

Moeller, Kathryn, 141

Monica (EE programming director; pseudonym), 21, 25; and asset-based ideologies, 50; on asset-rich perspective, 96–97, 98; departure from EE, 109, 110, 117, 182; and EE culture, 59, 60, 155; on EE culture, 159; on EE existence beyond physical, 190, 193–195; on framing, 169; hiring of, 53; on leadership changes, 118–120; on relationships, 151, 166–167; on representation, 179–180; and Richard, 43; on Youth Lead, 87

Moynihan, Daniel Patrick, 115

A Nation at Risk (1983), 17

neoliberalism: and after-school programs, 26–27; and charter schools, 82; and community-based educational spaces, 208; and education reform, 30; and EE culture, 157; and gentrification, 31–32; and Gina's leadership, 180; and leadership changes, 146–147; and outcome-based education, 83; and philanthropy, 45–46; and privatization of public education, 81–82; and race, 195–196; and racial framing, 14–18; and racism, 205–206; and shifts in public education, 80–82; as threat to youth work, 173–174, 175–176

neoliberal reforms: and after-school programs, 12, 100–101; and charter schools, 78; at EE, 179; and EMOs, 79; and leadership changes, 121–122

New Orleans: closure of public schools in, 81, 207–208

No Child Left Behind, 81, 91

nonparental adults, 63

nonprofit industrial complex, 135

Obama, Barack, 30

Obama administration, 81, 95

Omari (S2C coordinator; pseudonym), 21, 55, 93, 217, 228n73

Parable of the Sower (Butler), 35
parents: and community-based
    educational spaces, 10, 207; and
    competitive high school admission,
    77; and education system, 38; and EE
    admissions, 19; and EE promotional
    video, 89; and framing, 219; as viewed
    by Board of Directors, 144–145
paternalism: and leadership changes, 191;
    and Leah-Richard power struggle,
    43; and neoliberalism, 210; and
    persistence of race, 195–200; and
    philanthropy, 45, 96; and racial
    discourse, 18; of Richard, 7, 116–117,
    134; and white supremacy, 28; and
    youth workers, 25
patriarchy, 17, 68, 116–117, 198
Patrick (EE development director;
    pseudonym): and Board of Directors,
    144, 146, 163; on deficit framing,
    144; on donor wishes, 90; and EE
    structure, 20, 55; on funding trends,
    92–94; and leadership changes, 122,
    124–125, 155, 156, 169; and promotional
    video, 89; on turnover, 185–186
Pattillo, Mary, 32
pedagogy: asset-based, 50; and charter
    schools, 78; and context, 62; and EE
    leadership changes, 173; and framing,
    67, 74, 204, 215; and humanizing, 99;
    and social justice youth development,
    196; and youth-centered classes,
    58–59
philanthropy: and community-based
    educational spaces, 207; and EE
    culture, 139–140; and power
    dynamics, 135, 198; and racist
    paternalism, 45–46
Planned Parenthood, 44
police violence, 29, 71, 170
popular culture, 93
positive youth development, 48–49
postracial discourse, 115

praxis, 62–63
pregnancy, 73
privatization: and accountability, 203;
    and competition for funding, 94;
    at EE, 6; and EE narrative, 110;
    and neoliberalism, 14; of public
    education, 7, 81–82; as threat to
    youth work, 175–176
privilege: and gender, 170; and Gina's
    leadership, 142; and hiring practices,
    168; and neoliberalism, 30; and
    pathological discourses, 212;
    Richard's failure to understand,
    116–117; and social identity
    development, 44
psychosocial growth, 11
public discourse, 12, 16, 30, 205, 207
public education: and Black youth, 18;
    and external political pressures,
    199–200; and market-based
    approaches, 7; and neoliberalism,
    14–15; and neoliberal reforms, 33–34,
    203–204

race: and achievement gaps, 93; and EE
    culture, 167–168; and leadership
    changes, 181–190; and neoliberal
    educational policy, 197–198; and
    search for Davis's replacement,
    119–120; youth workers'
    understanding of, 67–68
Race to the Top, 81, 95
racism: and color-blindness, 30; and
    neoliberalism, 14–15, 17; Richard's
    failure to understand, 116–117; and
    white supremacy, 134; and youth
    work, 11. *See also* structural racism
relationships: among youth workers,
    150–155; and leadership changes,
    166–167; and power dynamics, 198;
    and social networks, 188; and
    students, 190; and youth-centered
    classes, 58–59

representation, 179–180

respectability politics, 41, 71, 74, 177. *See also* dress codes

Richard (EE founder; pseudonym): and deficit framing, 38, 41, 98, 144; and EE culture, 161; and EE founding, 19, 37; as EE's owner, 196–197; and EE structure, 55; and expansion, 126, 131–132; increasing control by, 122, 133–134, 153; and leadership changes, 6–7; and Leah, 43, 109, 113–117; and power dynamics, 171; and pregnant students, 73; and pressure on EE staff, 86, 150; and pro-abstinence curriculum, 44; racial attitudes of, 45, 46–47, 128–129, 135, 138, 191, 197–198; and search for Davis's replacement, 120–121

Rick, John Martin, 80

S2C (Step 2 College): described, 20–21; and EE culture, 155, 160; and EE demographics, 170; and EE structure, 55, 56; and former students, 192

Samira (S2C coordinator; pseudonym), 123–124, 135–136

schools: and after-school programs, 12–13; and Black youth, 58; culture of, 132; and neoliberal reforms, 16, 80–81; reproduction of inequality within, 8

segregation, 70, 78–79

self-determination, 26, 47, 177, 201, 207

settlement spaces, 9

sex education, 44

slavery, 29

social capital, 10–11, 63, 77, 167

social context: and charter schools, 82; and community-based educational spaces, 10–11, 177, 210; of EE, 36–38; and EE Golden Era, 134; and ethnographic research, 22; and funding, 145; and neoliberal reforms, 100; and youth work, 168; and youth workers, 48–49, 175

social identity, 21

social identity development, 44

social justice youth development (SJYD), 48, 90–91

social mobility, 8, 17–18, 32, 40, 66, 102, 204

Solomon (EE instructor; pseudonym): background of, 66; departure from EE, 188–189; on EE culture, 162, 163, 163–165; on EE ownership, 199; and EE structure, 55; on Leah's departure, 195–196; and pro-abstinence curriculum, 44; and respectability politics, 70–71; on Richard, 134–135, 138; on Richard's racism, 46–47, 198; on social development, 87; on structural forces, 72–73; and students, 65; on Terry's isolation, 166; workshops by, 21

Standard American English, 69–70

standardized testing: and funding, 91; and limited course offerings, 84; and market-based approaches, 7; and neoliberal reforms, 80, 176; and pressure on EE staff, 86–87

Stanton-Salazar, Ricardo D., 63

state-sponsored violence, 70–71

stereotypes, 5, 96, 145

structural inequality: and Black youth, 74; and bootstraps rhetoric, 39–40; and critical consciousness, 191; and framing, 44, 182; and neoliberalism, 206–207; and philanthropy, 141; and resource hoarding, 204–205; as state-sponsored violence, 70–71; understanding of, 179–180, 186; and white rescue trope, 208; and youth of color, 197; and youth work, 68. *See also* inequality

structural racism, 17, 18, 68–69. *See also* inequality; racism

student-centered learning, 42
students: basic needs of, 33; and charter schools, 78–79, 93–95; and community-based educational spaces, 5–6, 10, 27, 208; and competitive high school admission, 76–77; and curriculum changes, 44; and deficit framing, 12; demographics of, 3, 52–53; and education system, 38, 83; and EE admissions, 84–85; and EE culture, 4, 34–36, 65–66, 136–138, 148–150, 156, 159–165; and EE expansion, 122–127, 129–133, 146–147, 157, 200, 203; and EE Golden Era, 196, 201–202; and EE programs, 19–21, 56–61, 86–92; and EE staff, 54; and expectations, 39–42; framing of, 96–104, 142–143; and funding, 145; and gentrification, 32; and Harlem Children's Zone, 29; and inequality, 8; labeling of, 17; and leadership changes, 7, 140, 158; and Leah-Richard power struggle, 117, 134; and neoliberalism, 14; and neoliberal reforms, 80–82, 176; and outreach, 51; and poverty, 141; and race, 168–172; and racial representation, 119–120, 179–180; and relationships, 166–167, 184–190, 193; and respectability politics, 67–73, 177; and Richard, 46–47; and Richard's demands, 128, 198; and school system, 49; and turnover, 188–189; and youth workers, 13, 24, 50, 62–64, 74, 152–153
Summer Experience, 131

teacher education, 7
Teach for America, 93
Terry (EE program director; pseudonym): and accountability, 85–86; on aging out of youth work, 71–72; background of, 54, 82; on

Board of Directors, 127–128; described, 20–21, *216*, 222; on EE culture, 159; and EE culture, 164; and EE structure, 55; and expansion to Bayside, 131; and expectations, 49–50; hiring of, 53; isolation of, 166; and leadership changes, 111, 113, 122, 124–125, 137, 163, 165, 182–184; on relationships, 152–153; and Richard, 134, 135
Trump administration, 81–82, 207
21st Century Community Learning Centers (21CCLC), 9–10, 11, 12

underachievement, 40–42, 46

Waiting for Superman, 93
Walidah (HA director; pseudonym): background of, 54, 82; and Bayside expansion, 129–135; on Black Americans, 49–50; on Board of Directors, 128; and competitive high school admission, 76–77; described, 20; and EE structure, 55; on expansion, 123–124; on framing, 169–170; hiring of, 53; on internal politics, 180–181; on leadership changes, 113, 119, 165; and leadership changes, 187; on racial power dynamics, 129; on shifts in public education, 78–79; on Terry's isolation, 166; and youth-centered classes, 58
War on Drugs, 9, 37
Washington, Carl, 107–109, 117
Watson, Vajra, 13
white liberals, 39
whiteness: gaze of, 68, 74, 196; and Gina's leadership, 142; logics of, 145; and paternalism, 28; and philanthropy, 135; and private schools, 16; Richard's failure to understand, 116; as standard, 172; and structural racism, 134

white privilege, 116–117
white supremacy: and Black youth,
    28–29; and double-consciousness,
    74; and EE students, 128–129; and
    savior mentality, 144–145; and sense
    of self, 68; and youth work, 12
whole child development, 42, 47–48,
    58–59, 67

YL (Youth Lead): and Faith Davenport,
    112; described, 21; and EE culture, 59,
    61, 160, 201–202; and EE structure,
    56; and funding, 95–97; and HA, 20;
    and social development, 87–92; and
    turnover, 186–187
YMCA, 37
Young, Alford, 15
youth development, 90–91, 92, 96–97
youth workers: and age gap with
    students, 71–72; background of,
    82–83; and Board of Directors, 128;
    on charter schools, 95; concern for
    EE's direction, 184; as cultural

workers, 204–205; described, 62–63;
    dialogue among, 49–50; and
    education reform, 27; and EE culture,
    158, 160–161; and EE engagement,
    51–52; and external political
    pressures, 201; and framing, 67;
    and framing of students, 4–5; and
    gentrification, 32–33; heterogeneity
    of, 10; and individualized
    intervention, 63–66; and leadership
    changes, 6, 25, 109–110, 149–150, 165,
    177–178; and neoliberal reforms, 16;
    and pedagogy, 13; and police, 35; and
    power dynamics, 135, 191–192;
    professionalization of, 40–41; and
    racial awareness, 168–169; on
    relationships, 150–155; resistance to
    neoliberalism by, 102, 103–104; and
    Richard, 43–44; on shifts in public
    education, 78–79; and social capital,
    11; and social context, 36–38; and
    social reproduction, 8; and turnover,
    121, 188–190